Tradition and Unity

D0231648

Other titles of interest:

THE CANTERBURY PAPERS
Essays on Religion and Society
Edited by Dan Cohn-Sherbok

TRADITION AND UNITY

Sermons Published in Honour of Robert Runcie

Foreword by Lord Hailsham

Edited by Dan Cohn-Sherbok

Bellew Publishing
London
1991

First published in Great Britain in 1991 by
Bellew Publishing Company Limited
7 Southampton Place, London WC1A 2DR

The collection copyright © Bellew Publishing 1991

All rights reserved. No part of this publication may
be reproduced, stored in a retrieval system or transmitted,
in any form or by any means, electronic, mechanical,
photocopying, recording or otherwise without the prior
permission of the publisher

ISBN 0 947792 62 7 (cased)
ISBN 0 947792 61 9 (limp)

Phototypeset by Input Typesetting Ltd, London
Printed and bound in Great Britain by
Billings & Sons Ltd

All royalties will go to The Canterbury Oast Trust,
of which His Grace The Archbishop of Canterbury is patron.

Contents

Part II   One Church

Part III   One World

Foreword

I commend this book without hesitation. Owing to the immense antiquity of both offices, Archbishops of Canterbury and Lord Chancellors inevitably find themselves often in each other's company. Their Court precedence brings them close in all grand processions, State Banquets, and at other ceremonies in which attendance of both becomes necessary. So, without affectation, I can honestly claim Robert Runcie as my friend, and I am proud to do so. He was decorated in the War, characteristically for saving the life of a comrade-in-arms from a burning tank. His spirituality is plain to be seen by any person of perception. His sermons are always thoughtful, and, when appropriate, extremely moving. Obviously the duties of the office, whether as Archbishop, or titular head of the Anglican Communion, are extremely difficult, at times even verging on the impossible. He has few, if any, coercive powers outside his own diocese. He cannot possibly please all the factions and opinions within a communion representing all, or almost all the divergent opinions of a rapidly changing Christian theological world. He has maintained and extended our corporate unity together, and our friendships with other Churches. He has never lowered his immense personal dignity, his fine presence, or compromised his humble heart and his deep sense of personal loyalty to Our Lord. We all owe him a great debt of gratitude. I shall miss him greatly, both as Archbishop and for the loss of the opportunity of contact which our widely different offices enabled us to maintain. I shall also miss the unfailing kindness and occasional company of his loyal, talented, and always entertaining wife.

HAILSHAM OF ST MARYLEBONE

Preface

I would like to acknowledge my indebtedness to all those who have contributed to this volume of sermons in honour of Robert Runcie. In various ways they testify to the regard and the affection the contributors have for him. Some of them have known him for a long time; others have a much more limited acquaintance. But in all cases – as the introductions to the sermons illustrate – it is clear that the Archbishop has exerted a formative influence on their lives and thinking. In particular his own aspiration to seek a wider communion for all human beings has had an important impact. Firmly rooted within the Anglican tradition, he has reached out not only to Christians of all denominations but also to those of other faiths in the quest to create unity among individuals and countries. For this reason the book is entitled *Tradition and Unity* and is divided into three sections: One God, One Church, and One World. Never more has humanity needed wholeness – and in his ministry Robert Runcie has shown us the way forward.

DAN COHN-SHERBOK
University of Kent,
Canterbury

Part I
ONE GOD

God's Love

Desmond Tutu

Archbishop Robert Runcie is a deeply pastoral and caring person. He cares enormously about people because he believes deeply that we are each of infinite worth in the sight of God, and that explains his passionate concern about human rights and his support of those members of the Anglican Communion who have experienced harassment through a violation of their human rights.

Robert Runcie has made us in the Anglican Communion outside the United Kingdom feel cherished and cared for in an extraordinary manner. He is held in very high regard in that part of the Communion, and we have been shocked and deeply dismayed to see how he has been vilified and belittled in the British press. We have experienced him as a warm-hearted pastor. Terry Waite is languishing in Beirut as a hostage because the Archbishop has helped so many through Terry to be freed from their captivity. We in the Church in South Africa have experienced his caring through sending envoys such as Terry Waite and the Bishop of Lichfield at times of particular stress in our individual and corporate lives because of the awfulness of apartheid.

We give thanks that Robert has lived out his belief in a God of love and of grace who loves us not because we are lovable, but because we are lovable precisely and only through His love for us.

Jeremiah 1:5

Soon after I first came to Britain in 1962, I went to a garden party. I do not know why but we were expected to pay for our tea. I offered to pay for someone I had just met at the party. He was perfectly entitled to refuse and say, 'No, thank you'. You could have knocked me down with a feather when he retorted, 'No thank you – I won't be subsidised'. Well, I never. Thinking over that incident, I realised that it reflected in perhaps a mild form, the affliction of most of us. We have been brought up on the achievement, success ethic. We must prove ourselves in order to be acceptable to our contemporaries. We have come to accept the codes of the rat race, and we work ourselves into a frazzle, and now we think that stomach ulcers are really a status symbol. What matters in our culture is that one succeeds. It does not much matter what you succeed in as long as you succeed. The worst thing that could happen to anyone would be to fail. We have come to believe that our worth is a matter of our achievement. That we are valued because we deserve it since we have earned it.

Perhaps there is some validity in this thinking in the way we have ordered things. To qualify as a doctor you must work hard and impress your examiners who will, depending on your performance, pass or fail you. The tragedy is that we have thought that the same rules apply in our relationship with God. We have been brought up, it seems, to believe that we must impress God, we must be good or virtuous in order for God to love us, to accept us, to value us. And so too many of us refuse to be 'subsidised', even by God. What a horrible distortion of the Good News and what a tragic toll it has taken of our lives.

I have always had a soft spot for Jeremiah, who seemed destined to fail in a calling which he had shown the greatest possible reluctance to accept. He was a sensitive, retiring soul who knew just what being a prophet would entail, and who balked at the prospect of speaking words of doom to a people he loved dearly but whom he knew were as hard as adamantine in their stiff-necked disobedience and wanton disloyalty. I love reading the account of his call and commission which serves as the text for my sermon.

God does say what on the surface seems quite odd, 'Before I formed you in the womb, I knew you' – and we are tempted to say that God does not seem to know a great deal about human biology. How could you know someone before he or she had even been conceived? Actually, God was making an astounding assertion about Jeremiah and about each one of us. God sought to reassure this shy and gentle person that he was no divine afterthought. It was not as if God, looking at the plight of the people of Israel, scratched His head in puzzlement and then exclaimed, 'Ah, I know what I shall do – I will call Jeremiah to be a prophet'. No, God was saying to Jeremiah, 'You have been part of my divine plan from all eternity. Indeed, you are an indispensable part of that plan. No one else can love me as you can love me; no one else can apprehend my ways as only you can; no one else can understand me and misunderstand me as only you can; for you are unique and something wholly irreplaceable would be missing if your kind of loving, your kind of apprehending, your kind of understanding and misunderstanding were to be missing.'

It is an incredible assertion about each one of us, which almost all of us find difficult to accept. It seems too good to be true. But it is a truth wholly consonant with other truths about God and God's dealings with us. The doctrine of the Trinity among other things assures us that God's home life is not a kind of divine solitary confinement of the Alone contemplating the Alone. But God is a pulsating *koinonia*, fellowship of love, that flows from the Father to the Son and back again. This bond of love is God the Holy Spirit and so God is love from all eternity; long before there was any creation, God was love.

Poor Hegel got it all wrong when he said, 'God without the world is no God'. Without God there would be no world, there would be nothing. Creation is the result of God's overflowing love. St Augustine puts it thus: 'These things you have made not of any need, but out of the fullness of your goodness.' (*Confessions*: XIII.2) Creation is an act of divine grace. It has come about freely, gratuitously.

You exist, I exist, *because* God loves you, loves me. We are the result, each one of us, of the divine love. Consequently the most important fact about you and about me is that God loves us. Period. That is the most fundamental fact about us. Therefore we do not need to try to earn God's love. It is freely given. Everything else about us flows from this fundamental fact. That is the Good News Jesus tried so desperately to instil in his followers. Do not be anxious for the morrow. Your Father loves you and will provide for you. You are of more value than the sparrows and yet not one of them falls to the ground without the Father's knowledge. The very hairs of your head are numbered. You are known intimately by name, loved as if you were the only human being on earth.

And God's love is unchanging, eternal. God staggeringly loved me from all eternity and God loves me now and God will love me forever world without end. God's love for me will not change, cannot change. It is a love that will not let me go. It is a prevenient love – a love that goes before. It cannot be earned. It does not need to be earned. It is freely given. Before we were conceived, God knew us and loved us and created us and so invested us with an incalculable worth, with an infinite value creating us in His own image, so that to treat one of such creatures as if they were less than this is not only evil, not only painful as it often is to its victims, it is positively blasphemous. It is to spit in the face of God, for we are God-carriers, the temples of the Holy Spirit, those who are indwelt freely, gratuitously by God the most holy and blessed Trinity.

Often people malign the Old Testament and say it is legalistic – meaning thereby that it purveys a religion of achievement through fulfilment of the law. It certainly contains a great deal of legal material but that does not make it legalistic. The religion of the Old Testament is a religion that at its best is a religion of grace in Exodus 20. The Decalogue, we are reminded, is preceded by an important preface which introduces God who has already delivered a rabble of slaves utterly undeserving, long before they had done anything to earn or deserve that deliverance. There is a 'therefore' which is missing which we should supply: 'I have already delivered you *therefore* thou shalt not . . . ' Grace precedes law. The Exodus comes before Sinai and that order is important. God is a God of grace. The law is God's gift to help His people to express their gratitude for what God has already done.

We come to understand what the writer of Ephesians was saying when he spoke about how God chose us in Christ before the foundation of the world – we could not deserve or earn that election. It is freely bestowed. We should be liberated to enter our heritage, to enjoy the glorious liberty of the children of God. You know God loved us so deeply that, 'While we were yet sinners, Christ died for us'. God did not wait until we deserved to be redeemed. He would have waited until the cows came home. It was while we were God's enemies, while we were in our sins, that God demonstrated His love for us.

One of my former professors at King's College, London, Dennis Nineham, once preached on the present theme in the College chapel. And I remember how he referred to what Bishop Goudge said of our misinterpretation of the parable of the Good Shepherd. Our conventional pictures of the Good Shepherd reflect this misinterpretation. Our pictures usually show the Good Shepherd carrying a fluffy snow-white little lamb. Now fluffy little lambs do not usually stray from their mother ewes. The sheep that is likely to stray is that obstreperous old ram which will have had its fleece torn and dirty and it may have fallen into a ditch full of stinking water. That is the sheep the Good Shepherd will go after, leaving ninety-nine perfectly well-behaved sheep behind. It is this one which when He has found it He will carry home on His shoulders and then invite His friends for a party to celebrate its recovery.

Oh, how we could transform the world if people could but know this good news. They would not be overwhelmed by a sense of self-hate and disgust in a culture that tells people they do not count if they are poor or unemployed. The world would be revolutionised, for a great deal of the aggression in the world is due to those who feel insecure, inadequate and who want to affirm, assert themselves like bullies and say, 'Notice me, I am here, I am someone, I count'.

Students in examinations often produce so-called howlers with inappropriate answers. Once in a Bible-study exam the question was asked, 'What did John the Baptist say to Jesus when He came to be baptised?' This particular student answered, 'John the Baptist said to Jesus "Remember you are the Son of God and behave like one!"' Yes, remember you are a child of God, loved and cherished and affirmed by God from all eternity and forever. Behave like one. The world would be revolutionised.

Share Your Bread

Frances Dominica

*On one of my first encounters with Robert Runcie I introduced him to a
fourteen-year-old boy. The boy's disease had left him with no speech or sight
and minimal movement; he could communicate only with the fingers of
one hand, his smile and his infectious laughter. (He was most comfortable
lying on a mattress on the floor.) Almost before the introduction was
complete the Archbishop was stretched out on the floor beside him, and the
two became absorbed in a 'conversation'. It would have been intrusive for
anyone else to remain in the room and so no one knew what passed between
them. It became apparent that both were football enthusiasts but there
must have been more to it than that because the boy was both elated and
peaceful after the visit. He died a few days later.*

*Here was an Archbishop whose compassion was both prayerful and
practical, a pastor who combined humanity and holiness. The boy had a
new friend, a companion on the way.*

Isaiah 58:7

> I was hungry, and you formed a Humanities Club and discussed my
>   hunger.
> I was imprisoned, and you crept off quietly to your chapel in the cellar
>   and you prayed for my release.
> I was naked, and in your mind you debated the morality of my appear-
>   ance.
> I was sick, and you knelt and thanked God for your health.
> I was homeless, and you preached to me of the spiritual shelter of the
>   love of God.
> I was lonely, and you left me alone, to pray for me.
> You seem so holy and so close to God – but I am still very hungry, and
>   lonely, and cold.
>
> 'Listen, Christian' – *Social Justice Newsletter*

The teaching in St Matthew's Gospel, chapter 25, is so familiar that
we run the risk of being lulled into complacency, and this twentieth-
century interpretation leaves us feeling uncomfortable. But our
Lord's actual words allow for little complacency. You and I are
surrounded by the hungry, the thirsty, the stranger, the naked, the
sick and the prisoner. We do not need to go to Calcutta or Central
America to find them, though for some that is indeed God's calling.

Nearly a quarter of a century ago, when I was completing my

nursing training, I hoped to be accepted by one of the voluntary agencies to work abroad, to go perhaps to Vietnam, as some of my friends had done, to nurse war-wounded children. God had other ideas, and before I knew where I was, I found myself walled-up in a convent less than an hour's drive from home, working part-time in the small home we ran for disturbed, maladjusted children. Family and friends were horrified at what they saw as the shameful restrictions I had placed on myself. But suddenly I knew that if, in my lifetime, I could reach through to even one of those children in love, it might mean far more than anything seemingly heroic I might achieve in Saigon, at least in God's sight. All that mattered was that I should listen and know where God wanted me to be and then give myself wholeheartedly wherever that might be.

We do not need to go to faraway places. People in need are here all around us – the abused child hungry for someone to trust; the alcoholic business man thirsty for self-respect; the immigrant of different colour and different tongue aching for home; the dosser, wearing two pairs of trousers, a jacket, a raincoat and an overcoat, all tied round with a piece of string, needing to be clothed; the person with AIDS, the modern-day leper, asking only to be touched; the petty offender, rendered hopeless by the chains which hold him to his past, pleading for release.

There is a children's song which goes like this:

> Si tous les gens du monde
>   voulaient se donner la main
>   on pourrait faire une ronde autour du monde . . .
>   Si tous les gens du monde
>   Voulaient se donner la main . . .

> If everyone in the world would reach out and hold hands
>   we could make a ring around the world . . .

Instead we form small circles which, by their very nature, exclude others. Can the church exonerate itself from such a criticism? I believe those people I have just listed have many things in common. They can be described as marginalised – on the very margin of the circle of society; or as outcasts – thrown outside that circle. Experience has led them to believe that they are unacceptable because they are abnormal, different from the rest of humankind. In 1 Cor. 12:26, we read, 'If one part is hurt, all the parts share its pain.' Such people feel quite literally 'out on a limb' and cannot believe that the rest of the body is aware of their existence, let alone shares their pain. What do they ask for? To be drawn into the circle, to be led back from their terrifying isolation, to have living proof that we are all parts of one body and that they are no exception. What can we offer? If you are like me, you are often left feeling totally inadequate to the task; afraid perhaps. Faced with the vast ocean of human suffering or even the immense suffering of one other person, what can I do that will make any difference? A picture comes into my mind of a small boy pulled out of the crowd by Andrew and brought to stand in front of Jesus. He clutches a snack for himself and his brothers, some bread and two small fish. He hears enough of the grown-ups' talk to understand that everyone is very hungry. What possible use can his snack be to all these thousands of people? But amazingly Jesus does seem to want what he has brought. The little boy holds it out in an attitude of eager anticipation. Only a child could be so ridiculous – there were five thousand hungry people to feed . . .

Bread and fish – simple basic things, nothing out of the way, the food of ordinary folk. Like the small boy, we are in the place where Jesus is; we possess just what he needs to feed the hungry. What does he need?

- that we should care, care enough to want to do something;
- that we should have compassion, feeling with that other person, listening more readily than speaking;
- that we should be kind – 'O Jesus, how one misses a bit of loving-kindness, instead of this god-awful welfare' – wrote a long-term prisoner in a letter to *The Times*;
- that we should be willing to draw alongside and offer companionship.

The word companion comes from the Latin 'to share bread'. Bread is symbolic of that which we need for survival, a basic food. I believe that you and I are called to share bread with others. We can all do that. We have exactly what Jesus needs to perform miracles, just as the little boy had. We just have to have the courage to offer what we have.

Tim was five when he died. Two-and-a-half years previously his baby sister had been found dead in her cot. His mother not only lost two of her children, but her father and her sister, in the space of those two-and-a-half years. A year later she went to her doctor and said, 'I'm depressed'. He looked back in her medical records and commented that all that had happened a long time ago. He gave her anti-depressants and referred her to a psychiatrist. Six weeks later, she swallowed the contents of a bottle of aspirin. Someone found her in time; they pumped her out and got her on her feet again. Within two days she was back at the kitchen sink. 'I didn't want anti-depressants or a psychiatrist,' she said. 'What I wanted was the odd neighbour who would drop in unannounced on her way to the shops and have a cup of tea. What I wanted was that, when I took the other children to school, the mums at the school gate wouldn't scatter as if I had two heads or a contagious disease or something.'

Not anti-depressants or a psychiatrist, just a fellow human being who would share life as it really was and would call in for a cup of tea. Share your bread.

A loving and faithful priest who had had years of anxiety over the behaviour of one of his children said that countless people had said to him, 'I'll pray for you'. 'But you know', he said, 'it's just not enough.' It's not enough. Not enough if we think we've done our bit once we've 'referred' it to God. If we really pray, then it involves far more than that. J. Neville Ward wrote, 'To bring the world before God in prayer is to stand where you can hear most clearly the most tragic voice in the universe, God's despair of man. "Whom shall I send and who will go for us?"' If we really pray, we take a big risk because by so doing we are saying, 'Here am I, send me.' God may take us at our word. Sometimes this will lead to practical action, however simple, like dropping in for a cup of tea. Even this can be a costly gesture, because by the very act of coming alongside someone who is suffering and laying ourselves open to their pain, we almost inevitably absorb some of that pain. In praying for a person experiencing black depression, we should not be surprised if we find ourselves rocked for a time by that same experience of blackness.

We could go on enumerating all too familiar examples of people who have been left outside the circle of humanity, not least by those of us who call ourselves Christians:

- the father, whose handicapped teenage son had died two hours previously, seeing people walking up the garden path, said, 'Oh, they're from the Church. What a pity they didn't come before. He loved company, you know. They did say they were praying for him.' All this was said without a trace of rancour or even surprise;
- the members of a church congregation who prayed regularly, Sunday by Sunday, for the homeless, but who were the first to protest when there was a proposal to establish a drop-in centre in their neighbourhood;
- the convicted murderer who broke down and cried like a child because someone thanked him for the kindness and concern he had shown for them – 'in seventeen years, no one has suggested I was anything other than a monster who should never have been allowed to exist'.

'If one part is hurt, all the parts share its pain, and if one part is honoured all the parts share its joy.'

Caring is about glorying in the fact that we are fully human and that it is in and through our shared humanity that we can reach out to others. It is in and through our shared humanity, the humanity Jesus himself shared and shares, that God can work.

It has been my experience in working with families whose child or children have suffered with fatal illness that tragedy often transcends the usual barriers we erect, barriers of race, religion, education, background, politics and so many others. In tragedy, such barriers have no place. Stripped of sophistication and complexity, we share the most basic experience of what it means to be who we are. Sharing bread in the midst of suffering, we enable one another to lift the heavy mask of pretence we so often wear. What is revealed is beauty, goodness, truth, nobility and love – yes, in every child, woman and man, whatever their appearance may have been before the mask was discarded. And then maybe, just maybe, it begins to dawn on us that what we see in the unmasked face of our companion is the face of Christ. Has he not told us that we are made in the image and likeness of our Creator? Has he not told us that what we do for others we do for him? Let us pray, dear sisters and brothers, pray that each of us will recognise our calling to care; pray that each of us may believe that we possess in ourselves, just as we are, the very things God needs if we are to be the channels of His caring.

As we share bread together with one another and with those for whom we care, maybe our eyes will be opened and we shall recognise Jesus just as the two disciples did, those disciples whose companion on the way to Emmaus was their Lord.

On Really Believing in God

David Jenkins

I believe that one thing that people will notice when they come to reflect back on Robert Runcie's time as Archbishop is that, in his own way and style, he was quietly but constantly concerned with something much deeper than keeping the Church of England (and the Anglican Communion) together, although any Archbishop of Canterbury inevitably appears to be spending a great deal of his time and energy on that. The point of seeing this as a vocation lies, however, in an understanding of God and the Tradition which guides us in knowing Him, worshipping Him and learning about Him so as to be able to serve Him. The mystery of God requires that the Tradition must be received both faithfully and openly – hence by a diversity of responses which need to be kept in living relation with one another. Certainly, whatever he thought of my style and my timing, Robert Runcie always encouraged me in my explorations of this 'dynamic of God'. So it seems appropriate to offer a recent attempt to reflect further on this in a sermon I gave in May 1990 in Lincoln Cathedral at the Lincoln Theological College Festival.

The fool hath said in his heart, there is no God (Psalms 14 and 53)

I asked for the readings for our Festival Eucharist today to be taken from the ASB readings for the commemoration of a teacher of the Faith. I suggested that choice because I am sure that all of us who have had our preparation for ordination at the Chancellor's School at Lincoln, commonly known as Lincoln Theological College, and all of us who are now concerned with the training of ordinands, both at this Theological College and anywhere else, must have a central concern about what it is that is involved in teaching the Faith today.

What is supposed to be put over, in what way, to whom and with what hoped for effect? What is it to be a confessor and teacher of the Faith today? It is in connection with this question about teaching and confessing the Faith that I put forward my text from the Psalms. A famous one enough, 'The fool hath said in his heart, there is no God'. Now I know that the text can be positively expounded, both in its own context in the relevant Psalms and in relation to the use Anselm made of it in his so-called ontological argument for belief in God. But I think it can also be taken as a text that is typical of complacency, blinkeredness and concealed fear as displayed by the religious. Anyone who is an atheist, so it is claimed, is a fool – an empty person without weight, insight or reflectiveness, and immoral to boot, as the Psalm goes on to suggest. Or as you might put it, *Dixit insipiens* (as the common Latin version given as a heading to the BCP which some of us continue to use, puts it). Anyone who says in his or her heart that there is no God is the opposite of wise. He or she has no *sapientia*. And any truly *homo-sapiens* (which must of course include *mulier sapiens* these days) would acknowledge God.

Now surely, this is plain, complacent, conceited and insensitive nonsense. The case for there being no God is well nigh overwhelming and is underlined by the behaviour and history of religious persons, traditions and institutions, not least the Christian Church.

Just consider very briefly the pile of evidence which suggests that believing in God is bad for humanity. The history of Christianity is very worrying; it includes the Crusades, the Inquisitions and anti-Semitism. There has been, and there continues to be, great intra-Christian rivalry often conducted with bad temper, ill will and violence. Believers so often organise to display loyalty to God and the Faith by illiberality, bullying and persecution. Whether in matters of Faith or in matters of morals, religious commitment seems to be an excuse to be nasty to people who are alleged, shall we say, to have queer ideas or follow queer practices. These habits are not confined to Christianity, but are endemic in Religions. Islam rejoices in its Jihads, has quite a record of forcible conversions and shows a pretty ugly face in much of its current revivalism; and its treatment of women is very troubling. Not that Christianity is entitled to any self-righteousness here. The ambiguities of the Jews, Zionism and the nation state of Israel are alarmingly obvious. The Intifada is troubling, persistent and miserable. We can see if we follow the newspapers how elderly Rabbis controlling small, deeply committed religious parties can block the formation of any secular government to deal with devastatingly pressing problems of peace and living together. We see fanaticism feeding political incompetence and personal misery. Then there is the nearly overwhelming realisation that the Jews, the Christians and the Muslims all claim to worship the one true and only God, and therefore, necessarily, the same God whose alleged heavenly demands are supposed to justify hellish behaviour. One has to spend very few days in Jerusalem (as I have recently done) – that Holy City – before one finds oneself not on the edge of, but in the middle of, practical atheism. Is not all this simply tribal warfare directed by self-interest? Self-interest in this world conveniently linked to a belief that we (always the 'we' to which *we* belong) are chosen for benefit and privilege, not only in this world, but also in the next. This is clearly a spiritual con-trick.

Religious people and institutions are therefore strong and persistent contributors to the case for atheism. But the case is very much there on what we might call more secular grounds. We now know about the space–time scale of the universe. Does not this trivialise and randomise us and call in question any notion of a personal presence, possibility and promise, who is God overall, in all and through all? Suppose one replies (as I personally do) 'no', it is not the time–space scale which is the ultimate clue, but our human capacity for knowledge, value, wonder and love. We are in the image of God and so can, and do, pick up the echoes and offers of God.

If one replies like this, then we are confronted by what this so-called image of God actually does. We are multiplying the poor, using up the earth and continuing our wars and our greed, after a long (from our point of view) history of wars and greed. If there is a God, and He can properly be thought of as a Creator, surely we are His mistake? And if He makes mistakes like that, how can He be God, or indeed, be at all – especially and finally, when the world is so full of the realities of torture and so many torturing realities?

I have begun to think that we men and women of religious faith know only too well how strong is the case for atheism. We are therefore full of more or less concealed anxiety and fear, and so we play games to keep ourselves whistling in the dark. This is why we get so worked up about internal religious disputes. Disputes over the ordination of women, changes in the liturgy or angry controversies about doctrinal or biblical interpretations. First, these are matters which only religious people would get really worked up about. And, second, we get worked up about them so neurotically, angrily and ungraciously. In fact, our disputes, and especially our manner of conducting them are, I suspect, displacement activities. If you read about animal behaviour you will see that chimpanzees under pressure, and when confused, first of all take to mutual nit-picking (which actually continues to bind them together as a fellowship) and then, as the trouble gets worse, start growling at one another and biting one another. Displacement activity. As we know – and you have only to go to General Synod! (But that is by the way. It is right not to take this solemnly because sin will not have dominion over us, but it has to be taken very seriously.) As we know our Faith is threatened, and as we strongly suspect that the threats are more powerful than the Faith, we displace our fears, anxieties and self-deceits on to one another. We are not sure in our hearts and souls about the reality of God and His Gospel, so we tend to argue with one another about what is proper evangelism and what is not. Much easier than trying to get on with it. More energy is put into arguing with fellow Christians about whether our version of the Faith or your version of the Faith is right and proper, than is put into common efforts expressed in a variety of ways to share in the sharing of God with a hostile, indifferent or difficult world. The odds are thus alarmingly against there being a God, and our Christian behaviour by and large shows that we actually and persistently share that alarm.

So the question for all of us who hold ourselves to be called to be teachers and confessors of Faith in God, in the name of Jesus Christ through the power of the Spirit, is how to teach in the face of, and in the context of, all this. Of course, behind that question lies the sharp, simple and profound question: 'Do we actually believe in God?' Or perhaps better: 'What is it to believe in God, and are we on to it or part of it?'

Here the critical issue seems to me to be: can we and do we worship? Can we and do we worship? Or at times do we long to worship and hope that we shall be able to worship again? For it is no use pretending that we always feel worshipful or always find that worshipping is immediately full of attraction, joy, purpose and meaning. It is a question of an underlying meaning, commitment, purpose and hope. This is a conviction, purpose and hope about worth. A worth which is so worthwhile that it is infinitely worth living for and therefore absolutely and obviously worth dying for. (Not that one is living up to the worth in one's actual life, nor that one could be clear that one could die for it if the need arose. But the worth engenders the hope of grace to live up to it and of power to die for it.) This worth is God; God who is the source and end of all 'worth-ship'. He is the offer of worth beyond all measure and yet within the gracious possibilities of enjoyment and sharing by His Will and gift. This is the God who is, so to speak, behind, beyond and within the dynamics of the biblical revelation – the God who is as he is in Jesus. The God who shares with us in the immanence and intimacy of the Spirit. He is the power, the presence, the possibility and the promise who has been encountered in the midst of all things that argue against Him. He is the God who persists in getting through to men and women who have emerged in His image, and continues to do so despite all they do – all we do – to forget Him, flee Him, spit in His face, demean His image and distort His word. This is the God who is so sure of His work and commitment to worth, which is Holy and steadfast love, that He will risk His all in being Jesus. The God who risks His all in passion and crucifixion. This is the God who will persevere with the wretchedness and stupidly conceited faithlessness of the Church in the simplicity of Sacramental gift, shared fellowship and the possibilities of prayer. This is God, Father, Son and Holy Spirit, greater than great in his mysterious transcendence, more loving than love in the particularity of His Incarnation and persistent offering, closer than close in the persevering and painstaking intimacy of the Spirit. The response to this God – the very possibility of believing in this God, the continuing hope of serving and sharing this God – lies in worship. A lively worship together in the name of the Trinity. A worship which celebrates and rehearses what has been learnt of Him and is focused in His Sacramental gifts, combined with a lively personal discipleship which seeks worshipfulness. A discipleship which lives and longs to become part of this God's worth, part of the work of His worth, of the longing and of the persevering of this worth. This is what the Lord's Prayer is about. To be part of the coming of His Kingdom.

So, our teaching must be informed by worship, given its form, its direction and its spirit by worshipping. Like the God we worship, and by His intimate grace, we must teach in full openness to all that is going on – including all the sins of religion and all the threats of the world. God risked openness in Creation. He demonstrated that this costs passion and death in the Incarnation. He asserts Himself as love and life in the Resurrection. He continues to live, work, plead and promise in the Spirit. So our teaching must be open, wrestling, suffering, engaged, passionate and always hopeful. Always hopeful – no matter how much it sometimes has to be given in the depths and when we are in the dumps. Teaching must open people up. Open them up to God, to their best selves, to the world. Godly teaching informed by worship cannot restrict, confine or distort. It is so dreadful when people get religion and become less than themselves.

However, such teaching will, of course, challenge, confront, disturb and sometimes terrify. For Godly love which is passionately striving for the worshipful worth of all, must often be received as wrath, judgement and threat. Love is wholly against the destruction of worth. But the wrath of love is for repentance of the sinner and for the fulfilment of love. Consider how Jesus in New Testament terms is to come as the Judge, but it is the Saviour who is the Judge and the Judge who is the Saviour. Judgement is for salvation, but salvation comes through wrath, Godly fear, repentance and change. So teaching can be tough but it must be informed by worship and grace. It cannot be one up, strident, moralistic, self-righteous and rather enjoying telling people off – this brings us back to religious perversion and betrayal of God the Holy Trinity.

Godly teaching can go only with confession of Faith, in commitment of life, persistent daily discipleship, sustained learning and simple worship. It is in the simple worship of God the Holy Trinity, Father Son and Holy Spirit, that there can be glimpsed from time to time the sheer folly of saying, 'there is no God'. Of course God is, as Father, as the Son in Jesus and as the Holy Spirit. All the depths, heights, struggles, hopes, passions and sufferings of men and women in the world, and of the very world itself, are full of Him – although in hidden and surprisingly humble ways. For God seeks to share the worth of His love through the risks of Creation, the distortions of sin and the mysteries of freedom. God offers us teachers the chance, the grace and the worship to be fools for

Christ's sake; not to be religiously superior to people who have more reasons than enough to be atheists.

So let us pray that in our Ministries we do not add to the case for atheism, but that we can be of some service to God and our fellows because we glimpse the Glory of God, Father Son and Holy Spirit. Amen.

Breadth and Sanity

John Habgood

*This Sermon was preached on All Saints' Day 1989 in All Saints',
Margaret Street, London as part of the commemoration of a volume of
essays entitled* Lux Mundi, *first published in 1889. The title was given
to me.*

*Lux Mundi was a milestone in Anglican theology. It represented a
major attempt by the catholic wing of the Church to move into a more
liberal and questioning intellectual atmosphere, and it forcefully reaffirmed
an incarnational and sacramentally rooted faith. Its editor was Charles
Gore, who went on to be Bishop of Oxford and was much associated with
Cuddesdon.*

*Robert Runcie, I believe, stands in this liberal, catholic tradition. The
particular aspect of it, breadth and sanity, which was set me as my task
describes not only the tradition, but the man.*

*Robert Runcie is catholic in the true sense of that word, a man grounded
in a large tradition, and with large sympathies, able to embrace and to
convey something of the richness of our Christian heritage with the kind
of balance and common sense which such a rootedness makes possible.*

*It would be untrue to claim that I wrote the sermon with him in mind,
but I immediately picked it out when asked to contribute to this volume.*

The late George Woods, a charming and gentle Christian philosopher, once remarked that we tend to take sanity too much for
granted. It is quite an achievement to be sane, he said.

I thought of him when I was asked to preach this evening on
breadth and sanity. They sound such comfortable virtues – calcu-
lated, in the immortal words of Willie Whitelaw, 'to stir up world-
wide apathy'. How can one get excited about being broad and sane?

Perhaps they are harder virtues to acquire nowadays than in
the days of *Lux Mundi*. Perhaps not. We live among competing
fanaticisms. We are conscious of the strength of the hard and narrow
line in a world where much has grown soft and shapeless. Many
are disorientated by relentless change.

But in 1889 Gore and his companions also felt they were living
through a time of crisis. They, like us, had to face the problems of
articulating a sane and truly catholic faith which took seriously the
intellectual ferment in which they were living. And it is fascinating
to see how in Scott Holland's opening essay on 'Faith' he was

anxious to expose himself to all that world of ferment and new discovery.

How, he asked, is a steady faith possible when all the old land-marks are being removed? How can we hold to faith with integrity when the great advances in knowledge require openness, uncom-mittedness, a readiness to revise one's most cherished opinions?

Don't panic, he said. And don't retreat. Faith is not a theory. It is not some addition to knowledge on a level with scientific knowl-edge. It is our primary consciousness of being related to God. It is the condition of our knowledge, not the fruit of it. In Scott Holland's words, 'it lies *behind* our secular life, secreted within it'. And it comes out into the open through the long history of religion which he described as 'the story of its slow and gradual advance in sanity and clearness, until it culminates in that special disclosure which we call Revelation'. He goes on: 'If religion means this coming forward into the foreground of that which is the universal background of all existence, then we cut ourselves free from the perplexity which benumbs us . . . ', we can begin to see the sanctity and worth of the whole natural world. 'All of it is God-given, God-inspired, God-directed; all of it is holy. But the *fact* of this being so is one thing: the *recognition* of it is another; and it is this recognition of God in things which is the essence and core of religion.'

I have quoted Scott Holland because his essay on 'Faith' in *Lux Mundi* sets the tone for the rest of the book. And it is broad, all-embracing, open to new knowledge, not afraid of change, because it is rooted in a reality which does not change – in a living relation-ship with God through Christ. Religion has a history, and that is why we need to take our Christian tradition seriously. But the object of faith is not religion, not a set of ideas, not the creeds, not even the Bible. It is Christ and him alone. And in him lies true health of soul, true sanity.

Breadth and sanity are indeed proper themes for this celebration. But to celebrate them on All Saints' Day feels at first a bit odd. Sanity and sanctity are not natural bedfellows. In fact many saints have been distinctly strange.

Were Joan of Arc's voices schizophrenic, or did she really hear the voice of God? Were the Middle Eastern ascetics who sat for years on the tops of pillars praying and eating nothing but beans, mad or marvellously holy? Were those hundreds of eager evangelists who rushed off to distant parts of the world in the nineteenth century, to die within a few months in fever-ridden swamps, fools or heroes? Sometimes it is hard to tell the difference. There is a deep foolishness in being Christian at all, as St Paul himself well understood.

Saints are uncomfortable people, at times terrifyingly single-minded, absurdly indifferent to what the world counts as sane and reasonable.

> Blessed are the poor in spirit . . .
> Blessed are they that mourn . . .
> Blessed are the meek . . .
> Blessed are the pure in heart . . .
> Blessed are you when you are persecuted . . .

This is not a recipe for comfortable sanity. This is about turning the world upside down; about a kind of madness which proves in the end to be the only true wisdom.

Saints are often highly tensile people, people who live at the edge, who have looked in the abyss, and whose very brokenness allows God to possess them more fully. There is an extra petition in the litany which runs, 'From living saints, Good Lord deliver us'. Awkward people to have around.

Fortunately there are also less dramatic forms of sanctity, quiet and good people, filled with the love of God, who just get on and live their lives without fuss, radiating God's presence. I think of All Saints' Day as especially for them, and in them sanctity and sanity are not such an ill-assorted pair.

But we can't escape the holy fools, and the foolishness of faith itself. A broad sane religion which misses out on this aspect of faith has lost its bearings, has ceased to be faith in a crucified Christ – to the world utter foolishness, but in reality the power of God and the wisdom of God.

Perhaps we can get nearer to the heart of Christian sanity by thinking for a moment about insanity. Some insane people are terrifyingly rational, trapped in a system of delusions which it is impossible to penetrate with counter-arguments, sometimes they are alarmingly plausible, yet all our instincts tell us they are out of touch with reality.

There are religious systems like this, closed circles, accessible only to those who surrender all powers of criticism on stepping inside, radically cut off from so-called normal assumptions and perceptions. Sane or insane? It is not always easy to tell, and when we think we know, the unexpected presence of real sanctity may surprise us.

It is easier to see the insanities in the world at large. What are we to make of a so-called rational civilisation trapped in a lunatic search for happiness and self-fulfilment through things which can never satisfy it? Trapped in a kind of logic which excludes all that is most humanly precious? We watch millions die of poverty and starvation because the logical constraints on our behaviour don't allow us to help them. In such a world, a bit of foolishness may be the only true sanity.

Or think secondly of the roots of madness in deep and unresolved hurts. We are told that inside every insane person is a crying and frightened child. So what is sanity? The facing of pain. The acknowledgment and resolution of conflict. The rejoicing in forgiveness. The acceptance of self, because the self is accepted by God.

Here are the roots of that inner security, that unchanging foundation of life which Scott Holland identified as faith. It is a faith which, if truly centred on God's gift of Himself through Christ, frees us from self-preoccupation to explore and accept the world in all its wonder and breadth.

We live in a hurt world which needs the healing touch of Christ. Only so can it become sane.

A third and final feature of insanity, all part of this picture of closed logic and inner hurt, is its loneliness and isolation. To be mad is to live in one's own world, a narrow, self-made, self-contained world, reflecting only one's own obsessions.

To live in difficult times can induce a sense of isolation and self-pity. Sometimes the forces against us seem too strong. Sometimes our faith can seem beleaguered and we are tempted, as Elijah was, to cry out to God, 'I, even I only, am left'. In such moments remember God's answer to Elijah, and take courage from All Saints' Day. The great things about this particular celebration of sanctity are the sheer weight of it – 'a great multitude which no man can number' – and the sheer variety of it – 'of all nations and kindreds and peoples and tongues'. We need this great company of people, and we need their diversity, if we are truly to be ourselves as God would have us be.

Sanity and breadth belong together. Thank God then that He has set us within a broad, a catholic, Church. Thank God that we can find our true selves and give our true selves within a great stream of devotion, whose boundaries lie beyond our horizon, and which flows into the limitless sea of God's love. Yes sanity *is* an achievement: a triumph of God's grace.

The God Within

Don Cupitt

In the autumn of 1980 my book Taking Leave of God *appeared and caused much controversy. Bishop John Robinson, the Dean of Trinity College, had been through it all before. He gave me encouragement, and invited me to preach in the College Chapel. The sermon that follows shows that in those days I was still close to Kant and Kierkegaard in outlook.*

I cannot pretend that Robert Runcie (my own former College Dean) liked the book. He didn't. But he has stood for a liberal and spiritual conception of religious belief, he has argued that academic theologians need freedom of expression, and he has manifestly not gone along with those who want to turn the Christian faith into a rigid and repressive ideology. He has been a true Anglican, and for that we salute him.

During these last few weeks there has been a small commotion over a recent book of mine which teaches a version of Christian existentialism. It says that to believe in God is simply freely to impose upon oneself an infinite requirement, the task of becoming spirit. The implications of the thesis are made rather explicit, and the book has been called atheistic. One section of the Church press is praying for me and another, less charitably, is demanding my resignation. So I imagine you may be expecting to hear what I have to say for myself.

The book is called *Taking Leave of God* and is an attempt to write a modern spirituality – a risky business. The title echoes a line from the medieval mystic Meister Eckhart: 'Man's last and highest parting comes when, for God's sake, he takes leave of God.' I understand that to mean that in the end we must give up objectivity and external guarantees, because the highest religious truth is inward. The summit of the religious life is pure spirit without distinction of subject and object.

This introduces the point that the book is a long critique of excessively objectifying or realistic views about God and religious belief. Many people's religious ideas are very literalistic. They think it essential to faith that one should first of all accept a long series of supernatural facts – assertions about supernatural beings and supernaturally-caused events. These supernatural facts, these objective dogmas, are seen as the *sine qua non* of faith. Unless they are true, religion is illusory, and unless you accept them, you are not a believer at all.

I have brought forward many arguments against this idea. One obvious one is that under present conditions it is, to say the least, not easy to establish the truth of even one of these supernatural beliefs. In almost every possible way they are topics of sharp controversy and shrouded in doubt and obscurity. How could we ever rationally commit our whole lives on the basis of such uncertainties? Can it be right to set such strict – and indeed impossible – intellectual conditions for honest entry upon the Christian life?

Put it the other way round and we may ask ourselves, 'Is the Christian life worth living for its own sake?' Surely, 'Yes'. For Christian holiness requires of us purity of heart, inner integrity, active love and complete unselfishness. These qualities of character not only *may* but positively *must* be sought disinterestedly and for their own sakes. But in that case acceptance of the supernatural doctrines and motives cannot be the necessary basis for holiness in quite the way people suppose. Holiness must in the end be pursued for its own sake and be its own reward.

I think people are already seeing this point. In modern times the fear of Hell has suddenly disappeared as a motive for living the Christian life. We no longer seem to need it. It seems that we are already making the transition to a more adult and disinterested religious outlook.

These and other considerations lead me to propose a switch in the way we see religion. I want to put spirituality and the lived life of religion first, and then treat the doctrines as symbolic expressions of the spirituality. I do not say, '*Because* the supernatural doctrines are first descriptively true, *therefore* it makes good sense to live the Christian life.' I say instead that the spirituality, the ethics and the ritual of religion come first. They are what attract us in the first place, and they must be pursued for their own sakes. The doctrines need to be interpreted symbolically. They communicate to us what the religious ideal is and how to attain it. We join in the language of worship by way of pledging our allegiance and deepening our commitment to the Christian life.

So I am led to a symbolist and regulative view of religious truth. God symbolises the religious ideal and its claim upon us and guides us in the spiritual life. I must confess that I am quite uncertain about the objective metaphysical reality of a personal God as a distinct individual being, though the book retains the possibility of a hidden Transcendent God. But so far as the day-to-day life of religion is concerned what I mean by God is something like the Pearl of Great Price, the religious ideal that guides us and is our goal.

At this point I want to introduce the second theme of the book, which is an attempt to synthesise the modern spirituality of liberation with the traditional Christian spirituality.

I mean this: for a long time now the basic drive of modern people has been a struggle for personal freedom and autonomy, a struggle that has involved rebellion against all traditional authorities whether political or religious. People passionately demand liberation and self-possession. They want to control their own lives and they want to become free, self-expressing, fully-conscious spiritual subjects. The ideal is to become fully oneself, in full control of one's own life.

This modern drive for liberation and individual human rights is so strong that the Churches have at least partly endorsed it. Yet it is plainly difficult to reconcile with the traditional Christian outlook. For the language of Christianity is steeped in a masters-and-servants vision of the universe, in which our highest happiness is to serve One above us whose will is our law and our destiny. Traditional Christianity (understood literally) seems to have a colonialist view of man as someone who needs to be ruled from outside by a superior Power, whereas what modern man above all desires is autonomy. Traditional Christianity offers only the discipline of being someone else's servant. It proposed 'the handmaid of the Lord' as the ideal believer.

So is it possible to reconcile Christianity and freedom? Can Christianity offer anything to the modern autonomous person in his or her quest for liberation? On my account, 'Yes', for I emphasise that religious commitment must be a free and self-imposed acceptance of the religious demand for holiness, our own highest spiritual fulfilment. God's call to holiness *exactly* coincides with my will to freedom.

In support, I point to the theme of internalisation in the Bible. Instead of being constrained by an external Law that cannot save, people will be filled with a new spirit. Hearts of stone will be replaced by hearts of flesh. The external Temple and external circumcision will be replaced by inward equivalents. The movement from Letter to Spirit, outward to inward, is a powerful biblical theme.

I have also used the phrase 'Christian Buddhism'. I do not mean that I am a Buddhist. I just mean that Buddhism is an inner discipline, it stresses autonomy, and it exalts spirituality above theological doctrine. Similarly, I would like to see Christians turn away from their obsessive attempts to convince themselves and others about objective supernatural facts. Even if we had them I do not think they would really help much – and I do not really think we can get them. Instead, more attention should be paid to ethics and spirituality, for religious truth is in the end subjective, not objective.

At any rate, I attempted in the book to achieve a *tour de force*, a synthesis of the spirit of Christianity with the spirit of freedom, so that a fully-secular person might think it possible to pursue the Christian path to sanctity for its own sake. It was a bold idea – perhaps too bold. Some people are dismissing it as merely destructive, as atheism, and in general as of no value. If they are right, then it's back to the drawing-board for me. I tried to demythologise dogma into spirituality and to claim that the spirituality can be pursued for its own sake. I looked for an undogmatic Christian faith. If I was wrong, then it should at least be noted that the problems I was trying to deal with still remain to be solved.

In closing, I should add that I love Christian prayer and worship. But I think it vital to see that the language of worship is poetic and expressive rather than technical and descriptive. Worship is a way of acting out and deepening our commitment to the Christian life and it teaches us spiritual values in symbolic language. In former days people used the language of myth and symbolism with unconscious ease. But nowadays critical thinking makes us aware of the merely metaphorical and human character of our own ideas, in religion as in other matters. This new self-awareness has involved a certain fall from innocence, but it cannot be helped, and I am arguing that we can profit from it.

However, since I am so cautious about all doctrinal questions I cannot have any very strong itch to undermine other people's convictions. So if what I have said has offended you, disregard it. Just allow me to say that for the people of the Bible the commitment of the will to the new life of personal integrity and unselfish love was at least a very large part of faith. In Jesus' name. Amen.

The Hinge of Faith

Angela Tilby

The book of Job is endlessly fascinating. One of the themes it considers is the scope and limitation of practical wisdom. Job is a patriarch, a God-fearing man of the world, whose judgements are universally considered to be sound and sane. Perhaps it needs such a man to bear what Jung calls God's trial of human courage. Perhaps only through such a man could the frailty of human endeavour be exposed.

I offer this sermon, which was preached before the University of Cambridge in May 1990, to honour the retiring Archbishop as a man of practical wisdom and courage. I am sure there have been periods when he has felt that courage tried by the world, the media, and the Church itself. Within the trial I suspect there may also have been an encounter with the mystery of God. As he will know, and as he has often implied, God cannot answer all our questions, but He is Himself the resource by which we learn to live more creatively.

Job 40

There are people, and I am one of them, who see the book of Job as the pivotal book of the Bible, a horizontal hinge on which the whole divine and human logic of our Christian faith swings open and shut. A theological and spiritual catflap, if you like.

Job tells an odd story. The hero is a great patriarch who is singled out by God to be *tested*, to discover whether his faith is based on self-interest or not. In the course of the test Job loses all his possessions, wealth and family (except his wife, who is rather a trial to him. It is a very patriarchal book). The opening scene makes it clear that Job is the victim of an unnerving bet between God and Satan, who is cast here in the role of the heavenly policeman, spy and assassin.

Job responds with exemplary resignation and patience, so much so that a second test is arranged in heaven with the result that he is afflicted with a dreadful skin disease. Three friends, experts in moral theology and pastoral counselling, come to console him. In different ways they all urge him to seek the cause of his sufferings in his own character and actions. They know what all the religions know, that this universe of ours is a moral cosmos, founded on laws that cannot be broken. They also know that we reap what we sow.

Their task with Job is the task of moral and psychological analysts, to help him see where he has gone wrong. According to Stephen Mitchell, who has produced a splendid new translation of the book, their argument goes like this: God is just. Suffering comes from God. Therefore Job is guilty. They urge him to confess his frailty and repent. This Job steadfastly refuses to do. He will not accept the role that has been allotted to him, but insists on his integrity and unswerving fidelity both to God and to the laws of God. *His* argument, again, according to Mitchell, goes like this: Suffering comes from God. I am innocent. Therefore God is unjust. This conclusion causes him enormous pain. He is on the knife-edge of blasphemy. On that knife-edge he stays for thirty-six chapters, breaking out frequently in bitter and suicidal anger against life and God, and demanding that God explain Himself. There is no answer from heaven. The friends patiently continue their counselling session, while Job continues to behave as if he is in a law court marshalling forensic evidence. His mounting desperation is paralleled by a growing confidence in the justice of his case – and then in the 38th chapter God appears, out of the whirlwind, to stun and amaze Job with a series of impossible questions. Job is silenced. He withdraws his charge against God, and acknowledges that he is satisfied with God's answer. God vindicates Job; and criticises his friends for speaking incorrectly about God and His ways. Job's fortunes are restored, and he dies, as a great patriarch should, in good old age.

This tragedy, farce or black comedy (and part of the problem is that we don't know which it is) has comforted and infuriated Jews, Christians and sceptics for over 2,000 years. If Job is some kind of moral hinge then the 40th chapter is the hinge on which the hinge rests. Here is the climax of the book. The encounter between God and Job. God from the whirlwind, Job from the dung-heap. A series of impossible questions from God, Job's awe-struck response and lapse into silence, and then another battery of questions from God, ending with a description of the great Behemoth. Well. I don't expect the examiners for the theological tripos in the University of Cambridge would be unduly impressed if, faced with a searingly difficult question about the aetiology of evil, one were to respond with a description of the red hippopotamus.

But God is God. And one of the things about this apparently rather unsatisfactory encounter is that God and Job are clearly *themselves*. Neither speaks through solicitors. God conducts His own defence. And Job, who thought he was the defendant and finds he is the prosecutor, is appalled into silence both by the likeness which enables them to communicate and the difference, which is never relieved.

I know this enounter is painfully difficult for us. It is all so profoundly unhelpful. We look for consolation in our sufferings and what we seem to meet here is a divine trick, a harshness and abrasiveness, which moves our heart on behalf of Job and against his odd and violent God. Yet the exasperation we feel with the character of God is very much a modern phenomenon. Earlier ages read Job differently. They wanted it to be a book of consolation and encouragement, and that's what they found – even though it required them seriously to distort the story and the two main characters. Never mind. It kept intact a religious framework which made meaning out of the experience of suffering and enabled people to bear it bravely. 'You have heard of the patience of Job . . . ' says St James in his epistle, exhorting his readers, who seem to have been victims of greed and injustice, to wait patiently for the coming of the Lord. And since then everyone has believed that Job was patient in spite of the fact that his patience runs out at the end of Chapter 2 and there are 36 very impatient chapters to follow. So Job has not been heard in our tradition; at least only part of him has been heard. Why should this be? Many scholars believe that the author of Job took an old pagan myth of a patient man tested by a god, and injected into it this passionate moral dialogue, in order to question the assumptions of the myth itself. But what is remembered is the myth, not the protest.

Gregory the Great lectured endlessly to his retinue of monks on Job. He felt it was a suitable text for troubled and disturbed times. And for him Job is a type of Christ, an example of faithful endurance. He has read the book, but he knows that the literal meaning of a text is not the most important meaning, and so when Job shows signs of impatience or of an urgent desire to be dead, or when Job describes God as his enemy, or cries out against the heavenly archer, the malevolent watcher of men, Gregory warns us that to read the text in its plain sense can only engender error. He knows what the book means and he's not going to be disturbed by actually reading it. (Of course, in fairness to Gregory, he was probably working from a very poor and inaccurate text.) So Gregory acknowledges that Job's complaints are somewhat harsh to readers of little experience, but insists the Lord permitted Job's testing in loving-kindness, that even a good man remains insipid unless he is struck down and crushed by the divine hand. What a tragic picture Gregory gives of the relationship between humanity and God. In it we are truly vile; and our vileness serves to protect the untouchable beauty and integrity of God. It is a shining framework of meaning, and it has inspired some of the most sensitive and intelligent spirits in Christendom to astonishing feats of moral endurance. But it is not what the book of Job is about, or can be about for us. Job is a hinge, opening a door between earth and heaven. Gregory's reading of it makes it an electrified fence, keeping earth and heaven apart.

The reformer John Calvin reads the book with more understanding. He somehow knows that Job's story is crucial for us and for our salvation: 'The book written here shows us how we are in God's hand.'

Calvin also is delighted to find clear support for the doctrine of the supremacy of grace: 'Job is arguing a good case . . . he understands that God does not ever punish us according to the measure of our sins.'

Calvin sees all too clearly where the friends of Job go wrong. They have tied God into a moralistic framework which God Himself has overthrown. But he is deeply puzzled by Job. Calvin was a Christian gentleman and scholar, and he was attempting to found a new kind of Christian state of thoughtful, theologically sound, well-educated, cautious businessmen, and Job's behaviour does not impress him. Though his case is good, he says, it is badly handled. And he notices the fact that 'those who undertake the evil case have goodly and holy sentences . . . ' whereas 'Job ranges beyond his bounds . . . ' Job, in other words, rather loses his cool, and Calvin finds this reprehensible. So he sets out to put him right. When Job curses the day of his birth in Chapter 3 Calvin responds delightfully by praising the goodness of birthdays in general and offering a prayer thanking God for His past mercies. It seems, he concludes worriedly, 'that Job would pervert the whole order of nature'.

Poor Calvin. Yet many of us share his problem. We want assurance from religion; identity, meaning, purpose. On the whole we are prepared to pay a price for it. The price is sometimes to believe that we are wholly bad, sometimes to believe that God is arbitrary and tyrannical, sometimes to allow that God is loving in a rather wet sort of way, but has nothing to do with the problems that beset us. In the worst of our fantasies God Himself is as ignorant and confused as we are. Job's author confronts that one in the Prologue, where it is clear that God *needs* Satan, the heavenly traffic-warden, to roam around the earth looking for the trouble that He can't see Himself. In the 40th chapter there is no mention of the court of heaven. The whole panoply of heaven has rolled up and disappeared, like a cumbersome stage set, and we are left alone, vulnerable to the whirlwind, to the voice in the whirlwind and the unseen face of the Holy One within. How little we want this encounter, how much we dread the face of the Alone. For we know that the sight of that face will strip us of our fantasies and leave us with the illogical logic that we knew all the time. God is just. Suffering comes from God. Job is innocent. What is missing is the 'therefore'. In the closing chapters of the book God presents to Job a whole video display of life on earth. It is vivid, exuberant, full of surprises. The fierce and the foolish, the wise and the wonderful all have their place. The creatures are strong, funny, forgetful, violent, handicapped. And God says to Job, your moral universe with its causes and effects and its guilty ones and innocent ones and its judgements and its 'therefores'; you go and run it if you can. Be a big and powerful God like you want me to be, and abase the proud and condemn the rich, and stamp on the wicked with your great divine foot. And just to start you off, how about putting a ring through the nose of this red hippopotamus and taking him for a walk?

This is not the answer of a power-crazed divine monarch, the celestial judge of our dark and fearful imagination. It is the reply of one who has brought into being an astonishing world, and looks after it with gentleness and humour and compassion. It is not a disordered world, but it is in a sense an untidy one. It is not an immoral world but it is not quite a moral one either.

It is not the world of the great ordered religions, either of East or West, with their hierarchies and codes, rewards, punishments and ladders of perfection, in which our free choice is the pivot that raises us up or casts us down.

In Job's world we are not as important as that, and we are loved though we are not necessarily all that important. We may be dangerous and exploitative and God will talk to us because He loves us, but God also loves whales and insects, monkeys and giant pandas, and we have our place within this fascinating and evolving cosmos, but it is not the only place. Job's world is strange. And yet it is surprisingly close to the world of chance and necessity, and the space–time continuum: the world that modern science reveals to us in all its order and paradox, a world where God, as Einstein puts it, does not play dice, a world whose Lord is not malicious, but is subtle. Job is in the end a book of wisdom – and the universe that it presents is a world that interlocks. There is both a total outpouring of creative energy and a total cost in death and destruction. Yet the moral balance between death and life is not paid in the way that the law would incline us to suspect. Our interdependence goes deeper. The forgetful ostrich always has God's ultimate care. The holiest one in the universe pays the final price of it all. It is not law or karma, but a more subtle transaction on which our life is poised. 'Dying each others' life, living each others' death' is the red strand of sacrifice that runs through it all. In this sense Job is, as Gregory foresaw, a type of Christ, and his struggle with God is the struggle of all of us with the form of the mystery in which our life is set – to argue with the mystery until it reveals the face of love. For the hinge of Job is nailed to the one who says to us now and always, 'I am the door, if anyone enters by me, he, she, will be saved'.

The Resolution of Fear

Donald Soper

I have received many blessings from the church over which Dr Runcie presided. Not the least of them was the welcome continuously offered, and which made me feel at home in the church of John Wesley despite all the separations of the last 200 years. That sense of belonging to a communion, which so often seemed almost irreparably divided ecclesiastically, owes much to my personal and official relationships with Dr Runcie. The theme of this sermon is not specifically directed towards a particular concern that I shared with him. It is the opportunity to say thank you for a sense of fellowship which he inspired. Not least, I was able to preach it from an Anglican pulpit – at St Martin's-in-the-Fields, London, 26 March 1979.

The first broadcast I ever made from an Anglican pulpit was a very long time ago in the days of the beloved Dick Sheppard. I can remember, as if it was yesterday, the onset of fear. Fear that I might break down, or not find the words in which I was endeavouring to preach. I was afraid that the notes to which I was unaccustomed would disappear; I was afraid that my voice would falter; and I was afraid also of a number of things less worthy than that – that Dick Sheppard and others might think badly of me. What are the marks of that kind of fear? It is a lively apprehension of danger. We have just been singing a hymn, and incidentally it is a coincidence that when the declaration of war was made that Sunday morning in September 1939 we in Kingsway Hall were singing that hymn, 'Fear him ye saints and you will then have nothing else to fear'. I realised then that that very proper apprehension of danger which is the beginning (but not the fulfilment) of wisdom is very different from that anxiety which is an unworthy reflection upon faith. There is a world of difference between Christian fear and craven anxiety. I want to say something about that fear as it has its rightful and important place in the conduct of the would-be Christian.

Our point of reference is inevitably Jesus himself. I have lived long enough, and talked loudly and long enough, to know how important it is that when we are thinking about Christianity we stand a little askance, shall we say, from the prelates of the Church and consider that the roots of our Christian faith are not found in the behaviour pattern even of the most godly and apostolic Christian: our faith is Jesus. Archbishop Booker wrote, I have no doubt, many sermons and I came across the other day one of his phrases. It is this, 'God was kind to us in Jesus Christ'. Now in our modern translation of the word 'kind' we think of God's benevolence, His loving kindness and tender mercy. That is not quite what Booker meant, for he was an Elizabethan and he was talking in the language of Shakespeare, and the word 'kind' there has more to do with mankind than it has to do with loving kindness. And what Archbishop Booker was saying was that in Jesus Christ God came to us in our own kind. That is why I have professed for so long that if you can be sure of the humanity of Jesus his divinity will look after itself. But the imperative thing is to see Jesus as the human photograph of God – God comes to us in our own kind. Therefore, it is perfectly reasonable that we should look at the way in which Jesus faced the world, the world fundamentally the same as the one we face, and in particular tonight to enquire how Jesus looked at and dealt with and, indeed, overcame fear.

In the first instance, it was a lively sense (that seems to have been denied so many living in a permissive society) that sin is highly dangerous. In fact, it is mortally dangerous. You will allow me, an old man, to draw from reminiscences from over the years listening to questions and talking to people who have little use for Christianity and oppose it rigorously, if not very intelligently. What they say is a comment on the extraordinary fact that the world in so far as they have come across it, apart from the wickedness of other people, is one in which the edges of sin, suffering or appreciation of good and evil have been largely blurred. So much is done for the giggle, so much is reputed to be the consequence of environment. Fear is one of the constituent elements in the proper evaluation of what is good; and I wish so heartily that people would be afraid of doing what is wrong, not because of the penalties that the law or society or their friends may impose upon them, but for the old Platonic reason that it is a killing disease. And it was the purification of the intentions of Jesus, symbolised supremely, I suppose, when he accepted baptism from John, which was the clear-cut recognition that Jesus, like everybody else, has to flee from the wrath which comes to those who disobey. A very right and real fear of evil, of sin. I have it. I do not pretend for one moment that I necessarily respond as I should, but I know when I have done wrong and I am afraid of the consequences. I know that evil is not another word for circumstance; it is something deeply rooted, and the reality with which Jesus bids us escape from this net of power and of contingency – this is a word in season for us. 'Ye that do truly and earnestly repent of your sins and are in love and charity with your neighbours, draw near with faith, as we have done tonight, and take this holy sacrament to your comfort.'

But the fear of Jesus was also a fear of ignorance. The terrible consequences of even the best intentions when they are not married to intelligent purpose. That is why sentiment is no substitute for goodness, and in so many cases the road to Hell is paved with good intentions, because good intentions, unless they are fortified and strengthened by real knowledge, are false paths – deceptive byways. Many of the people who have said to me over the years that they see no reason for going to church, and are not much impressed by those who do, are really victims of this kind of mistake. They are not malevolent, they are just wrong, because they believe that if your intentions are peaceful, if you want to be good and not hurt other people, if you want to live in friendship with your neighbours, if you want to behave according to the dictates of the law – that is what is required and that is what will be done.

Now look at Jesus. Jesus says, 'We must find some guide-lines – you will find some guide-lines to your own behaviour patterns, which when they are extended and amplified belong to the Kingdom of God.' This is what the Sermon on the Mount is all about; and I repeat what I have said to some of you many times: Why don't you read it? Don't tell me you have, perhaps you have. Most people have not read it – all they have read are passages from it. How long ago was it since you sat down at the place where it says, 'And seeing the multitudes', and read straight through to the place where it says, 'And not as the scribes'? For in that parcel of words is the elucidation – not the Good News, not the Gospel – the Gospel is the Cross – but the substance of our understanding. Nothing is so dangerous, nothing should be feared more ardently than the uninstructed way of seeking the Kingdom of God. That is why Jesus told the parables he did. They are, of course, not as the schoolboy said, 'Heavenly stories with no earthly meaning'. The parables are explications in every-day language of what in our hearts and minds we would like to feel is true. Jesus explains and explicates in those tremendous utterances about the Prodigal Son and the Good Samaritan, and Seed sown in the ground. Jesus bids us learn. Some people assert that knowledge is not the prerogative of any group; certainly that is true, but they despise the more simple aspects of wisdom. I know a great many clever people who regard themselves as polymaths whereas, as a matter of fact, they have been educated rather above their intelligence. Wisdom is that perception of the ultimate truth by which you can make your way along many tortuous paths to real profundity.

And finally, and here we pass from that which is deducible, shall we say, from the teaching and spirit of Jesus to that which belongs to the higher reaches of our own senses. It is fear as something which promotes awe. One of the things that I most dislike about so many aspects of the modern world is how commonplace it is and how little people are affected. They do not genuflect in awe, shall we say, before the craftsmanship of the true poet, they only sneer at the craftiness of his words. Fear, which is the beginning of wisdom, becomes the instrument then of true adoration, and that is an element of the ultimate Christian virtue of love without which love can become meaningless. How can I love God? A very proper question to ask. I love my wife – and, bless her, she loves me – but then I can stretch out my hands to greet her, I can put my arms around her. I can sit with her and converse – she is there. And my loving, such as it is, is a caring process which has very definite and proper physical connotations. How do you love a hungry man? By giving him something to eat. How do you love somebody who is sick? Well, I have been in hospital and I know what love is; the rigorous tender care of those who minister to you; that is love. Love is a ministry. How can I love God? I have never seen Him, I cannot touch Him. And let it be said, how can I love Jesus? I would have given so much to be present as the disciples were. I sometimes think how much easier faith would be if we could hear Jesus talking. The jingle, 'He walks with me and he talks with me.' It is not strictly true. I sometimes wish that we parsons would not be so 'broadside on' in our claims that these loving conditions are possible. A better word is the word 'adore' and it is the way in which we come to love God – though we are, of course, seeing God in our fellow creatures and becoming the body of Christ, as it were, sacramentally.

There is another aspect and it is the only other aspect I can talk about tonight. It is when we are filled with a sense of fear which is compounded of awe and wonder. Let me tell you of one experience in which I was filled with that sense of adoration and awe. Many years ago I was travelling by flying boat to the Far East. Those of you who are familiar with air travel will know that sometimes the sky is filled with awesome beauty. I shall never forget the feeling when, as I looked out of the window of the plane, I looked along a great corridor of blazing awesome wonder. Mercifully for those who were around me I did not want to say anything – it would have been banal so to do, but I know what adoration means and I know that fear, that sense of aweful excitement of mind and spirit. I remember how clearly I felt that I should be on my knees that I should take my shoes from off my feet, for this was the reality of which so much of life is a show and substitute.

I have said nothing about the way in which unreal and unchristian fear should be faced and overcome, because I finally believe in what I think the psychiatrists have been telling us for a long time in their better moments – the expulsive power of a new affection. And it seems to me that the final overcoming of that fear which is so natural in this world of violence and wickedness, and in our hearts and minds, and in a society which seems to be tottering totally today – the proper answer is not to battle with fear as if that is the terrain upon which victory can be won, it is to be so sure of that kind of holy fear which we see in Jesus Christ that there is no room for that craven substitute.

So lift up your hearts. The fear of the Lord is the beginning of wisdom, that wisdom which takes us through understanding to the foot of the Cross and to meet our Lord on resurrection morning. It opens the Kingdom of God to all.

The Beauty of God

Richard Harries

Ever since that horrible man, King Henry VIII, stole the Church's money to enrich his lay friends, the Church of England has been in a state of decline. The loss of power, position, wealth and influence in the life of the nation compared to even fifty years ago, is dramatic. During the Archbishopric of Robert Runcie the Church has been lively and newsworthy. Nevertheless the decline in strength and position has continued. This is no cause for dismay. On the contrary, it brings members back to the Church of the early centuries when Christians were a vulnerable, powerless minority; it brings us back to the Cross of Christ.

Now, thank God, we cannot bully people into belief by the fear of Hell. Nor, thank God, can we force people into faith through fear of the social and economic consequences of failing to conform. Far from being fashionable, the Church of England is continually reviled by the semi-cultured despisers who shape so much of our public consciousness. Within this context the faith has to shine in its own clear light or not at all. Robert Runcie's manner and style has been entirely appropriate for this new context. He has not been proud. He has not presumed. He has been natural, disarming in his self-mockery, warm and humane.

Today when there are so many interesting distractions to fill people's lives, when every conceivable need can apparently be met by one social agency or another, the Church must offer something different, distinctive and profoundly spiritually attractive. If all props have been taken away then everything now depends upon the spiritual drawing power of the faith and its adherents. So I offer this sermon, on the beauty of God (given at Oxford University, January 1989) because in the end it must be the sheer spiritual attractiveness of the divine, shining through us, which will win followers.

Out of Sion hath God appeared in perfect beauty (Psalm 50:2)

The beauty of God is one of the most neglected themes in recent Christian theology; indeed it has been largely overlooked since the Reformation in both Catholic and Protestant thought. Why such neglect? At root, I suspect there is a fear that the beautiful will cut loose from the ethical and a theology based on beauty will quickly degenerate into mere aestheticism. Christianity, we know, is about sinking our will in the will of God and going out in the service of others, especially the unlovely. What place is there here for the beautiful, even in God? Yet it was not always thus. Radiating at the heart of Augustine's *Confessions* is the one he addresses as 'O thou beauty most ancient and withall so fresh'. Or, to take just one example of earlier theologians, Gregory Palamas in the twelfth century, whose theme is the uncreated light, the fullness of divine beauty, which no one has ever seen but by which we are destined to be transformed. He writes of 'the superluminous splendour of the beauty of the Archetypal the very formless form of the divine loveliness, which defies man'. Again he writes: 'We are to be made beautiful by the creative and primordial beauty, and illumined by the radiance of God.'

We neglect this theme to our serious loss. For the world is shot through with glory and as human beings we are capable of producing works of art of great beauty. Unless we have some way of integrating this capacity to appreciate and create beauty into a Christian perspective it will assert itself as an autonomous realm. Indeed this has already happened. For many people in our generation the natural world or the world of art, particularly music, has come to occupy the place that religion would have occupied in their lives in a previous century. No less crucially, unless we are capable of catching some contemplative glimpse of the beauty of God, what is to draw us out of ourselves to delight in reality for its own sake? Truth by itself can be bare and cold, mere acknowledgment. Truly to acknowledge is to behold and to behold God is to be transported. We are transported because the divine splendour has captivated and drawn us beyond ourselves. Rectitude can be hard. But the goodness of the Lord is sheer loveliness. The psalmist urges us to worship the Lord in the beauty of holiness. God is holy and that holiness has a beauty, which no less than truth or goodness is a fundamental constituent of being, of God Himself. In short, as Hans Urs Von Balthasar, the one great modern theologian who has placed beauty at the centre of his theology, puts it, 'We can be sure that whoever sneers at her name as if she were the ornament of a bourgeois past – whether he admits it or not – can no longer pray and soon will no longer be able to love'.

Beauty is about form. Cultural anthropologists suggest that art originates in basic dance-like movements to the drum beat, in rhythm and repetition, and although this evolves in endlessly varied and complex ways we are still, whether it is dance or music, painting or poetry, concerned with pattern and shape, balance and harmony of however subtle a kind. The forms present in works of art have their counterparts in nature. We need only look at a snowflake or a crystal under a microscope, or a leaf or a stratum of rock to discern patterning. For God, in creating the world, ordered primeval chaos. Indeed without the regularity and stability that we call laws of nature, we could not exist as rational beings. All works of art share, in one way or another, in that divine work of patterning chaos.

Yet when the psalmist says that, 'Out of Sion hath God appeared in perfect beauty', he does not primarily refer to reflection of the divine glory in nature. Rather, the beauty of the created world provides an analogy for the beauty of God. As the beauty of the world is to creation, so there is that corresponding to beauty in relation to the eternal splendour of the divine being; which indeed no eye has seen, but who has shone through in Jesus. For 'the word became flesh and dwelt among us, full of grace and truth; we have beheld his glory, glory as of the only Son from the Father' (John 1:14).

Christ is the primary form; he is the image of the invisible God; in his being radiates the light of God. For if God gives Himself to us as goodness and we receive His revelation as truth, the form in which He gives Himself is beauty; thus, to recognise His self-giving as truth, is from the outset to be enraptured, to be transported by His beauty.

Christ is the primary form of God's beauty. But there are the secondary forms through which He is expressed and received; story, poetry, image, concept and pattern. It is not surprising that Christ should have inspired such powerful secondary forms of beauty – not only in Byzantine and European civilisations but in the Bible itself. The Gospel of John is a sublime work of art; indeed we are more and more discovering that each of the Gospel writers is a creative artist. Nevertheless, it is the primacy of the spiritual form, the beauty of God in Christ, that is our concern. We see it, for example, in the story of the transfiguration, when the glory of God irradiated and broke through the being of Christ to shine on the three disciples present. It is not surprising that Icons of the transfiguration in the Orthodox tradition, with its sense of the glory of God, its grasp of the unity of the spiritual and the artistic, and its discipline that painting is inseparable from understanding and prayer, succeed so sublimely in conveying this scene. Yet even Western Art, at least until Giotto, seems able on occasion to convey the spiritual through the aesthetic.

Two objections to this emphasis on the beauty of God need to be explored more fully. First, the fitful sense that Christianity is really about the good and the true, and not the beautiful. So that if Christianity is true and if we are striving for the good, that is, the will of God revealed in Christ, the aesthetic is at best an irrelevance and at worst a hindrance. It was this feeling which exploded in the Iconoclastic movement during the eighth century, in the Puritans of the seventeenth century and in puritan tendencies in many ages. We find the tension behind this objection even in such a person as Evelyn Waugh. Waugh had a well-developed aesthetic sense, particularly a visual one. At school he designed bookplates, and he took some training to become an artist. But he was at pains to emphasise that his conversion to Roman Catholicism was in response to truth, as he saw it, in opposition to where his aesthetic inclinations might have led him. For he was quite clear that Roman Catholic trappings in the 1930s, the design of churches and their ornaments, the music and the liturgy were greatly inferior to the Anglicanism in which he had been brought up. Sometimes he takes an almost perverse delight in stressing the cheapness or tawdriness of some Roman Catholic artefact. Right at the end of *Brideshead Revisited*, at what is the culminating point of the novel, as Charles Ryder meditates before the blessed sacrament, Waugh writes, 'a small red flame – a beaten-copper lamp of deplorable design relit before the beaten-copper doors of the tabernacle'. Here the centre of faith, Christ in his sacrament, co-exists with the lamp of deplorable design, that design in no way undermining the truth of the faith. It seems we have a complete disjunction between beauty and truth. Yet would it not be right to say that the total Christian schema – the God who creates us out of love and for love of us becomes incarnate – has a wider, deeper beauty which, while it is natural for it to be expressed in works of art, has a compelling appeal that can come through even the most vulgar of expressions? Something of this is suggested, in a slightly dangerous form, at the beginning of *Brideshead* where Charles, then an agnostic, says to Sebastian about the Christmas story, 'But my dear Sebastian you can't seriously *believe* it all.' 'Oh yes,' replies Sebastian. 'It's a lovely idea.' Charles protests, 'But you can't believe things because they're a lovely idea.' 'But I *do*,' responds Sebastian. 'That's how I believe.'

From this exchange and the earlier quotation of Waugh I would want to draw two conclusions. The source and standard of beauty is the loveliness of God's love, conveyed so movingly for example in the hymn 'My song is love unknown'. And it is natural for this beauty to be expressed in works of great beauty, poetry, painting, music. So it is that the Christian tradition, at its best, has brought together divine beauty and human beauty in a harmonious whole. The Song of Songs is, in its context, a love song in response to human beauty. Yet in the Christian mystical tradition it has been used as a song of divine beauty. This in turn, as in the works of John of the Cross, has given birth to further works that contain mystical and artistic beauty. Secondly, however, this beauty can not only co-exist with, but can shine through, human situations of great drabness and ugliness.

This leads to a third point, which is also full of ambiguity, the capacity of art, as of love, to transfigure brute reality. This is not without its dangers. For crucifixion was one of the cruellest forms of torture invented by human beings. In endless crucifixes and paintings of the Crucifixion, not least those of Duccio, crucifixion has become a thing of great beauty. But in reality it was horrible. It has given rise to sublime poems and hymns but in reality it was torture. As W.H. Auden put it in 'Epistle to a Godson', 'Only the unscarred, overfed enjoy calvary as a verbal event.' Isaiah 53 is strangely to the point. For the servant of God there described 'had no form or comeliness that we should desire to look at him, and no beauty that we should desire him.' Yet the passage in which that description occurs is one of the most haunting in the Bible, which has decisively influenced Christian thinking about the meaning of the Cross. The Holocaust was horrible, horrible; yet out of it has come the writings of Elie Weisel and the novels of Primo Levi. I want to say that no work of art must allow us to forget that the horrible is horrible. To forget is to go down the road of the worst kind of falsely comforting fantasy. Yet, art does transfigure. And the Christian cannot avoid seeing here an analogy of the transfiguring power of the resurrection. In the light of the resurrection the tree of sorrows becomes the tree of glory. The capacity of art to transfigure brute reality is an analogue of that: The love of God, as our hymn suggested, forms heavenly beauty out of strife.

This leads on to the other area of ambiguity and tension, that between the ethical and the aesthetic; and more particularly, the imperative that we are to love the unlovely. Francis kissed the leper. Mother Teresa embraces those she brings in off the streets of Calcutta. The tenderness of such scenes should not let us forget the disease, smells and squalor of the reality. But if art's capacity to transfigure is an analogy of love's power to redeem, what we have here is the reality, to which art is the pointer. It is no accident that Mother Teresa, writing to Malcolm Muggeridge, before they were to make a film of her work, wrote: 'Now let us do something beautiful for God.'

Gerard Manley Hopkins, whose mind often dwelt on such themes, entitles one of his poems, 'To what serves mortal beauty?' It is dangerous, he admits, but indispensable, for 'it keeps warm men's wits to the things that are' – and the things that are, are men's selves. 'Self flashes off frame and face.' We are, however, not to linger on that beauty but own it, give thanks for it and go for 'God's better beauty, grace', to which all human beauty points.

'Out of Sion hath God appeared in perfect beauty.' So we, beholding the fair beauty of the Lord, seek His grace; grace to share in His work of transfiguring the squalid, the ugly, the demeaning. That we, with all, may be able to say with Miranda in *The Tempest*.

> O, wonder!
> How many goodly creatures are there here!
> How beauteous mankind is! O brave new world,
> That has such people in't!

Puzzling Reflections of Truth

Maurice Wiles

Politicians seldom admit the limitations of their knowledge or the possibility that they may be wrong. Not many actually believe in their own omniscience or inerrancy. It is just too dangerous to admit publicly what they – and we – know to be true. The traditional style of leadership in public life demands a false façade of omnicompetence and certainty. Archbishops are part of the public life of the country and are expected to conform. Even the media, while often delighting to expose the false confidence of politicians, complain when Archbishops do not adopt the prevailing style of unqualified assertion.

Robert Runcie has received more than his fair share of criticisms of that kind in the public press. Many members of the Church too have voiced their demands for firmer and more decisive pronouncements – a decisiveness that would often have had to contradict itself if it were to meet the demands of all the critics.

As I have observed the Archbishop as a spokesman of the Church in the face of such unreasonable pressures, I have done so with sympathy and admiration. He has not succumbed to the temptation to assume a false certainty of knowledge which so many have wanted him to display; but neither has he failed to speak the prophetic word of faith in season. To me that has given to what he has said a distinctively Christian force amidst the many strident voices in the public arena. It has come across as the fruit of a Christian faith, which holds fast both to the mystery of God and the revelation in Christ. That calling applies to us all, though few have to live with its difficulty in the glaring light of the public gaze as Robert Runcie has done. The sermon that I am offering as a contribution to this tribute to him is one that seeks to explore the strange character of faith as a way of knowledge that knows its own ignorance.

I held nothing back; I declared unto you the whole purpose of God (Acts 20:27)

Now we see through a glass, darkly (1 Cor. 13:12) or: At present we see only puzzling reflections in a mirror (REB version)

Those two sayings are both ascribed to St Paul in the New Testament. Yet they represent two contrasting ways of understanding the basic character of Christian faith. According to the first, God has clearly declared His purpose. The Christian is one who has accepted that revelation in faith. His or her responsibility, like that which Paul in his farewell speech to the elders of Ephesus claims to have discharged, is to hold nothing back but to declare that revealed purpose of God, whether, as it was said to the Old Testament prophets, people will hear or whether they will forbear. Christians know the truth because it has been revealed to them and they must declare it.

But the second sounds a more tentative note; it sees Christian faith in terms of a quest, a quest for the meaning of life, a search after truth. Christians believe themselves to have glimpsed puzzling reflections of that truth in the mirror of their Christian faith, and what they have to offer to others is rather an invitation to join them in the quest, to help them in their attempts to decipher those puzzling reflections in the mirror.

If we set those two contrasting approaches side by side, we are likely to look upon the former (whether we regard it as a viable form of faith for ourselves or not) at least as robustly faithful to Scripture and the main stream of Christian tradition, and the latter as a watered down version of it – a product of the Enlightenment and secularisation, a result of the impact of historical and scientific criticism.

But the possibility of rooting that second, more questing approach in those famous words of Paul from the hymn to love in 1 Cor. 13 should give us pause before we type-cast those two approaches in that way. Think again for a moment of the content of some, at least, of the more declaratory passages of Scripture.

In the book of Job, it is Job's friends who know the truth and simply affirm that suffering is due to sin and that Job's sufferings are evidence that, whatever the outward appearance, he must be a specially culpable sinner. The glass in which they look remains clear; it is Job's glass which is dark – for he insists that God, who must be righteous, has denied him justice and hidden Himself away. 'If only I knew where to find Him, how to enter His court', he cries in despair. But in the declaration which God Himself makes out of the whirlwind at the end of the book it is Job and not his friends who receive the divine commendation. Nor does that declaration of God remove the darkness of Job's glass. It gives him a sense of God's presence, but the most it gives him by way of understanding are some oblique clues to aid him in his wrestling with those puzzling reflections in the mirror. 'Where wast thou when I laid the foundation of the earth? Hath the rain a father? Who begot the drops of dew? Canst thou draw out Leviathan with a fish-hook?'

But more significantly think of Jesus himself. The two basic descriptions of his teaching according to the Gospels, the two things that most impressed themselves on the crowds, were that he taught with authority and not like the scribes, and that he taught in parables. His teaching had a declaratory character all right – not for him the carefully hedged legal opinion of the scribe or academic lawyer; but once again it was declaration of a curiously oblique and enigmatic kind. 'The Kingdom of God is at hand; repent and believe the Gospel'. But ask what 'Kingdom of God' means and no explicit answer is forthcoming; the answer that is given is given indirectly in a series of parables. Those parables were not a species of sermon-illustration, entertaining ditties derived from a collection of after-dinner stories to refresh the flagging congregation half-way through the sermon. Welcome though you might find such an illustration at this moment and ready though I might be to provide one were it a genre in which I had any expertise, that was not the *raison d'être* of the parables of Jesus. He spoke in parables because they are the most appropriate way of speaking about God. The Christian Gospel is something to be declared, but it is not something to be declared straight. What the parable helps us to do is to look at life from a new angle, one that may help us to focus better on those puzzling reflections, and to respond to them more adequately. The one thing it cannot do is to replace those puzzling reflections with clear and unmistakable pictures. And when the Church tries to do that, as it often does and as it is under particularly strong pressure to do today, it runs the risk of ceasing to point men and women to the true God, and pointing instead to itself or to the god of its own ideology.

Can a faith, you may ask, which acknowledges the blurred nature of its own vision, command our allegiance with the absoluteness to which religion lays claim? I would turn the question on its head and say that it is only such a faith, one which *does* acknowledge the blurred nature of its vision, which can rightly claim our full allegiance – because it is only such a faith which is pointing us to the true mystery of God and not enrolling us in the service of some lesser god of its own invention. In the Church of England Doctrine Report, *Believing in the Church*, one sentence stood out for me, and it was a sentence written by my erstwhile colleague, Canon McManners: 'As Christians, we have to get used to being totally committed to a faith that can only be provisionally stated.'

When Christians come together in their most characteristic way of meeting to renew and deepen their common faith, they meet not simply to declare and to proclaim that faith, nor simply to probe and to enquire. They meet in the context of an action with bread and wine, which has about it a firm and confident declaratory character: 'This is my body; this is my blood.' But the declaration is of an oblique, puzzling and parabolic kind. The words are not simple or straightforward in meaning. Had they been, they would not have been the occasion of so much controversy and conflict down the ages. No, they are too profoundly true for that. They point us to things that lie behind and beyond what can be clearly stated: a union of the divine and the human; a union of our present with the past life, death and resurrection of Jesus; they speak to us of how our ordinary, workaday lives can be the medium of God's presence; they speak to us of how our life with God and our life with one another are inseparable, because only as the body of Christ can we receive the body of Christ. Such words remain riddling words; the vision to which they can give rise remains a puzzling reflection in a mirror. But a reflection is a reflection of something, of something other than itself, of the ultimate reality of love in which our lives are grounded. And the basic declaration is that while the puzzlement remains, while the quest goes on, here we are being grasped by that ultimate reality, the God whom we know in and through Jesus Christ.

The Wounded Surgeon and the Dying Nurse

Graham Leonard

An Archbishop of Canterbury has, of necessity, to speak about the relationship between society and the Church. In an address to the Magistrates Association in October 1981 Archbishop Runcie spoke of the proper place which law must have in society if it is not to descend into barbarism. At the same time, he said: 'For a civilisation to achieve spiritual maturity, to be on the road to eternal life, the limiting logic of law-making and limit-defining is never enough.' When Pope John Paul II visited Canterbury Cathedral in 1982, the Archbishop spoke of the way this has to be achieved when he said: 'The Kingdom spoken of by Our Lord Jesus Christ is built by self-sacrificing love which can turn even places of horror and suffering into signs of hope.' When I was asked to preach in Worcester College, Oxford, in February 1989, on the theme of T.S. Eliot's 'Idea of a Christian Society', I sought to examine, in the context of Eliot's thought, how, while a rightful place is given to law, love can be the mainspring of the life of the Church.

In 'the Idea of a Christian Society', T.S. Eliot said, 'I am not at this moment concerned with the means for bringing a Christian Society into existence; I am not even primarily concerned with making it appear desirable; but I am very much concerned with making clear its difference from the kind of society in which we are now living.'

Of the essential difference he had already written some five years earlier in 'The Rock'. Some lines in that piece of dramatic writing reflect the 1930s and Betjeman's 'Metroland' set against the world slump and the rise of dictators.

> In the land of lobelias and tennis flannels
> The rabbits shall burrow and the thorn revisit
> The nettle shall flourish on the gravel court,
> And the wind shall say 'Here were decent godless people:
> Their only monument the asphalt road
> And a thousand lost golf-balls.

There are other lines which speak to us today with sharp precision and penetration in words of judgement for the Church in our time, mesmerised as it seems to be, certainly in the West, by the efficacy of secular remedies for our condition.

> Why should men love the Church? Why should they love her laws?
> She tells them of Life and Death and all they would forget
> She is tender where they would be hard, and hard where they would
>   be soft
> She tells them of Evil and Sin and other unpleasant facts.

These words have a hollow ring today when the Church so often fails to speak of Life and Death, Evil, Sin and other unpleasant facts. And the lines which follow, applied by Eliot to the world, describe in an uncomfortable and disturbing way the attitude of the Church of today.

> They constantly try to escape
> From the darkness outside and within
> By dreaming of systems so perfect that no one will need to be good.

Yes, systems, whether secular or ecclesiastical, political policies or ecclesiastical schemes.

In 'The Waste Land' Eliot spoke of various kinds of despair, reflecting his own inner tensions ' – for lost youth, lost love, lost friendship, lost value'. Yet that poem offered some possibility of renewal – not readily recognised at the time – glimpses of the primordial and eternal truth that the way to life is death – glimpses which drew on pagan rites, other faiths as well as the Christian belief in resurrection. The bankruptcy of seeking life by human activity alone, expressed in 'The Hollow Men', is again conveyed by lines in 'Burnt Norton':

> The strained time-ridden faces
> Distracted from distraction by distraction
> Filled with fancies and empty of meaning
> Tumid apathy with no concentration.
> Internal darkness, desperation
> And destitute of all purpose.

Throughout Eliot's writings, side by side with the expression of the agonies and perplexities of the human scene, runs the recognition that man is not a solitary being. He is part of the community of creation, a dependent being, drawing upon, living by and contributing to the culture and civilisation of the world. So in 'The Idea' he reminds us 'that whatever reform or resolution we carry out, the result will always be a sordid travesty of what human society should be – though the world is never left wholly without glory.' He rejects both what he calls the neo-Ruskinian view which insists that the only salvation for society is to 'return to a simple mode of life, scrapping all the constructions of the modern world that we can bring ourselves to dispense with', and the view that we must 'accept the modern world and simply try to adapt modern Christian social ideals to it'. The latter resolves itself into a mere doctrine of expediency, and it is a surrender of the faith that Christianity itself can play any part in shaping social forms. 'Human kind cannot bear very much reality', says Eliot in 'Burnt Norton'. He forbids us from trying to make the burden tolerable by solutions which accept only the collectivist or individualist view of man.

Nevertheless, there is an unfinished quality about 'The Idea of a Christian Society'. As Peter Ackroyd says, 'He avoids any detailed account of his own position and relies upon the denunciation of alternative arguments and a shrewd analysis of contemporary truisms.' I would put it less negatively. What he does is to set the social and supernatural side by side – as in 'The Waste Land' or 'The Family Reunion', allowing the reader to discern the truth by their juxtaposition. At the same time, his awareness and expression of the primordial truth that death is the only way to life becomes more and more explicit, finding its fullest expression in 'Four Quartets'.

The Church must tell of evil and sin and other unpleasant facts. If we are to be faithful to our Christian discipleship we must take the measure of the forces against us. The problems of the world are not, in the last resort, simply caused by ignorance or bad administration. We face problems of violence, poverty, bad housing and war because men are violent, grasping, unjust, greedy and bitter. While, as Christians, we must do all that we can to take our part in remedying the situations which arise because of what is in man, we must also proclaim boldly and without fear that the real solution lies in the re-creation of men and women in Christ. It is when we do this that we become conscious of St Paul's words: 'We wrestle not against flesh and blood but against the principalities, against the forces, against the rulers of this present darkness, against the spiritual hosts of wickedness in the heavenly places.' We must stop 'dreaming of systems so perfect that no one will need to be good' and face the need for atonement, and to know that we must understand ourselves as we are. It is a mark of our time to look back to the past and to try to discover in our history explanations and excuses for our present condition. Although the atonement took place in a moment of time on the Cross of Calvary, it is also ever effectual, which is merciful, for as T.S. Eliot says at the beginning of 'Burnt Norton':

> Time present and time past
> Are both perhaps present in time future
> And time future contained in the past.
> If all time is eternally present
> All time is unredeemable.
> What might have been is an abstraction
> Remaining a perpetual possibility
> Only in a world of speculation.
>
>   . . . If we look back we are disappointed,
>
> Footfalls echo in the memory
> Down the passage which we did not take
> Towards the door we never opened
> Into the rose garden. My words echo

> Thus in your mind.
>   But to what purpose
> Disturbing the dust on a bowl of rose-leaves
> I do not know.

It is here and now that we need atonement and the Cross has happened. So in the second of 'Four Quartets', 'East Coker', we read:

> The wounded surgeon plies the steel
> That questions the distempered part;
> Beneath the bleeding hands we feel
> The sharp compassion of the healer's art
> Resolving the enigma of the fever chart.
>
> Our only health is the disease
> If we obey the dying nurse
> Whose constant care is not to please
> But to remind of our, and Adam's curse,
> And that, to be restored, our sickness must grow worse.

In no way does it detract from the uniqueness of the 'one oblation which Christ offered of himself, a full, perfect and sufficient sacrifice, oblation and satisfaction, for the sins of the whole world', to say that atonement is a two-way process. The meaning of the word makes that clear. It is the restoration to a relationship of those who were estranged. In any broken human relationship there is a price to be paid, a cost to be met if it is to be restored. Such is the case even in a casual relationship. If I collide with someone accidentally, I must say, 'I am sorry', if the proper relationship between two persons is to be restored and we are not to go on our way in a sense of alienation. If the relationship which has been estranged was a deep one, the cost will be greater and it will not be borne equally. The greater cost will be borne by the better of the two. Because he is a more loving and holier person, he will understand more truly the meaning and significance of the estrangement which has occurred and will appreciate the cost of reconciliation. Perhaps the other man will not accept the cost at all, and rejects attempts to effect reconciliation. In that event, the better man must bear the cost of rejection while continuing to love and desire reconciliation. In a human relationship neither party can know the full reasons or the real depth of what has caused the breach, to which, perhaps, past experience of one or the other, say in childhood, may have contributed, or which may have arisen because of misunderstanding or ignorance. How often do we say, 'I am sorry; if I had known that, I would have understood how you felt'?

In our relationship to God, He knows the whole situation. He knows the ultimate significance of our sin, which alienates us from Him. He knows what we are at this moment, our past with our expectations for the future. For Him, this and every moment is the 'point of intersection of the timeless with time'. As we come to Him

He meets us as we are, and we can be reconciled to Him with our past and our expectations for the future, though the past, if need exist, can be exorcised and our expectations transformed.

For He bears the cost. God was in Christ reconciling the world to Himself. He bears the cost not only of our personal reconciliation and the forgiveness of our own sins; but that is too individualistic a way of looking at our redemption. It is the intolerable burden of the sins of the whole world, of which our sins are part, which Christ bears on Calvary. The cost of forgiving all sin is borne, and so the reconciliation is effected for the whole world for all time in Christ. 'It is love, the wounded surgeon, who endured the fire on our behalf and provides the fire that energizes us with the divine Spirit to begin again, to live anew and then to join the dance at the still point, participant in eternal life.'

Let us return to the Church in which we live. T.S. Eliot describes it as the 'dying nurse', which may seem surprising. Surely, some will say, the Church should live in the joy of the resurrection with the experience of eternal life. Yes indeed, but there was no resurrection without the Cross. The risen life demands both a daily dying to sin and the ability to suffer creatively. The Church is above all the sacrificial body, the body that has been slain to rise again, dying the death to rise in glory, the body set in the world through which the 'wounded surgeon' continues his work. By being the sacrificial body, the Church can be the community in which redemption takes place, in which hatred is replaced by love, in which forgiveness is offered and received, in which all life is consecrated in truth to God.

It is by the Church that we are restored to health, for living in Christ, as members of his body, we know that we must die to live, both for our health and for the health of all mankind. If we are to die to live, we must live with the wounded surgeon by our side, who brings diagnosis and healing, judgement and grace. So prays a monk of the Eastern Church:

> You are present when I sin
> And you remain in me, silent
> Your very presence condemns what I do.
> Yet at the same time, you know and understand my sin
> More profoundly than I understand myself.
> For you are more in me than I am in myself
> You do not judge me from a distance.
> And yet, at this moment, you contradict what I am.
> But your presence envelopes me in boundless mercy
>
> . . .
> You have no need of formal sentence.
> Your presence alone, Lord
> Is the judgement which condemns me.
> But your presence is also grace.
> There could be no word of grace
> If there was no word of judgement.

Failing to Satisfy the Examiners

Lavinia Cohn-Sherbok

Before I went to West Heath, for seven years I taught at the King's School, Canterbury. Robert Runcie was the official Visitor to the school and took the annual Confirmation service. It was a particularly awkward assignment. He had to preach a sermon which was suitable not only for the boys and girls, but also for their friends and relations. Many of the adults present were not regular church-goers and I knew from experience how difficult an audience the young could be. Many of them were only there under sufferance and, even at the best of times, they were highly critical of any religious speaker. The Archbishop always rose to the occasion magnificently. His sermons were models of clarity, wit and thoughtfulness and he even knew when to stop. As a token of admiration for his skill on these occasions, I offer this sermon which was also preached to a school-boy congregation.

The race is not to the swift nor the battle to the strong (Eccles. 9:11)

One of the duties of headmistresses is to entertain visiting preachers and this of course means listening attentively to their sermons and discussing them intelligently afterwards. So it is particularly nice to be preaching at someone else's school and to know that my old friend, your headmaster, is all attention. Now if this establishment is anything like West Heath, a very common theme for preachers is the responsibility of success. The script runs something like this . . . 'You at this private boarding school are privileged to be receiving an excellent education. You are among the élite. But such privilege entails the responsibility to serve. You're not here just to get three As in your "A" levels so you can go off in a burst of glory to University, admirable though academic success is. You are here to learn to contribute to society. You must help those less fortunate than yourselves.' But this morning I don't want to do that. I want to talk not about success but about failure – about missing the boat, about being off-target, about failing to satisfy the examiners.

Not so long ago I failed to satisfy the examiners. You may have noticed that I arrived last night in a taxi. That is because I have never succeeded in passing my driving test. Now I don't want to make excuses, but believe me, that test isn't easy. I've always been quite lucky when it comes to passing examinations. After all you only have to get about 70 per cent in 'A' Level to score an A grade. In other words you can get more than a quarter of it completely wrong and still land the top mark. But the driving test isn't like that at all. For some reason I never learnt when I was your age and when, a couple of years ago, I felt that I really should be able to drive a car, I went at it with determination. I wasn't leaving anything to chance. I realised early on that this was an area where I had little aptitude. Those wretched three-point turns and reversals round corners drove me demented. But I persevered. I had more than fifty lessons, two hours a day for a month. It cost a fortune and I really was getting better. Well, the day of the test arrived. I turned up at the Centre trembling like a leaf. I was introduced to a robot who turned out to be the examiner and off we went. I thought I did pretty well. I read the number-plate correctly in front of me. We didn't bump into anything. I stopped for pedestrians. The round-abouts were exceptionally traffic-free. I hardly rolled downhill at all when I did my hill start and my clutch control was a miracle of precision. I distinguished between the sign for a 30 mile per hour speed limit and one which indicated that the end of the motorway was nigh, and really I was feeling quite complacent. And do you know what the robot said? He told me my signalling was faulty. Apparently I indicated I was going right when in fact I went to the left. And that was it. Failure. No second chance. No compliments on the excellence of my emergency stops. Nothing. Just failure. Not competent to drive a car.

I felt dreadful. I walked back home nearly in tears, envying all those carefree motorists who seemed to be able to change gear without even thinking about it. It appeared that I was the only person in the Western world who couldn't drive a car, and life didn't seem worth living. Now of course this is a very trivial failure and I am sure you have all had similar experiences. Perhaps some of you have failed to make a particular team; others may not have passed their GCSE exams, or failed to get the part they wanted in the School Play. And what of the future? There are probably a few here, a very few, sitting in this Chapel today who will never achieve a Grade C in GCSE mathematics, no matter how hard they try. Others will fail to get the 'A' level grades they need to go to University. Still others will be deeply disappointed at not getting into Oxford or Cambridge. Still others will get poor degrees. And even if you do achieve your First, you still may find it impossible to land the particular job you want. So there you are – failure and misery, disillusionment and unhappiness. Much more than success, failure is a universal phenomenon. Even though here in this school you have been pro-tected as much as possible, have been given every chance, have had the benefit of an expensive education, there is no way you are going to avoid it. Failure is part of being human. All of us, in various ways, have failed and will continue to fail to satisfy the examiners. All among you, on the right and on the left, in front and behind, in this sea of respectable school uniform, are secret sorrows and hidden disappointments, in school work, on the playing fields, at home and even in love.

In the Judaeo-Christian tradition, the recognition that failure is an inevitable feature of life is of central importance. In the lesson which was read to you earlier, you heard the prophet Isaiah's description of the Suffering Servant of God. 'He was despised and rejected of men, a man of sorrows and acquainted with grief . . . he was despised and we did esteem him not.' Now what are we to make of all this? Is there any way to come to terms with failure and suffering? You remember how the passage went on, 'But he was wounded for our transgressions, he was bruised for our iniquities, the chastisement of our peace was upon him, and by his stripes we are healed.' What on earth is being said here? How can healing come out of pain?

The Jewish interpretation of this passage is that the Suffering Servant is the people of Israel. As you know, throughout history, Jews have been despised and rejected, persecuted and murdered, and they have partially come to terms with this miserable catalogue by understanding their role as that of chief actors in God's divine plan of redemption. Christians have interpreted this passage rather differently. Jesus is the suffering servant. He died on the Cross as a common criminal so that all humankind could be restored to God. As the old hymn puts it, 'He died that we might be forgiven, he died to make us good.' In the Christian faith, the death of Jesus is seen as the perfect sacrifice, an act by which God participated in the suffering of all people.

But how does this help us? What difference does it make when we have bruised feelings after failing to make the cricket team, failing French GCSE yet again or even failing one's driving test? Well in the first place, we can recognise that our situation is not unique. We live in a troubled and troubling world. That's the way it is and failure is part of the penalty we pay for being alive in it. It does help to know that other people are also experiencing it. Think of the last time you did badly in an exam. No doubt it was embarrassing, even humiliating. Probably you wanted simply to disappear so as to escape the rebukes and disappointments of your parents and teachers. But having had such an experience, you should be better able to empathise with others in similar circumstances. Remember when you last failed to get into a team. It was miserable. But again, if you can look beyond your own frustration, it is possible that you will learn to sympathise with others in the same predicament. Or being unsuccessful in love can evoke compassion for those equally distraught. From disappointments then, from failing to satisfy the examiners, can come human concern and caring. Through fellow-feeling, all of us who endure major and minor tragedies can discover a greater depth in our own natures. We can find an understanding and compassion which we did not know we possessed.

Now there is a temptation here. You may decide that failure is so miserable that you'd rather not risk it. Who cares about developing human compassion for other people anyway? Isn't it preferable to stay in your right tight little world and protect yourself as far as you possibly can from anything threatening or challenging? Better to try for the Third rather than the First Eleven. You'll have no trouble being accepted there. Better not to be vulnerable and open in your relationships with other people, then you won't have the risk of being rejected. Better not to audition for the School Play, better to refuse to join the new chamber orchestra, better to announce that you don't *want* to be a prefect. There are plenty of people who do this. They refuse any sort of challenge and, in order to minimise the risk of failure, they try to wrap their lives in a cocoon of mediocrity.

Now I believe this to be a fundamentally mistaken attitude. It's certainly true that if you refuse to run in a race, you will avoid the disappointment of not winning. On the other hand, you're never going to be much of a runner either. In order to get better at something, you have got to open yourself to the possibility of failing. You've got to recognise that that is the deal. Even though trying hard is no guarantee of success – look at me and my driving test – you can be quite sure that without effort, commitment and vulnerability, there is no possibility of success at all. And I would go further than this. I would argue that there are also some positive benefits to be found in the experience of failure. Through failure you are given the opportunity to grow and develop as a person. As you pull yourself out of the slough of despond yet again, you grow stronger and more compassionate. You find it easier to understand the difficulties and problems other people face. You become more loving and therefore more lovable. As your sympathy develops, you will become more and more the kind of person you were originally created to be. Through gritting your teeth and working your way through the disappointments and rejections of life, you are given the chance to grow in charity and magnanimity, strength and integrity.

I'm not going to pretend that it's easy to pick yourself up after failure. But if you are prepared to learn from your experiences, you will begin to appreciate the vast potential in other people, the extraordinary courage, humour and generosity which is to be found in them. You will find that the human race is not merely self-serving and mean. Through the battles of life, they are also funny and noble and kindly and true. As your sympathy and understanding becomes larger, you may even get a glimpse of what the writer of Genesis meant when he declared that human beings are made in the Image of God.

There is enormous pleasure to be had in winning a contest, in capturing the best part, in earning your Oxbridge place. But there is something to be learnt from failure too. My prayer for you is that through your disappointments, you will grow in knowledge, compassion and love, so that when you look back on your life you will be able to agree with the writer of the Book of Ecclesiastes, that the race is not always to the swift, nor the battle to the strong. It is then you will discover that it is in our failures rather than in our successes that true wisdom and understanding is to be found.

'In the End, God'

Nicolas Stacey

I am pleased to dedicate a sermon (preached at the Founders' Day Service of Ashford School for Girls, July 1990) to Robert Runcie on his retirement as Archbishop of Canterbury.

He is an intelligent, sensitive, caring and committed man, and although our 'careers' have taken different routes he must share with those of us whose work has taken them into the secular structures a deep sadness, pain and disappointment about the state of the Church of England today. Robert, like a number of us who were ordained after the 1939–45 war, was influenced by his war experiences to believe in the Christian faith. We were motivated to try to make the world a better place and believed the Church of England could be fashioned to be a mighty instrument in the building of the Kingdom of God on Earth.

Now, forty-five years on, the Church appears to many to be a marginalised and declining religious club. Robert has presided over this, unsupported by a quarrelsome synod and amid a barrage of personal criticism – much of it unfair – for the last ten years. It must have been a searing experience, because as all of us who understand how the Church of England works know, through no fault of his own and despite his valiant efforts, he has been powerless to turn things around in the face of a culture which is no longer 'Gospel Friendly'.

Yet in spite of it all – perhaps because of it – he still is able confidently to proclaim: 'In the end, God'.

It was a Hell's Angel who was asked what he would think about if the motorbicycle he was riding got into a skid and was heading for a brick wall. 'Sex,' he replied. 'Why sex?' the enquirer asked, 'At what might be your last moments on Earth?' 'Because I am always thinking about sex,' was his reply.

Some of us have more wide-ranging interests and occasionally think about other things. There is particularly another thought, or rather a question, that bugs us. And the question is: is there any meaning in life at all? Was Ginger Rogers right when she said, 'Life is just one damn thing after another'? The question is rarely on the surface of our minds. The hopes and aspirations, the fears and frustrations, of busy, interesting lives occupy most of our thoughts and time. But in the silent hours of the night, or when we have some traumatic experience, like a death in the family, it comes to the forefront of our minds. In the brochure on your school there is a section on aims. You can't fault them. They are all highly desirable, but I would add a further one – 'This school tries to help girls make sense of life!'

What are we to make of life? Every newspaper and every television programme illustrates the irony and paradox of our human situation.

On the one hand, one is appalled by both the immense complexity and speed of life, and by the fantastic folly of men and our power-lessness to alter things. There is so much that is ludicrous, so much folly, so much futility, so much absurdity, so much greed, that the whole proposition of *homo-sapiens* is in doubt. There is also so much knowledge, wisdom, so much love and self-sacrifice, so much that is good and beautiful. There are times when one feels that this is the most thrilling of all periods of the history of the world in which to be alive.

There is longer life and better health; there are wider interests and greater opportunities. But there is also more neurosis, more mental illness, more frustration, more bloody-mindedness, more insecurity, more alcoholism and drug-taking, and, among the young, more crime. People have the feeling that every institution in the land to which men in the past have looked for leadership, inspiration and guidance is discredited. Each new report and commission investigat-ing the life of this and that seems to tell the same story of bungledom and lack of imagination, of incompetence and sometimes plain dis-honesty. And the Church is no exception. It increasingly looks like a marginalised and declining religious club with its members arguing about the sexual orientation of male clergy and the ordination of female ones.

Statesmen belt from conference to conference in jets and mouth platitudinous clichés to press conferences at airports, and one won-ders whether it isn't all a sick game, with the world rushing forward with nobody in control. One feels like one does in a jet, with the beautiful, but frigid air hostess, who gives the sense that she is wrapped in cellophane like the tasteless sandwiches she distributes with the gin and tonics, and there we sit, strapped in our seats, without the faintest idea why we are in the thing at all and even less idea as to where it is going.

Change, speed and complexity are all underpinned by uncer-tainty. This is the world which you in the next few years have got to learn to come to grips with and to make sense of. It is a daunting prospect, made more so by the fact that many of the values which the school is trying to introduce you to, such as integrity, truth, fair-mindedness, the discipline of enquiry, are contradicted by the brash, slick, make-a-quick-buck, superficial nature of so much of our society. What one hears in the classroom or in the chapel is contra-dicted by the clamouring seductiveness of what one sees in the colour supplements, advertisements and TV commercials.

There are, I think, a number of ways one can react to this situation. The first is to try to escape from the reality of it all. Gin, obsessive money-making, and promiscuous sex are all popular but self-defeating and ultimately self-destructive cul-de-sacs down which we bolt. For my generation it might be booze. For yours perhaps it is more likely to be drugs.

Second, one can have a nervous breakdown. One can be so overwhelmed and so confused that one's mind just runs around in small circles and one lives in a state of constant intellectual dither, changing one's ground with each new book one reads or each new friend one makes. One can drop out in sheer confusion and despair. And this is what happens to some of the most intelligent and sensitive young people.

Third, one can shut one's mind, fall back on tradition and huddle together with one's peers to give oneself a sense of safety and security. This may be particularly tempting for a middle-class community like this. The close-one's-mind brigade are really retreating from reason, and for an intelligent young person to have a closed mind is a real tragedy because it prevents that growing in depth, that sensitivity, that understanding and that humility which are the hallmarks of an educated human being. I do not for one moment underestimate the attractions of back-to-the-paternalistic, back-to-the-womb approach to life. It may be cramped in the womb, but it is warm and cosy and at least one knows where one is.

Fourth, there is I believe another possible reaction. One can learn to face reality, to keep one's intellectual integrity, to keep one's mind open and at the same time to hold a few fundamental facts and beliefs about God and man and life which make sense because they measure up to one's own experience of life, and because they answer more of the questions than anything else on the market.

The more I struggle to come to grips with life, the more I find myself believing more and more in less and less. But the few things which one does believe help one to make some sort of sense about those many things for which, for the time being at least, I must remain uncertain. In our lifetime at least, Christians are going to have to travel very light. We will make our stand that *in the end God* – that ultimately God has got everything under control and that love in the long run will win.

One can believe that God did reveal Himself in Christ and with this Christ, men can have some kind of personal relationship, and that this need in him for a relationship is fundamental because he is ultimately a worshipping animal, and if he does not worship God with a capital G, he will find some other little gods to worship. It is the little gods who always let one down.

Some may say this is a very truncated gospel compared with the great dogmatic superstructures of belief which the Churches have built up over the centuries. Maybe it is, but I believe with all my heart and soul that for your generation at least this is as far as we are going to be able to go. But I believe it is enough for us to be getting on with and it can change our lives. It gives a focus, a purpose, a hope, and a vision to life; it gives a new dimension. It can give a life-transforming power. The Spirit of the Living God is available to us as it was to the disciples of old. But today to be a believer is unfashionable. To stand out against the money-mad, materialistic culture in which everybody wants to make a quick buck, and one is judged by the size of one's salary, takes courage. Our culture is not Gospel Friendly. This is not new. As St John says, 'He was in the world. The world was made through him, yet the world knew him not. But to all who received him, who believed in his name, he gave power to become Children of God.' – and that is my prayer for you all, Pupils, Parents, Teachers and Governors.

The Touch of God

Rowan Williams

All public figures in the religious world have a good deal to do, directly and indirectly, with the deeply disturbed. They know the flavour of the various ways in which religious tradition can warp and injure the human mind all too well. Anglicanism has not been very familiar with the stranger voices of religious utterance; it tends to rely on vague assumptions of good sense and balance. But the wisest Anglicans know that this is an evasion. Listening to what may seem disturbed and disturbing voices has to be part of allowing the unexpectedness of God to reach us, beyond the constraints of cultural taste, and even what we regard as sanity. Robert Runcie, quintessentially Anglican in so much of his background and formation, has worked with exemplary courage at listening to strange voices – the Christianity of other cultures, the voices of passion and unpredictability within our own church and society. This sermon (given in April 1990) is a meditation on all in religious commitment that is not covered by taste and balance.

The Revelation of John is written in two scripts. Some of it is chiselled in stone, with the deep and clear lines of some Roman inscription, still arresting after all the centuries. 'I am the first and the last and the living one'; 'Behold, I have set before you an open door'; 'I saw a Lamb standing as though it had been slain'; 'God will wipe away every tear from their eyes'; 'Seal up what the seven thunders have said'; 'Alas, alas for the great city': 'Behold, I make all things new'; 'They shall see his face, and his name shall be on their foreheads. And night shall be no more'; 'Let him who desires take the water of life without price'. These are the words etched upon the Christian imagination for centuries; they have the simplicity, the nakedness, of all 'revelatory' poetry, the sense of a fusion between word and world. They *embody* what they talk about.

And then there is the other script: tightly written, pen driving into cheap paper, page after page of paranoid fantasy and malice, like the letters clergymen so frequently get from the wretched and disturbed. 'They were allowed to torture them for five months, but not to kill them'; 'Let him who has understanding reckon the number of the beast'; 'The smoke of their torment goes up for ever and ever'; 'all the birds were gorged with their flesh'. And, this morning, 'I gave her time to repent, but she refuses . . . I will throw

her on a sick bed . . . and I will strike her children dead.' Goodness
knows who 'Jezebel' in Thyatira was or what she taught; perhaps
she was just an inoffensive liberal who had read something like
Romans 14, and wouldn't see what all the fuss was over eating meat
bought at the temple butcher's stall. But whoever she was, it is the
wild venom of John the Divine that has given her her unwelcome
immortality. Throughout the seven letters to the churches at the
beginning of Revelation, the tone swings disconcertingly between
vitriol and a language of haunting authority whose images – the
tree, the crown, the white stone and the morning star – have the
mysterious solidity of a conceptual Stonehenge.

Revelation has been the quarry for mystics and fanatics alike. The
script of paranoia and of revengeful fancy is a lot easier for most
people to write, and this book has touched deep and diseased places
in many psyches, and unlocked streams of violence and obscenity
and plain madness. Easy to forget that Scripture in its entirety is the
Word we must hear, and to attach the label 'God's Word' to this or
that fragment – as the curious rubric of the 1980 liturgy instructs us
to do. If there is a Word from God to hear in John's Revelation –
and if there isn't, it's a waste of time reading it aloud when we
might be reading something less troubled and troubling – then it's
to be heard in the very tension between the two scripts.

The average, the prosaic human mind cannot strike hard enough
to cut so deeply in stone ('Behold, I make all things new', 'Take the
water of life without price'). Our language is not used to speaking
for God – that is, speaking of some restoration and grace, some
resource of beauty and transfiguring strength, greater than the sum
of all things visible and invisible; some promise of wholeness that
can stand like Stonehenge through all the gales of horror and failure
that blow in the world. To speak like that is the result of having
had one's own speech interrupted, having been thrown off course.
John tells us about it at the beginning of Revelation: 'I turned to see
the voice that was speaking to me . . . When I saw him, I fell at his
feet as though dead' (notice the disorientated imagery of *seeing*
voices). John has seen something lethal to his ordinary perceptions,
and his mind is opened to the impress of rhythms far below the
surface of ordinary speech.

Yet to say this is at once to grasp how vulnerable the speaker of
such words will be. The poet or seer speaks from a fractured sensibility, following rhythms below the surface; but those rhythms are
not only the shapes of a reality creating and nurturing us: they may
also be the intermediate layers between the conscious mind and its
maker, the rhythms set up by our injuries or our inner diseases.
When the sensibility is fractured, it isn't only God who comes
through the fissures in the surface. The poet or seer may present
appalling contradictions – disturbed and destructive behaviour, the
capacity to say insanely wounding or cruel things. In our century,

the poet who, for many believers, comes closest to 'writing in stone', T.S. Eliot, could write what Stephen Spender called 'poetic death sentences' on tracts of experience that he feared or longed to ignore, not to mention the absurd and horrible anti-Semitism of some of his earlier work. His own mentor, Ezra Pound, offers a still more dramatic example of tragi-comic contradictions. A sensibility sufficiently blown off course to be able to speak for more than a pragmatic and conventional wisdom is a mind at risk.

Perhaps, as we read the Revelation of John, we should let its ugly and diseased elements speak to us in this way. The very disorder, the madness and vengefulness, of certain passages can help us to hear more clearly the depth and authority of others. Whatever we have here, it is not just the voice of common sense. Do we or don't we decide to recognise, among the fractures of this language, this imagination, some opening into the scale of God's language ('an open door, which no one is able to shut')? If we do, it will be because we have been jolted out of our good sense by this speech – by its disorders as well as its glimpses of God's order, God's rhythms. If there is to be some real communication from God, we might well expect to recognise it in a mind that has been forced beyond itself, for good and ill.

And this suggests a troubling but necessary reflection on the whole idea of revelation. The touch of God *is* dangerous, in that it can be a light too sharp to be borne without hurt or breakage; and when the perception is skewed and redirected, it may run close to the destructive and the hellish. Jonathan Smith, the great anthropologist of religion at Chicago, remarked some years ago about the horrific mass suicide of the sectarians who followed the prophet Jim Jones, that at least it reminded people that religion wasn't automatically 'nice'. For God to come near us is for God, it seems, to 'risk' God's own integrity, in the sense that God puts Himself into our hands to be appallingly misunderstood, to become the justifier of our hatred and fears, our madness. And it is to put *us* at risk, since the disorientation we thus experience can unleash some very dark things in us. Revelation itself, as the Church's history shows, is bound up with tragic possibilities.

But this is not to romanticise religious irrationality; only to say that the diseases and injuries of the mind that revealed religion seems so often to produce are the price paid for some perception of what is irreducibly beyond the whole world. For the Christian, that perception is that the world is sustained by mercy and generosity without limit, by a giving God ('take the water of life without price'); and that is not by any means a deduction of common sense. It *is* bought at a price – the price of the madness of violence unleashed in the Cross of Jesus, the price of the fracturing of the imaginations of a John or a Paul; and then the further disturbing price of the violence justified in the name of the Cross of Jesus and the distortions, the fury and hatred, that may be set free in the bruised mind of the prophet. But it is that Cross and that bruised mind that set before us the universal scale of a power of mercy: those things that touch and stir our diseases are also the things that finally show where our diseases are to be judged and healed. The rantings of John the Divine about his theological rivals are part of the by-product of the very vision of the Living One that shows these ravings for what they are, by showing the radical and unconfined purpose of God in Jesus Christ. Not all the Lord's people are prophets. Quite properly, our worship sets out to remind us of covenant and faithfulness, the reliability of God's mercy, and we don't expect to be blown off course by these reminders. Cathedral Matins are not very like congregations known to St John the Divine, hot quarrelsome groups jammed into someone's front room in the less savoury quarters of Turkish towns, intermittently praying and weeping together and screaming at each other in the tone of voice we hear in this morning's second lesson. We have learned how to build the disorientating vision of the First and the Last, the Living One, who was dead and is alive for evermore, into a tradition of grace and quiet and beauty. And we can come to think that the vision of God is natural to us (no one habitually falls on their face as if dead during Anglican worship, at least outside the more dramatic bits of the charismatic movement), and that grace and quiet are an appropriately low-key acknowledgment of this. But our worship does continue to set before us the memory that discovering the Living One is dangerous, and that we would know less of it without the fractured and disturbed languages of people like John the Divine, and their contemporary equivalents – sometimes even those people who write their strange and painful fantasies to clergymen and other public figures. We aren't called to believe and endorse all they say, only to ask ourselves what we are taught here about the strangeness and sometimes the terror of the Word of God to fragile minds. We at Matins, who may not think of ourselves as fragile, but are not likely to think of ourselves as prophets either, need to pay our debts to those scorched by their closeness to the One we observe from a polite distance. 'He who has an ear, let him hear what the Spirit says to the churches.'

The last word rightly belongs to the fractured awareness of the poet – Annie Dillard, the young American writer whose poetry and prose have taught many people to see the natural world and its maker with something of the terror and newness of revelation (Revelation). Here she is on going to church:

> Why do people in church seem like cheerful, brainless tourists on a packaged tour of the Absolute?
> The tourists are having coffee and doughnuts on Deck C. Presumably someone is minding the ship, correcting the course, avoiding icebergs and shoals, fuelling the engines, watching the radar screen, noting weather reports radioed in from shore. No one would dream of asking

the tourists to do these things. Alas, among the tourists on deck C, drinking coffee and eating doughnuts, we find the captain, and all the ship's officers, and all the ship's crew. The officers chat; they swear; they wink a bit at slightly raw jokes, just like regular people. The crew members have funny accents. The wind seems to be picking up.

On the whole, I do not find Christians, outside of the catacombs, sufficiently sensible of conditions. Does anyone have the foggiest idea what sort of power we blithely invoke? Or, as I suspect, does no one believe a word of it? The churches are children playing on the floor with their chemistry sets, mixing up a batch of TNT to kill a Sunday morning. It is madness to wear ladies' straw hats and velvet hats to church; we should all be wearing crash helmets. Ushers should issue life preservers and signal flares; they should lash us to our pews. For the sleeping god may wake someday and take offense, or the waking god may draw us to where we can never return.

Watch With Me

Cicely Saunders

This address, given at an Annual General Meeting after Archbishop Lord Fisher laid the Foundation Stone of St Christopher's Hospice in 1965, was developed from a sermon delivered in Coventry Cathedral earlier that year.

It seems appropriate to offer it to this collection as I think of Archbishop Runcie's visit to St Christopher's, the other times he has made opportunity to see a hospice and its patients and his Presidency of Help the Hospices. He pauses to give each person, patient, family or staff member a few moments of total pastoral attention, while his ability to see to the heart of a problem has made his addresses concerning hospice work both encouraging and challenging.

No challenge can be more demanding than an effort to face another's emotional and spiritual pain. We have witnessed in him a readiness to watch with many apparently insoluble problems in hope, and we have been grateful.

We can think about the foundation of St Christopher's in various ways. We can say that they consist of all the interest and the money that has been given and promised and that have made the building and the laying of the foundation stone possible. We can think about them as all the work that has ever been done in this field in the past by people other than ourselves and on which we will build our own work. We can think about them as the people who have gradually joined in thinking, praying and working for St Christopher's ever since the vision was first given more than seventeen years ago. I think you all know that I like best of all to think of St Christopher's as being founded on patients, those we have known and who are now safely through this part of their lives. One used to speak for all of them each time I told her of some meeting, as she said, 'I'll be there'. Now I want to look at our foundations by taking one particular phrase which I believe expresses our ideals concerning St Christopher's.

Ideals and Aims of St Christopher's

I am sure the most important foundation stone we could have comes from the summing up of all the needs of the dying which was made for us in the Garden of Gethsemane in the simple words 'Watch with Me'. I think the one word 'Watch' says many things on many different levels, all of importance to us. In the first place it demands that all the work at St Christopher's should stem from respect for the patient and very close attention to his distress. It means really looking at him, learning what this kind of pain is like, what these symptoms are like, and from this knowledge finding out how best to relieve them. It means continually gaining new skills, developing those already learnt from St Luke's Hospital and the writings of its founder Dr Howard Barrett, from all the work of St Joseph's Hospice and from discussion with many other people both here and in the USA. I have not found any individual place concentrating on these problems alone but many have helped to shed light on different facets of them and all this we want to bring together and develop into new skills in an area that is very greatly neglected.

'Not only skill but compassion also'

We want to plan and carry out research in the relief of distress such as has not been done anywhere else, so far as I have been able to discover. It is often easier in a specialist setting to go on learning in this way, and by building what we think is an ideal unit we hope to be able to help not only our own patients but to raise standards generally and also to stimulate others to think about these problems. A patient comes to my mind here, a young woman who said, 'You seem to understand the pain from *both* sides'. Our aim in learning such understanding is to give the kind of relief described by another woman who said, 'It was *all* pain but now it's gone and I am free'.

Seventeen years ago a young Pole died and left me £500 to be 'a window in your Home.' This was the very beginning of St Christopher's. I also remember his saying, 'I only want what is in your mind and in your heart'. This was echoed years later by another Pole who said to us, 'Thank you. And not just for your pills but for your heart'. I think both of them showed that they wanted not only skill but compassion also. They needed warmth and friendship as well as good technical care. I think our understanding of what real watching means must include this. We have, indeed, to learn what this pain is like. Still more we have to learn what it feels like to be so ill, to be leaving life and its activity, to know that your faculties are failing, that you are parting from loves and responsibilities. We have to learn how to feel 'with' patients without feeling 'like' them if we are to give the kind of listening and steady support that they need to find their own way through.

Here again comes a key phrase I have often quoted – 'I look for someone to look as if they are trying to understand me'. These patients are not looking for pity and indulgence but that we should look at them with respect and an expectation of courage, a heritage from seeing people like the woman who said to me, 'You can tell them all that it was *all right*'. She was not going through a strange, dramatic or just unlucky experience, to be written up as such with sentimentality or sensationalism, but an all-too-common experience such as ordinary people have always faced and somehow managed to come through.

'I don't *want* to die'

We will be seeing patients who go along the path which leads from the honest but wistful plea – 'I don't *want* to die, I don't *want* to die', to the quiet acceptance of 'I only want what is right'. We will not only see acceptance but also a very real joy, the true gaiety of someone who has gone through doubt, fear and unwillingness and come out the other side. I remember coming away from the bedside of a man who had come along that difficult path just about an hour before he died and saying to myself – 'He looked *amused*' – and he really did. Certainly we are going to see hard things, but we are also going to see rewards and compensations and insight given to our patients here and now and we will see an extraordinary amount of real happiness and even lightheartedness.

Planning an ideal unit is not enough to interpret all the meanings of the word 'watch' if teaching is not a vital part of what we do. We want St Christopher's to be a place where all kinds of people can join us to learn from our experience and learn from our patients with us. This does not mean burdening the patients with the demands of continual bedside teaching. It does mean that you can give them an interest I know they enjoy if it is done in the right way. It can also reveal a new purpose in what is happening to them and what they are doing themselves. Certainly they are not all going to be saints. Some will be, indeed, and we will be very honoured and helped by their coming to us. Others will be splendidly maddening and I have no time to suggest the various crises with which we are going to have to cope. But who is to say who does the best – the person whose last weeks are the crown of a life of devotion, the young girl who makes the whole ward into a party for months on end and never shows you how much it costs her, or the old man who just manages to stop grumbling for his last ten days or so? Certainly we will never fail to learn from them, and some of the things that we will learn may surprise our future staff. Work here will not just be solemn. Rather I would just say it will be real and reality is gay and funny as well as serious. Above all, it will never be dull.

Being There

'Watch with me' means, still more than all our learning of skills, our attempts to understand mental suffering and loneliness and to pass on what we have learnt. It means also a great deal that cannot be understood. Those words did not mean 'understand what is happening' when they were first spoken. Still less did they mean 'explain' or 'take away'. However much we can ease distress, however much we can help the patients to find a new meaning in what is happening, there will always be the place where we will have to stop and know that we are really helpless. It would be very wrong indeed if, at that point, we tried to forget that this was so and to pass by. It would be wrong if we tried to cover it up, to deny it and to delude ourselves that we were always successful. Even when we feel that we can do absolutely nothing, we will still have to be prepared to stay.

'Watch with me' means, above all, just 'be there'. I remember the patient who said of the people who had really helped her, 'They never let you down. They just keep on coming'. I also remember she described the way God had met her by saying, 'He sends me people'. I am quite certain that St Christopher's has to learn to be a place where people do not let you down but instead give the feeling of reassurance and safety that comes from faithfulness.

I think from this need especially stems the demand that we should grow into a real community. It is very important that we should be a group of people who have confidence in each other and that St Christopher's should be the kind of family and home that can give the welcome and hospitality of a good home, where people are accepted as themselves and can relax in security. It must also be a place where everyone knows that the individual contributions matter and that there is no hierarchy of importance in what is done. Who will know what or who matters most to an individual patient as his manifold problems are dealt with by various members of such a group? There is a kind of compassionate matter-of-factness that develops in such a place and in this the hard-pressed worker is not overwhelmed by her own responsibilities.

The Community of all Men

Above all, I think it is here that we see the very great need for a religious foundation. We must remember that we belong to the much wider community of the whole Church, to the whole Communion of Saints and, indeed, to the whole community of all men. It is because of this that St Christopher's is ecumenical and unde-nominational. We will welcome people of all sorts and kinds and be of all sorts and kinds ourselves. We are not emphasising that there is just one way but rather that there is one Person coming in many ways.

The same words, 'Watch with me', remind us also that we have not begun to see their meaning until we have some awareness of Christ's presence both in the patient and in the watcher. We will remember his oneness with all sufferers, for that is true for all-time whether they recognise it here or not. As we watch them we know that he has been here, that he still is here and that his presence is redemptive.

Re-interpreting an old Truth

We do not help patients through this part of life by denying that it can sometimes be very hard. We do not see it truly if we just think somewhat vaguely of immortality and 'going on' rather than of death followed by resurrection. Dying followed by rebirth has been a dominant theme of man's religion from the very beginnings of belief. For Christians this has once and for all been summed up and made truth in Christ himself. I believe that it is very important that this message should be shown at St Christopher's in every possible way, for it has hardly any meaning to a great majority of people in Great Britain today. This stands out with sad vividness in Geoffrey Gorer's survey, *Death, Grief and Mourning in Contemporary Britain*. It is a truth which needs to be re-interpreted in terms that are relevant to all those who will come to us, to the patients, to their relations and to all the visitors. Perhaps we may have a contribution to make to the 'new theology' as we learn about this very simply, seeing this truth, this Person, meeting people today.

Through Symbols and Sacraments

Christ will be present in all the skills that we learn and in symbols and sacraments of all kinds. These will include the sacraments of the cup of cold water and the washing of the disciples' feet. All these things will speak silently to the patients about God's love for them. So too will the whole planning and decoration of the building itself, thought out over a very long period with our architect and carried out by him with great insight and imagination. Especially, I think it will be shown in the planning of the chapel and in all the pictures, the symbols and the sculpture that are being created specially for us by artists who share this faith with us. It is very important that this message should be shown in these different ways. I have seen again and again how receptive patients are to the things they look at when they are not able to bear with talking any longer. Often it is important that very little should be said at all because it is so easy to interrupt a real message.

So much of our communication with people is done without words but I think this is especially so with the very ill. The patient who says soon after her admission, 'It is marvellous to begin to feel safe again', has been met by the atmosphere and by the things she lies and looks at just as much as by the nursing and by the drugs and relief she is given. In a whole climate of safety she finds her own key and her own meeting. We will see patients able to listen, perhaps for the first time, to something that has been said to them all their lives but for which they have somehow never had time for real attention.

I have been impressed again and again at St Joseph's by the way patients will lie and look at pictures or a crucifix and how much these can say to them. I believe that it is very important that these should be works created now, by artists who are interpreting these truths in the context of the world today. I am especially glad that this growing emphasis on art for St Christopher's has given us connections with Poland once again, a link that has been there from the beginning and forged again and again.

'My bags are packed . . . '

I think all of us remember the words of Pope John when he said, 'My bags are packed and I can leave with a tranquil heart at any moment'. I think that this is how we pray for all the patients who will come to us. We remember that some of them are already ill, frail, lonely or despairing and pray for them now. Others are busy and have no thought of calamity. Perhaps only in calamity are they going to find the meaning of the whole of the rest of their lives. I think that we should pray that we will be able to make it possible for them to pack their bags with the right things, pack them with what matters, with what *they* need; that while they are here they will find all that they should of reconciliation, fulfilment and meaning as they go through this last part of their lives.

. . . to be silent, to listen, to be there

I have tried to sum up the demands of this work we are planning in the words 'Watch with me'. Our most important foundation for St Christopher's is the hope that in watching we should learn not only how to free patients from pain and distress, how to understand them and never let them down, but also how to be silent, how to listen and how just to be there. As we learn this we will also learn that the real work is not ours at all. We are building for so much more than ourselves. I think if we try to remember this we will see that the work is truly to the greater glory of God.

Artists and the Spirit

Alan Webster

Robert Runcie's theology has always leaned towards a reticent catholic humanism, derived in part from Michael Ramsey, who described himself as a Christian humanist. Since Robert Runcie's early days in the war and afterwards at Oxford, Cambridge and Newcastle, he has enjoyed the close friendship of many who searched for faith, rather than committing themselves to a party in the Churches.

As Dean of St Pauls from 1978 to 1987 I saw how lay people responded to a thinker who shared their quiet faith. Artists, such as those to whom this sermon was preached, would say that they had confidence in the Archbishop's tolerance and light touch. People paid tribute not only to his courage in the war, but to his insistence that the sufferings of the 'Inner Cities' should be faced by a wealthy country, and that in victory after the Falklands war we should pray for reconciliation and remember all the fallen, both British and Argentinian, even at risk of being accused of failure in patriotism.

Whether he was coming to one's wedding, or listening to a student or a priest puzzled or uncertain, he has always communicated a sense of the wonder and hiddenness of the God in whom we believe. He has not ignored the Scriptures or Tradition but has never been railroaded by them. Lay women and men outside denominational boundaries have responded by continuing to look hopefully to the faith of Christendom. Occasions such as the Royal Academy Varnishing Day Service (for which this sermon was given in 1989) or the 1989 Thanksgiving in the Dutch Church for religious toleration, attended by the Archbishop, sharing the service with a Free Church woman Moderator, a Roman Catholic Bishop, a Jewish Rabbi and a Dutch Minister, illustrate the opportunities he has encouraged. He has taken risks for God and encouraged his fellow Christians to look ahead in days of unprecedented change.

Surely thou art a God that hidest thyself (Isaiah 45:15)

God is not obvious: our religious tradition and our personal experience teach us this truth, put in more profound words in the book of Isaiah, 'Surely thou art a God that hidest thyself'. When we draw together such ageless and passionate human concerns as God and Art, there will always be mystery and room for disagreement. From those paintings in the Lascaux caves to the 1989 Summer Academy, the artist and God have shared a dance of creation. Sometimes religious know-alls have tried to dictate the steps of the dance. That's always a mistake. As the London theologian Frederick Denison Maurice said, 'We have been dosing people with religion, when what they want is the living God'. The artist and the hidden living God share the joy of creation.

The Academy's 1988 Exhibition of Henry Moore's work included the maquette of that 'Mother and Child' which is now in the Ambulatory in St Paul's Cathedral. The last time Henry saw it in St Paul's he was in a wheelchair, but we took him up the steps so that he could look through the Tijou gates. From a position in front of the high altar he said simply, almost bluntly, 'It's a great mystery'.

He may have meant the mysterious strength of birth and life, or the mysterious insecurity of Mary or Jesus Christ, or the disturbing mystery of his own creative art – the way his hands went on drawing when he no longer had the power to carve. Certainly it was a kind of Credo, a courageous life-affirming Credo.

A few weeks later a tourist nearly caused a disaster. He was caught sitting on top of the travertine marble with his foot on the head of the child. The curators naturally insisted that the statue should be safeguarded, railed off, so that no one could approach too close, let alone touch the marble. But Henry Moore refused. When I said over the telephone that it might be damaged, he replied with a direct Yorkshire assertion, 'If it's destroyed we'll make another'. The divine gifts to artists are not primarily niceness or cosiness, but in a phrase, energetic courage.

In her poems published this year, Elizabeth Jennings described the artist's courage. She was writing about Turner, surely an artist who ought to be in our mind on Varnishing Day, when he was accustomed almost to take charge in the Royal Academy, and certainly to throw his weight about. Our poet is describing his power as a painter.

> Turner could always see and recreate and celebrate this taut tension and power, like the turning wave, that spreads and streams along the shore.

And of the artists of the Tate collection, Elizabeth Jennings writes:

> An almost impossible peace may here be gathered, But it has to be won by a courage of total looking.

The courage of total looking, both in the artist and the observer should grant the possibility of a hidden God detectable in the work of art. Even the most learned art historians can miss this clue. In the Metropolitan Museum of Art in New York an exhibition earlier this year on Painting in Renaissance Sienna showed a set of small narrative themes painted by Sassetta, once on the predella on an altarpiece in the Carmelite Chapel. Miraculously the Met had reassembled from all over the world these tiny vivid scenes. One of the two which came from Britain is in the Bowes Museum at Barnard Castle in County Durham.

The learned New York critic, who wrote the captions, stated that the meaning of the story of this scene was unknown: a monk dying in hideous circumstances as he received the sacrament. In fact Sassetta was another courageous questioner, a fifteenth-century Bishop of Durham with the same message that we receive from Dr Jenkins: think for yourselves; is it credible or incredible to you; does God really want you to believe that? In Sassetta's painting, the question is whether the Mass is a sacrament, a communion of love, a Eucharist, or whether it is a dogmatic puzzle with deadly consequences if you fail to believe exactly as the Church taught. Another Siennese painter, Giovanni di Paolo, in his final Paradise scene introduced another questioning note of dark despair, a challenge to contemporary religious security. So often, because the message of painters is oblique and hidden, it is all the more powerful.

Neither the Royal Academy nor the Christian Church should feel flattered if people go away saying, 'What a very nice exhibition . . . what a very nice service'. For artists, for all of us, our hidden God should give us energetic courage to expect, to discover a God who can be disturbing, because He is a God who has shared the human capacity to suffer and to question. We could become a famished generation, dissatisfied with what is religiously and artistically comfortable, if we are not challenged by the artists, who can be so powerful and haunt our imaginations. 'Don't worry, be happy', may have been a good tune for a Presidential Campaign, but it won't do for the Royal Academy or for our cathedrals.

The earlier attempts to make God obvious, either in theology or in art, seem to lack credibility. For many of us the cold conscientious recital of creeds raises problems over truth, rather than leading us through symbols and poetry to our own understanding. Saints identified by haloes, as was common in the older paintings and the older sculptures, appear to us less than the saints who have been our contemporaries. It is for the artists to interiorise the halo. Van Gogh put it explicitly in a letter to his brother: 'I want to paint man and woman with that something of the eternal which the halo used to symbolise, but which now seeks to confer through the actual radiance of our colour vibrations.'

This spiritual humanism links reverence for life with reverence for the hidden God. The sense that within humanity there is something given from outside, not self-generated but a 'freshness deep down in things', as Gerard Manley Hopkins insisted. This is the artist's armour against the squalid or the commercially sensational.

For all his accuracy about the horrors of war, it was the assault on the human spirit which Goya condemned. His portraits brim over with hidden energy. The work of Francis Bacon has the same searching dynamism. Many artists offer to churches and cathedrals not sugary comfort but the blunt catharsis which we need in our violent and dangerous century.

For me, moving evidence of the artist's ability to portray the hidden God is the series of Rembrandt self-portraits. As the pouches grew and the hair disappeared, as the blotches darkened and the eyes gave the impression of difficulty and tragedy beyond my imagining, there is in picture after picture a sense of hidden love: love for his art, love and acceptance of himself. In Rembrandt's reticent tradition, he lived and died as one loved by a God who ` Himself knew crucifixion.

Through the varnish and brush-work, and in the carving, we shall again and again see energetic faith. The conviction, under which this Service is held, is that the Spirit is revealed sacramentally in the artist's offering, and that we are all concerned with a God who is not obvious but is hidden.

To that God revealed in love and beauty, in sacrifice and resurrection, be all praise and glory, from the artists and from the Churches, today and throughout all ages . . .

On Leaving

Anthony Phillips

Robert Runcie was Dean of Trinity Hall, Cambridge, from 1956 to 1960. I held that post from 1969 to 1974 before moving to St John's College, Oxford, for whom this sermon was preached in June 1986. There is probably no ministry more intellectually testing than that of an Oxbridge Chaplain. Not only is the population constantly changing, but all one says and does is open to a kind of critical scrutiny rarely found in other ministries. An Oxbridge pastor has to know not only for what he stands but also how to defend himself in Common Room and lecture hall. It is a ministry which of its very nature must be flexible. Ethical and theological boundaries are ever on the move and it is the undergraduate community which dictates the pace.

Robert Runcie's instinct for openness, freedom from dogmatism, total lack of fear in facing theological issues, and respect for the young, all derive from his undergraduate ministry. Year by year saying goodbye to those whom one has come to love is a wearing and demanding exercise. Saying goodbye to active ministry is no easier.

Unless a wheat grain falls into the ground and dies, it remains only a single grain; but if it dies, it yields a rich harvest (from the Gospel)

I have never liked the end of the academic year. For seventeen years as an Oxbridge Chaplain I have had to suffer annual bereavement as men, and latterly men and women, whom I loved left College for the world outside. Of course many have gone on to be close friends, and there was no happier evening this term than when so many of my old pupils came back for supper with Vicky and me. But there is always a risk in parting, the risk that one may not meet again, or worse still that when one does meet, personalities will not be the same, and what had once been a natural intimacy has become a necessary formality. Yet as pastor I know no more pathetic condition than the man or woman who cannot leave, who hangs on, fearful of what lies beyond, unwilling to embrace maturity, ever seeking the safety of the playpen. We have to let go, for what God calls us to is not so much to do anything but to be. And being always involves becoming. Life, as Shakespeare's seven ages of man proclaims, is a journey, and those who will not travel will not know what it is to live.

Now the boot is on the other foot, for along with some of you, I too must depart. A journey beckons for me. Many of my colleagues have found it hard to understand why it is necessary. Oxford offers the don who is priest so much. There is the time for academic work, the time to be pastor – even if the tensions make it seem at times that one is bad at both. But there comes a time too when one knows instinctively that where one is there can be no more becoming, when another's gifts must be applied to the situation if that situation is again to be creative. Staying on is an admission of defeat, a saying no to what might be, an allowing what is, to stultify and stagnate. As Jesus himself knew, it can be good to go away.

But that does not make it easy. Looking round this chapel so many memories flood in – of joy and darkness, of tears and laughter, of the struggle to believe, and of the affirmation of belief. For this has not been a chapel in which those who worshipped have sought an easy faith. Together we have ventured on our own theological journeys, not afraid to risk, but conscious that the God who is creativity bids us ever venture, that we may know more of the truth which His Spirit wills to reveal. This has not been a chapel for retreating from the agonies of a perplexed and divided world, but one in which those who confessed did so amid all the doubts, ambiguities and tensions which no honest Christian can deny. Security has not been our watchword, but abandonment. We have indeed made our text our motto: 'Unless a wheat grain falls into the ground and dies, it remains only a single grain; but if it dies, it yields a rich harvest.' One of you said of my future work: 'Anthony, I hope you do for them what you have done for us: refuse to confirm our prejudices.' No better summary of what I hoped I had achieved could have been given. I am more than conscious that there have been many Christians in this College who could not follow where we have gone, and that has been a constant wound which I have had to bear, more painful than they ever imagine. But that has been the necessary cost of my discipleship, for there must be those who are willing to be at the frontiers of faith, or faith itself will degenerate into that comfortable irrelevance which it is for the majority of this College.

And we who struggle to confess must ever have in mind those who have not joined the struggle, who daily pass this Chapel which for over 400 years has stood at the centre of this College proclaiming the possibility of belief and inviting entry. Its witness has never been strident, nor cheap. It is perhaps best characterised by the daily worship where two or three are gathered together. But it has ensured a continuity of faith which at the end of the day has made and makes possible a vision which gives a dignity to life as nothing else can do.

For over eleven years, God has allowed me to be the enabler of His grace in this place in the administration of His sacraments. As pastor I have shared the doubts, despair, anger and hurt of generations of students. I have witnessed success and failure, seen the impossible become possible, opportunities thrown away. I have known both rejection and love. And like those to whom God called me to minister I too have had my doubts, and despair, I have been angry and hurt, I have enjoyed success and suffered failure, seen the impossible become possible, and thrown opportunities away. As minister of His grace, I know my utter dependence on that grace which I receive in the sacrament of penance. But it is not our failures which prevent the coming of the kingdom: God provides a way for dealing with them. It is our refusal to risk.

But a faith which proclaims that God is love must risk, for risk is the very essence of love. To abandon oneself to the other is the most risky thing one ever does, provides the biggest opportunity for hurt there can be. God risked in His creation of man, and suffers both the love and hurt that results. So as the community of love in this place, we have risked, risked showing that love for each other, risked where our communion would take us. We acknowledge our failures as week by week we gather for Eucharist, to be pardoned by Him who again sends us out to risk for Him. And that will be our endless journey wherever God sends us. If through my ministry I have encouraged others to that journey, then for all my failures, I count myself blessed by God.

It is not easy to talk about the will of God, and those who do it easily, cheapen Him. When an opportunity presents itself, and you have to decide what to do, it is rare indeed that you can ever be certain of the way ahead, can be sure that God is in it. For my part there has been much struggle and after the decision made, uncomfortable cold feet. I have never been very good at waiting on station platforms and protracted goodbyes are a sophisticated form of torture. I will not pretend that I can know that I am doing God's will. God does not in my experience give us those certainties. I believe it is a risk in which I pray I may find His presence.

A priest moving on not only leaves people whom he loves, but the building which has been the very vehicle of his ministry and which becomes part of his most intimate self. I shall miss this chapel more than words can express. When I came from the Chapel at Trinity Hall – described in the guide books as a small drawing-room – to the much larger St John's, I was not at once bowled over by it. No one could claim that what we see around us is a gem. However, it has over the years come to mean everything to me and I dread the last time I shall leave those doors as Chaplain, for it will then become part – as it should become part – of another priest's personality. It will never again be the same for me. If you have ever left a house you loved you will know something of what I am saying. Of your charity do not invite me back too soon.

And what of you, you whom I love. Some of you know that it was reading Bonhoeffer's *Cost of Discipleship* which finally decided me to offer myself for ordination. In my blackest moments, I always return and read it and draw strength to continue. So it is with Bonhoeffer that I want to leave you. May God bless you in your several ministries, may you ever have the courage to risk, may you never be afraid of being vulnerable, may you laugh and weep wholeheartedly, may you ever die that you may become, become an invitation to others to follow you on the journey of becoming. Bonhoeffer writes:

> Nothing can fill the gap when we are away from those we love, and it would be wrong to try and find anything. We must simply hold out and win through. That sounds very hard at first, but at the same time it is a great consolation, since leaving the gap unfilled preserves the bond between us. It is nonsense to say that God fills the gap: He does not fill it, but keeps it empty so that our communion with another may be kept alive, even at the cost of pain.

A Sense of Wonder

Kallistos Ware

As an Orthodox Christian it gives me particular happiness to contribute to this volume. Robert Runcie, like his predecessor Michael Ramsey, has been a generous friend to the Orthodox Church. While a member of the Anglican/Orthodox Joint Doctrinal Discussions in the 1970s, I admired his challenging yet good-humoured leadership as chairman on the Anglican side. This sermon, however, deals not with Christian unity but with a different theme: the Christian significance of a university as a place for the cultivation of wonder and freedom. I develop here two seeds planted in my mind by the Archbishop. I shall always remember the garden maze in his enthronement address at Canterbury. For me a maze is not just a puzzle or muddle, but a path of initiation and discovery, a place of wonder; and it is of this wonder that I speak in my sermon. I was delighted, secondly, by his insistence, during the Oxford University Mission in February 1983, upon universities and colleges as places where freedom is learnt – a point of crucial importance to me as a university teacher. I am grateful to Robert Runcie for his consistent witness as Archbishop to these two values of wonder and freedom.

This sermon was preached, in slightly varying forms, at the commemoration services in All Souls College, Oxford (6 November 1988), and Malvern College (1 July 1989).

O Lord, how manifold are thy works! In wisdom hast thou made for them all; the earth is full of thy riches (Psalm 104:24)

The beginning of truth is to wonder at things (Plato, *Theaetetus*)

There is a service, striking in its symbolism, that members of the Orthodox Church perform at the start or conclusion of any major task or period; on the first day of the month, for example, or at the blessing of a foundation stone, and equally at the commencement or ending of the academic year. It is the ceremony known as the Great Blessing of the Waters. Water is placed in a large bowl, prayers are said over it, the grace and power of the Holy Spirit is called down upon it, and finally the Cross is plunged into the water.

This service of blessing is performed above all on 6 January, the Feast of Theophany or Epiphany. On this day the Orthodox Church is commemorating, not the three wise men – whose coming has already been remembered on 25 December – but the baptism of

Christ in the Jordan. The blessing is held if possible in the open air, by a river or spring or on the sea shore. I can vividly recall the occasions when I have taken part in the Epiphany Blessing of the Waters on the island of Patmos. The abbot of the Monastery of St John the Theologian – the monastery to which I myself belong – comes down with the monks and parish clergy to the harbour and the service is performed at the quayside, with the fishing boats, some thirty or forty of them, drawn up in a great semicircle. At the culminating moment, when the abbot throws a wooden Cross into the water, all the surrounding boats sound their sirens simultaneously, and the young men and boys dive from the boats, racing each other to see who will retrieve the Cross and return it to the abbot.

In an unexpected way this ceremony of the Great Blessing of the Waters helps us to understand the purpose, from a Christian standpoint, of a college or university. Christ's baptism is seen in the Orthodox tradition as possessing a cosmic significance, as embracing the whole created order. His baptism is in a sense the reverse of our own. In our case, baptism is a purification from sin. But Christ is sinless; why, then, should he be baptised? Such precisely is the query posed by John the Baptist: 'I need to be baptised by you, and do *you* come to me?' (Matt. 3:14). The Orthodox answer to this question can best be put in simple picture language. We are dirty; at baptism we go down into clean water and we come out cleansed. At our baptism, then, we are sanctified by the waters. But Christ is clean; at his baptism he goes down into the dirty water and himself cleanses the waters, making them pure. As we affirm in the liturgical texts for the feast of Epiphany, 'Today the Master has come to sanctify the nature of the waters'. At his baptism it is not the waters that sanctify Christ, but Christ who imparts holiness to the waters, and so by extension to the entire material creation.

If we speak of the waters as 'dirty', by this we mean that the world around us, while filled with meaning and beauty, is yet a fallen world, broken and shattered, marred by suffering and sinfulness. Into this fallen world God himself enters, accepting a total solidarity with it, assuming into himself the entirety of our human nature, body, soul and spirit. Through this act of assumption at his incarnation and through all that follows after it – through his baptism in the streams of Jordan, his transfiguration, crucifixion and resurrection – Christ cleanses and heals the marred and fallen world, effecting the renewal not of humankind alone but of the whole creation.

What we are doing, then, at each celebration of Epiphany, at every Blessing of the Waters, is to reaffirm our sense of wonder before the essential goodness and beauty of the world, as originally created by God and as now re-created in Christ. Nothing is intrinsically ugly or despicable; it is solely our distorted vision that makes it seem so. Through the power of God incarnate shown in his baptism in Jordan, all persons and all things can be made holy, can be transfigured and rendered Spirit-bearing. All things are capable of acting as sacraments of God's presence. As we express it in one of our Epiphany hymns:

> At thine appearing in the body,
> The earth was sanctified,
> The water blessed,
> The heaven illumined,
> And humankind delivered
> From the bitter tyranny of the enemy.

Water, earth, sky, the human body and the whole human person with its emotions and affections – through Christ's incarnation and baptism these are all reborn, transformed, hallowed. The Great Blessing of the Waters is in this way a proclamation that the universe around us is not a chaos but a cosmos. There is glory in everything; this is a world full of wonder.

All this has an immediate relevance for the work of a university. For a school or a university is precisely a place in which with rigour and discipline we cultivate our sense of wonder. As teachers and students we are here in order to pursue truth and knowledge; but truth and knowlege, as Plato recognised, are impossible without a sense of wonder: 'The beginning of truth is to wonder at things.' A university, then, is a controlled environment in which we are to develop our sense of wonder before the universe that God has made, before the human person whose vocation it is to serve as microcosm and mediator at the centre of that universe, before all that is conceived by the human mind or fashioned by human hands. It is a place where we are to discover how varied and unexpected is the world in which we live. It is a place where we 'lift up our eyes to the hills' (cf. Ps. 121:1), acknowledging with astonishment the broadness and generosity of our surroundings. It is a place where we are saying explicitly or implicitly, 'O Lord, how manifold are thy works! In wisdom hast thou made them all.'

Plato's insistence upon the link between wonder and truth is confirmed by the Cavalier poet Sidney Godolphin:

> Lord when the wise men came from farr,
> Led to thy Cradle by a Starr,
> Then did the shepheards too rejoyce,
> Instructed by thy Angells voyce:
> Blest were the wisemen in their skill,
> And shepheards in their harmlesse will . . .
>
> There is no merrit in the wise
> But love, (the shepheards sacrifice).
> Wisemen all wayes of knowledge past,
> To th'shepheards wonder come at last:
> To know, can only wonder breede,
> And not to know, is wonders seed.

'To know, can only wonder breede': the 'wisemen' at our modern universities cannot afford to dispense with the wonder of the shepherds. For knowledge and wonder go hand in hand.

Some months ago I had a dream. I was back at the boarding school where forty years ago I lived while at public school. A friend took me first through the rooms already familiar to me in my waking life. But then in my dream we entered the other rooms that I had never seen before – spacious, elegant, filled with light. Finally we entered a small, dark chapel, with mosaics gleaming in candlelight. 'How strange', I said to my companion, 'that I have lived here for years, and yet I never knew about the existence of all these rooms.' And he replied, 'But it is always so.'

Such exactly is the meaning of a school or college. It is a place where we constantly discover new rooms in the universe and in the human heart, in both macrocosm and microcosm; a place where we open the door to each other and invite one another to explore these rooms together.

There is also a second, connected aspect to the Christian meaning of a college or school. As a place for the cultivation of wonder and the pursuit of truth, it is equally a place for the cultivation of freedom. Wonder and freedom, truth and freedom – these things are essentially linked. Wonder can be evoked but not compelled; and truth, as Christ observed, makes us free (John 8:32). In any university it is our task to bear witness to what Kierkegaard said: 'The most tremendous thing granted to man is choice, freedom.' We are to resist all that erodes or diminishes freedom. If I am asked by my students at Oxford, 'What are you trying to teach us here?', then perhaps my best answer is to say no more than this: 'We want you to learn to be free.'

'Learn to be free': freedom cannot simply be assumed; it has to be *learnt*. Suppose that you ask me, 'Can you play the violin?' and I reply, 'I don't know, I've never tried.' You might feel that there was something odd about my answer. Unless I have learnt to play the violin through the exacting discipline of a musical training, I am not free to play Beethoven's violin sonatas. And so it is with every form of freedom. Freedom has to be learnt through the *ascesis*, the ascetic discipline, of precise observation and imaginative thinking; and then it needs to be defended with courage and self-sacrifice. As Nicolas Berdyaev observed, 'Freedom gives birth to suffering, while the refusal to be free diminishes suffering. Freedom is not easy, as its enemies and slanderers allege: freedom is hard; it is a heavy burden. Men often renounce freedom to ease their lot.' Yet if we renounce freedom, we become less than truly human; and if we deny others their freedom, we dehumanise them.

Freedom is not easy, and this means that in a university we are not seeking to offer either to ourselves or to others an easy path. We are never to forget that culminating moment in the Great Blessing at

Epiphany. The Cross has to be plunged into the waters. There is no other way of transfiguration. It can come about only through repentance, *metanoia*, a radical change of mind; and that means through the creative suffering of the Cross.

Such, in part, is the Christian meaning of a college or school. As a place for the cultivation of wonder, its vocation is summed up in words attributed to Christ in the Gospel according to Thomas: 'Let him who seeks not cease from seeking until he finds, and when he finds he will be troubled, and when he has been troubled he will be filled with wonder and he will reign over them All.' As a place for learning freedom, its role is well expressed in a Jewish saying recorded by Martin Buber in his *Tales of the Hasidim*. Rabbi Shelomo asked: 'What is the worst thing that the evil urge can achieve?' And he answered: 'To make someone forget that he is the child of a king.'

Justice Human and Divine

Peter Baelz

The Church of England is an Established Church and the Archbishop of Canterbury has a significant role in the affairs of both Church and State. His task in the latter is critical as well as affirmative. If he appears to some to resemble a member of Her Majesty's loyal Opposition, this is partly because criticism is of more interest to the media than affirmation, but chiefly because it is his duty to remind us all, governors and governed alike, that the only sure foundation of peace and prosperity is the truth and righteousness of God. It is the perennial temptation of those in power to imagine that the benefits of religion derive from having God on their side rather than from placing themselves on the side of God. The following sermon, preached before a congregation of judges, lawyers, police, prison staff, probation officers and others in Durham Cathedral, explores the relationship between law, order, justice and the judgement of God.

> Mercy and truth are met together; righteousness and peace have kissed each other (Psalm 85:10)

I cannot but feel that there is something faintly comic or even frankly Gilbertian about our solemn assembly here this morning. To say no more, we appear on parade in an extraordinary collection of bizarre and eye-catching costumes. In dressing up like this we are taking part in a kind of religious drama. Now the Greek word for play-acting, I need hardly remind you, is *hypokrisis*, 'hypocrisy'. But God, if God there be, is the God of truth. Here we are, then, acting out our little charade in the presence of the One who is, by definition, Being most real. Who, then, is kidding whom?

From one point of view, religion provides a kind of sacred canopy to cover the multifarious activities of society with a cloak of harmony and authority. Or, to use a different image, religion is a sort of ceremonial cement, binding together the rents and ruptures which threaten to destroy the social fabric. According to this view of religion, God's proper name is 'Lord Uhu'. But such is not the God whom we approach this morning. He is the creator of all that is, seen and unseen. He is the Lord, the holy One of Israel. Righteousness and equity are the habitation of His seat, and He requires truth in the inward parts. So I ask again: who is kidding whom?

If we would hear God's 'Yes' pronounced upon our human

institutions and activities, we must also be prepared to hear His 'No'. If we would appeal to Him for His grace and mercy, we must also be willing to submit to His truth and judgement. Archbishop Laud's prayer for the Church is equally applicable to the law: 'Fill it with all truth; in all truth with all peace. Where it is corrupt, purge it; where it is in error, direct it; where anything is amiss, reform it; where it is right, strengthen and confirm it; where it is in want, furnish it; where it is divided and rent asunder, make up the breaches of it, O thou holy One of Israel.'

As we come together, therefore, to affirm in symbol and ritual the significance in human life of order, law and justice, we do well to remember that there is a more profound and sobering dimension to what we are about. We come into the presence of the God who, the prophet reminds us, is apt to despise our solemn assemblies and regard our splendid robes as filthy rags, in order to confess our sin, to seek His forgiveness, and to pray that He will set our feet again firmly in the paths of His righteousness and truth.

With this in mind let us consider what it is that we wish to affirm and ask God to bless. First, it is something to do with order. There can be no world at all without its having some kind of order. However much chaos there may be, chaos is ultimately parasitic on order. The concept of absolute chaos does not even make sense. And what is true of the natural world is also true of the human world. No society can survive, let alone flourish, unless it is an ordered society. This is why we are inclined to think that any kind of 'archy' is preferable to no 'archy', or anarchy. Some years ago, when New York was suffering one of its periodic bouts of near-bankruptcy, there were prolonged cuts in the electric power supply. The street-lights were turned off. Not only did this lead to a rise in the birth-rate some nine months later, but it also coincided with an increase in crime. Perhaps it is going too far to suggest that, had he a ring of invisibility, the so-called just man would behave as badly as the so-called unjust man. However, it is a sad fact of human nature – call it 'original sin' if you will – that, given half a chance, we are apt to prefer darkness to light, easy self-gratification to a disciplined concern for the common good.

No society – not even a society of thieves – can survive for long without some kind of order. Those human propensities which lead to disruption, disorder and crime have to be subjected to a measure of control. Even so, I suggest, we should be unwise to dismiss out of hand the perverse utterances of the anarchist. His witness is a reminder to us that ultimately the imposition of order depends on the use of coercive power, and that, human beings being what they are, the exercise of power swiftly and all too easily corrupts. In an ordered society, therefore, room must be made for public criticism and protest.

From order we move on to law. The imposition of order may be arbitrary and cruel. The rule of law is one way of limiting the abuse of power and placing restraints on its exercise. Under the rule of law individuals and groups have some knowledge of where they stand and what they may expect. Without such an element of predictability human life disintegrates. Where nothing is predictable, human beings break down. This was one of the lessons of the concentration camp. Arbitrarily exercised power can produce some kind of order, but without law humanity is destroyed. A civilised and humane society requires both order and law.

Law and order, however, important as they are, are not enough. Laws may be unjust, and the administration of law the promulgation of injustice. It is possible, no doubt, to keep one's eyes close to the ground and to define justice in circumscribed terms of legality. But such a proposal is short-sighted. For one thing, it leaves no solid basis for criticising and, if necessary, amending the law. We may or may not wish to speak of a 'natural' justice, but such language does at least convey the truth that law itself must stand at the bar of fairness and equity. It is this 'natural' justice that is invoked to protect the individual from the worst excesses of those who hold power and make law, claiming for each human person what fairness and equity prescribe as that person's due. It is a symbol of the fact that, despite all our differences, natural and cultural, we share a common humanity.

But are even natural justice and common humanity enough? If they are to have a firm foundation, must we not press beyond them and speak of a divine justice and a God-given humanity?

A former professor of philosophy at Cambridge – with the appropriate name of Wisdom! – once wrote of our need as human beings for a deeper and more thorough judgement than that which deals only with surface appearances. I quote:

> Though we do make and need to make limited judgements we need again and again to call to mind how different they are from the divine judgement in which both easy forgiveness and easy condemnation are impossible. This is the judgement we ask for ourselves. For we ask that at our own trial counsel and judge shall proceed with infinite patience. We ask that they shall not judge a part of the picture without seeing the whole. We ask that they shall consider, ruthlessly but with understanding, circumstance beyond circumstance, wheel within wheel.

This picture of the judgement of God, ruthless but patient and understanding, needs to be borne in mind when, as today, we are affirming order, law and justice. In the presence of such a judgement we are all sinners. Our plea can only be: Lord, have mercy. Or, as Wisdom puts it:

> We know that action cannot always wait for such judgement. The law must take its course and rightly the sheriff's men ride hard behind the man who has broken it. But at times his case is such that we may take

leave to note with a certain satisfaction the unfaltering gait of the good beast that carries him 'beyond the ten commandments'.

'Beyond the ten commandments'? Must we, can we, really go beyond the law? Is there something even more fundamental in the ordering of the good life than justice? Let us put the question differently. If justice is concerned with giving us all our due, what is it that is 'due'? Is it what we deserve? Then who would escape a whipping? Is justice blind, not only in the sense that it is impartial and incorruptible, but also in the more dubious sense that it fails to take into account the full range of our humanity? Is it essentially backward-looking, when what we need is something which also looks forward to what, as God's creatures and under God's providence, we have it in us to become? Jesus' parable of the Labourers in the Vineyard is notoriously difficult to interpret if it is taken literally as a parable of justice. No industrial court would tolerate for one moment the employer's decision to pay the same wage to those who had worked for only one hour and to those who had borne the heat and burden of the day. But the gist of the parable is not about justice. Rather it points us beyond justice to the deeper reality of generosity. Those who had not been employed because they were unemployable were still human beings with human needs. God's dealings with His people spring from His overflowing generosity. His love embraces all His children. He sends sun and rain on good and bad alike. This love is not heedless of the claims of justice and truth. In Him, however, justice and grace cohere. His righteousness is a saving righteousness. Herein lies the mystery of the atonement. 'If we confess our sins, He is faithful and just to forgive us our sins, and to cleanse us from all unrighteousness.'

Human justice needs to be set in a context of divine justice. And divine justice needs to be set in a context of divine charity. Such charity is neither easy nor cheap. It combines the judgement of truth with the hope of forgiveness and renewal. It is the charity which, for our sin and our salvation, took our Lord Jesus Christ to the Cross, where the judgement of truth upon our all-too-human injustice and lovelessness was enacted and endured. It is the charity which, through resurrection faith, offers new life. It is the charity which makes justice bearable and gives miserable sinners hope. It is the spirit and life of God Himself, in whom mercy and truth, righteousness and peace, greet each other with a kiss.

So back to ourselves. When we dress up and meet in solemn assembly, as we do here this morning, are we only acting out a pretence? Or, through our acted symbolism, dare we also humbly approach the judgement seat of God, bring before Him our successes and failures, our hopes and our fears, seek His forgiveness and mercy, and pray that He will surround and support our striving for order, law and justice with the resources of His abundant grace?

Let Gerard Manley Hopkins have the last word and leave us with a vision of a justice that mediates the grace and graciousness of God:

> I say more: the justman justices;
>   Keeps grace: that keeps all his goings graces;
> Acts in God's eye what in God's eye he is –
>   Christ. For Christ plays in ten thousand places,
> Lovely in limbs, and lovely in eyes not his
>   To the Father through the features of men's faces.

The Creative Vision

Ursula King

My contact with the Archbishop goes back just a few years ago when I was invited to give the Fifth Lambeth Inter-faith Lecture in 1986 entitled 'Seeing the Divine in Hinduism and Christianity'. When this lecture later appeared in print (published by the Centre for the Study of Religion and Society, University of Kent), the Archbishop provided a kind foreword to it, and subsequently we had several opportunities to meet again over inter-faith matters, especially on the occasion of other Lambeth Inter-faith Lectures to which he always gave generously of his time and hospitality.

Another link between us have been the Teape Lectures, which are given annually, but alternate in their location between Cambridge and India and deal with comparative themes in Hinduism and Christianity. Like several other British scholars I was invited to give these lectures some time ago but it is worth knowing that Dr Runcie, when still a lecturer at Cambridge, went to India to lecture in this series.

There is not only the shared interest in inter-faith dialogue but another link concerns the value and importance of education. As is well known, Dr Runcie was a university teacher earlier in his career. His general interest in education relates to wider questions such as how to foster true understanding, insight and wisdom in individuals and communities, and how to put Christian principles into practice in today's world. I have selected a brief sermon given at the invitation of the Catholic Chaplaincy during the annual university service at St Emmanuel's Church, University of Leeds, in November 1988, as a small contribution in honour of Robert Runcie's work and achievements. In it I reflect on the right attitude of mind and heart, the creative and imaginative vision needed for being alert to the stirrings of the divine spirit within and without – otherwise all education amounts to nothing.

> Beware of the scribes who like to walk about in long robes, to be greeted obsequiously in the market squares, to take the front seats in the synagogues and the places of honour at banquets; these are the men who swallow the property of widows, while making a show of lengthy prayers. The more severe will be the sentence they receive (Mark 12:38–44)

In today's Gospel Jesus warns us not to follow the example of the scribes – the doctors of law – who see themselves as set apart and special; they walk around in long robes and take pride of place in secular and religious life, at banquets and in synagogues. The example of the rich who give freely but condescendingly and perhaps rather absentmindedly, is not the example Jesus holds up to us. No, it is the example of the poor widow who makes a real sacrifice through her giving, but remains humble about it.

This parable, like the reading, points to the importance of simplicity and humility. Can we be humble and give simply, wholeheartedly, without taking pride in what we do, without self-importance, just as the simple woman in the Gospel? Or are we like the scribes, the learned, who take false pride in their learning which gives them wealth and high positions from where they look down on their fellow beings?

On the occasion of the annual Academic Mass it seems appropriate to reflect on what our learning, the education we seek and find at a university, truly gives us – not in terms of achievement and success, but in our whole human development, and especially in terms of our spiritual formation.

Does our learning lead us into false arrogance and pride so that we are no longer humble and simple at heart, before God and our fellow beings? This raises the further question: what kind of education do we really receive in the university? Is it all external and merely instrumental, useful for doing things, for earning money, for acquiring a reputation and possessions – or does our education truly 'educate' us – bring out the best in us, so that we can be truthful, honest and loving – the way Jesus was, truly transformed by the power of the Spirit?

We must ask ourselves: how far does the education we receive and give perhaps lead to a neglect of the inner life of the spirit? How far does it lead us *away* from true insight and wisdom rather than towards them?

So many people today have a rather compartmentalised and impoverished notion about religion and spirituality, as something set apart and different from life as ordinarily lived. But we do not need to seek special religious experiences set apart from our ordinary experience; instead, we need to discover how to see our ordinary experiences in a new light so that we understand them all religiously, as possible entry and starting points for being transformed by the power of God's spirit. This is a very deep, enriching experience which also extends to our learning and search for knowledge.

We are all involved in education in one way or another, as students and teachers, learning to find their way. How can we understand – and transform our life as students and teachers religiously? How can our daily experience of learning lead to inner, spiritual transformation and strength?

This raises the question of how knowledge is related and must

ultimately be grounded in true wisdom. But does university education really enrich us, does it make us grow in insight, wisdom
and love – or is it merely linked to external quantifiable results, to
degrees, titles, honours and positions in an ever increasing hierarchy, so that we can swell ourselves with self-importance like the
scribes? Is knowledge not being commodified by the educational
and knowledge enterprise, as knowledge that can be traded as prop-
erty and possession, that is bought and paid for, and exchanged for
other goods? Much of our society's government, and industry's
dealings in knowledge is of this kind. The pursuit of knowledge
today is linked to heavy investments in both time and money, but
also in personal efforts and ambitions. But is this state of affairs,
this commodification and false externalisation of knowledge, not
really a betrayal – a betrayal of ourselves and of the truth, a betrayal
of the real goals of a truly worthwhile and fully human life, and
deepest of all a betrayal of our Christian life and its vocation to
become redeemed and transformed by the power of wisdom and
grace?

We have made an idolatrous thing of knowledge, based on the
split between a narrowly defined and poorly used intellect and the
powers of love – a split between our intellectual/rational life and the
affective, inner life deep within us.

We need not only educate ourselves; we need to *re*-educate our
faculties and vision to become sensitive to 'the stirrings of the spirit',
not only within us, within our own depths, but also without; we
need to become aware of the powerful presence of God all around
and amidst us, working and transforming people and situations.
That is true awareness leading to wisdom, to find the centre of our
identity not in possessions and honours, in the things we have
acquired and which rightly belong to us, but in an awareness grown
in response to a calling from the divine spirit which breathes through
all the events of our life.

Some people full of insight today say that we must learn to combine and fuse the spirit of modern knowledge, the spirit of science
with all its wonderful advances and achievements, with the spirit
of love, which alone can bring people together in true community,
so that we can use and share the best of our knowledge, the precious
gifts discovered and given, for the best of humanity.

Let us honestly ask ourselves why and what do we study for? For
a degree? A job? Because of the social pressure exercised by our
parents and peers to seek advancement, ostentation and power? Or
do we love knowledge and seek it with a sense of enquiry, a sense
of wonder, discovery and adventure?

Let us ask ourselves, do we ever look beyond the knowledge we
receive, and search for wisdom, a wisdom human and divine, a
knowledge understood as much larger and deeper that will lead us
to the wholeness that is God? If we enter that path, we have to walk

not just for three years, or five, or even ten, but we have to walk for the rest of our lives as true seekers, true adventurers of the spirit who remain humble till the last, for the more we know, the more we realise that the best insights and true wisdom are not acquired, but are gratuitously given by a power higher than ourselves. Seeing all knowledge, including higher education, from this perspective, means to be on a path to that Mount of Vision which is God. From there we gain a much larger perspective, a deeper, richer insight, which Melvyn Mathews in a fine, reflective book has called *Delighting in God*.

Can we so love a rightly understood knowledge – knowledge as rooted in and suffused with the spirit of wisdom – that we experience it as our path to the delight in God? That can give us deep strength and sustenance, even in the midst of affliction and suffering – it will give us a share of power in God's power, not power in the sense of domination and claim over others, but *enabling* power which will help, support and nourish us so we can share it in community with others. Such power drawn from spiritual experience and insight is truly transformative. We can greatly develop and strengthen it by the resources of the Christian faith, by looking at Jesus and the community of early disciples, by sharing the power of the spirit in communion and community. But in our search for knowledge, truth and life we can also look at the numerous witnesses to learning, insight and wisdom found throughout the long history of the Christian faith. Let us pray to God that we may all be strengthened to find the right knowledge and power that will not set us against each other but that makes us humbly share in the gifts we have received. Let us finish by asking the help of God's spirit and power in all our endeavours by saying the opening prayer of today's liturgy:

> God of power and mercy,
> protect us from all harm.
> Give us freedom of spirit
> and health in mind and body
> to do your work on earth.

Rethinking on Principle

Leslie Houlden

Robert Runcie has presided over Anglican life in a difficult period for theology in relation to the Church. Diversity has rarely seemed so obvious. Ignorance and stridency have rarely felt so assured. Subtlety and patience of thought have rarely felt so undervalued. Institutionally, the theology of the universities has lost its old close ties with the Church and there is much mutual suspicion. Religion in schools makes a third element, largely distinct from both universities and Church. No doubt new good will emerge, but it will be difficult when so many can think of nothing but dogged traditionalism in one form or another. Perhaps the unprecedented expansion of theological courses recently in church life is a sign of that good. In this situation, the Archbishop has helped to preserve sanity and moderation, refusing to condemn and holding doors open. It has not been an innovative role but it has been what the times most required and the best contribution that was possible.

This sermon was preached at Hull University Chaplaincy on Trinity Sunday 1990.

Thirty-five years ago today, Trinity Sunday, I was ordained to serve as a curate in South Leeds, on a stipend of £180 per annum plus keep, and paying one shilling per month in income tax. In the period since 1955, things have changed immeasurably (not least in clergy stipends) and unpredictably. The Victorian Gothic church in Hunslet, built in 1864 largely by the munificence of a wine importer, has been pulled down, apart from its spire, and replaced by a modern meeting-hall-style church; save for the pubs, the greater part of the parish has been demolished twice, first the back-to-backs and then the high-rise flats, and major new roads have made everything unrecognisable. In Church life in general, few in 1955 were agitating much for a new prayer book; scarcely anyone suggested that women might be ordained (though it was said to have happened in far-off Hong Kong); a few priests faced the people to celebrate the Eucharist, and ordinands would travel miles to gawp at the sight; and the sound of the guitar was not heard in our worship.

The changes may be welcomed or regretted, but they cannot be denied or wished away: they are there for all to see. But how about other, more abstract changes, changes in Christian belief? It is common to feel that somehow they do not change: they are enshrined in creeds or Scripture. They may go out of fashion or circulation, or they may lose steam, as belief in final judgement has lost steam compared with its vivid prominence in the nineteenth century; but they are still firmly there in the Church's faith. You might on this view land up in a situation where a belief was not actually held by anybody you could point to but was still the faith of the Church. Then the question is: would that make sense?

Let me put forward another, more historical, candid approach – and let me state it quite starkly. Beliefs do change – constantly and subtly. It is true that old beliefs never quite die: each phase of belief survives somewhere. A little thought may reveal that you have among your acquaintance ripe specimens of fourth-century or thir- teenth-century believer (though he or she is unlikely to keep it up thoroughgoingly, and if you know enough you can spot the flaws). But new ways of believing do constantly arise; including of course new perceptions of God himself. How could it be otherwise, as new cultural situations, new ways of thinking, come on the scene? Such new perceptions are the very condition of intelligibility, both for oneself and for any likely audience. Ye olde fourth-century believer is an isolated figure, likely to be a mysterious eccentric to those around, a puzzle to all except himself.

So to today's observance, Trinity Sunday. Here is a prime example of the two approaches I have just described. You can point to Church formulations which embody the Church's doctrine of God as Trinity. The classical ones come from the fourth and fifth centuries, but they have been the basis for much reflection since, yielding refinement of thought and clarity of exposition. They are couched in the lan- guage and thought-forms of that distant period. Not surprisingly, their language and thought are not natural to us now. In practice, scarcely anyone, clerical or lay, except a handful of professional theologians who specialise in the subject, can expound those formu- lations successfully. Even fewer can make them their own, that is (I take it) believe them in any real way. I heard a priest expound the doctrine with what I felt to be simplicity and accessibility to an audience of students – to be greeted with an irritated protest of mystification. Yet of course the belief remains on the official agenda. It is the Church's faith. And has it not been so from the start, at least in embryo?

There was a television discussion about the interpretation of Beethoven's Ninth Symphony. Two conductors put their views. One insisted that it should be played as Beethoven would have wished, that is, on early nineteenth-century instruments and using early nineteenth-century methods and style of musicianship. The other said that the symphony contained the seeds of future German romanticism: Wagner was latent in Beethoven. So it should be played in such a way as to demonstrate that potentiality, a way

Beethoven himself could not have seen consciously but might have recognised hazily if it had been pointed out to him.

So we may say that the full-blown, classical doctrine of the Trinity, set out in those fourth- and fifth-century formulations, is not to be found in the New Testament; but perhaps it is foreshadowed in the New Testament, waiting to be given substance. Or is it better to say that the Christian perceptions of God found in the New Testament (themselves diverse) are one thing, and belong to their time and are best appreciated so; while the Christian perceptions of God in the fourth century are another thing, best appreciated as such, in their own setting; *and* Christian perceptions of God now are another thing, to be understood in *our* setting? To point up the comparison with musical interpretation: while there is a tradition of musical development that is identifiable, and music does not simply lurch from one manner to another, each disconnected from what precedes and succeeds, there is much to be said for hearing each work in its own historical right.

Surely, then, there are connections between the various perceptions and styles of Christian believing. Surely there are common threads. Let us list some:

1. Christians believe in one God, not many deities: that is worth saying, though, with few exceptions, it is not controversial as it was in the early days, at least not in the old form.
2. Christians believe in God as creative, as the concerned ground of all things, for ever, relentlessly, for now, in the constant present.
3. Christians believe in God as saving, that is, as insistent on bringing us to great good, to the heights of well-being, in relationship with Him and with each other; yet through suffering and hardness, which are to make for good.
4. Christians believe in God as giving the key to these perceptions through Jesus. He set going or revived, by his life and death, modes of reflection, again diverse, in which we still share and to which we contribute as our lives enable us to do and make it our duty to do.

You may say that this comes out recognisably as belief in God as creator, redeemer and sustainer, and that 'Father, Son and Spirit' come out very nicely after all as symbols for these beliefs. Well and good, you can say that. But the convictions I listed are deeper and more constant in Christian life than the old fourth-century classical formulations of Trinitarian doctrine, which can now even obscure those convictions for us and lead us to think in terms of information about God when we should be seeking a vision of God. What is more, those convictions bring us into closer touch both with our Jewish roots and with other faiths (the quest of humankind for God and His for us), while the formulations can scarcely help separate us from them and historically have played that role. Indeed, their original purpose was to set fences and gates, albeit against benighted Christians as well as plain infidels. As I put them, the convictions venture to say nothing about the inner structure of the divine life and speak rather of our experience of God. That modesty is wise, for that is where our assurance lies. Even the apparently bold language of the old Trinity doctrine was always modified by recognition of God's essential 'ungraspability' by human minds – something which modern literalists forget or ignore.

The thing to do with God is, after all, not to analyse Him as if He were an object in our hands, but to serve His cause, to love and worship Him, the source and goal of all our good.

Part II
ONE CHURCH

The Path of Unity

John Paul II

On the Eve of Pentecost, 1982, Canterbury Cathedral was the setting for A Celebration of Faith to Welcome Pope John Paul II. This event has continued to fire the imagination of all who seek the unity of Christians. It was a celebration rich with hope for the eventual fulfilment of Christ's prayer 'that they all may be one' (John 17:21). The homily of Pope John Paul II develops a theological approach that has become characteristic of his teaching on Christian Unity. Anglicans and Catholics share a common baptism. They have already received the gift of the Holy Spirit and it is precisely the Spirit that will restore unity among Christians: 'Christ's promise gives us confidence in the power of this same Holy Spirit to heal the divisions introduced into the Church in the course of the centuries since that first Pentecost day.'

The passage which has just been read is taken from John and contains the words of Jesus Christ on the eve of his Passion. While he was at supper with his disciples, he prayed: 'That they may all be one, even as thou, Father, art in me, and I in thee, that they also may be in us, so that the world may believe that thou hast sent me' (John 17:21).

These words are marked in a particular way by the Paschal Mystery of our Saviour, by his Passion, death and Resurrection. Though pronounced once only, they endure throughout all generations. Christ prays unceasingly for the unity of his Church, because he loves her with the same love with which he loved the apostles and disciples who were with him at the Last Supper. 'I do not pray for these only, but also for those who believe in me through their word' (John 17:20). Christ reveals a divine perspective in which the Father and the Son and the Holy Spirit are present. Present also is the most profound mystery of the Church: the unity in love which exists between the Father and the Son and the Holy Spirit penetrates to the heart of the people whom God has chosen to be his own, and is the source of their unity.

Christ's words resound in a special way today in this hallowed Cathedral which recalls the figure of the great missionary Saint Augustine whom Pope Gregory the Great sent forth so that through his words the sons and daughters of England might believe in Christ.

Dear brethren, all of us have become particularly sensitive to these words of the priestly prayer of Christ. The Church of our time is the Church which participates in a particular way in the prayer of Christ for unity and which seeks the ways of unity, obedient to the Spirit who speaks in the words of the Lord. We desire to be obedient, especially today, on this historic day which centuries and generations have awaited. We desire to be obedient to Him whom Christ calls the Spirit of truth.

On the feast of Pentecost last year Catholics and Anglicans joined with Orthodox and Protestants, both in Rome and in Constantinople, in commemorating the First Council of Constantinople by professing their common faith in the Holy Spirit, the Lord and Giver of life. Once again on this vigil of the great feast of Pentecost, we are gathered in prayer to implore our heavenly Father to pour out anew the Holy Spirit, the Spirit of Christ, upon His Church. For it is the Church which, in the words of that Council's Creed, we profess to be the work *par excellence* of the Holy Spirit when we say 'we believe in one, holy, catholic and apostolic church'.

Today's Gospel passages have called attention in particular to two aspects of the gift of the Holy Spirit which Jesus invoked upon his disciples: he is the Spirit of truth and the Spirit of unity. On the first Pentecost day, the Holy Spirit descended on that small band of disciples to confirm them in the truth of God's salvation to the world through the death and Resurrection of His Son, and to unite them into the one Body of Christ, which is the Church. Thus we know that when we pray 'that all may be one' as Jesus and his Father are one, it is precisely in order that 'the world may believe' and by his faith be saved (cf. John 17:21). For our faith can be none other than the faith of Pentecost, the faith in which the Apostles were confirmed by the Spirit of truth. We believe that the Risen Lord has authority to save us from sin and the powers of darkness. We believe, too, that we are called to 'become one body, one spirit in Christ' (Eucharistic Prayer III).

In a few moments we shall renew our baptismal vows together. We intend to perform this ritual, which we share in common as Anglicans and Catholics and other Christians, as a clear testimony to the one sacrament of Baptism by which we have been joined to Christ. At the same time we are humbly mindful that the faith of the Church to which we appeal is not without the marks of our separation. Together we shall renew our renunciation of sin in order to make it clear that we believe that Jesus Christ has overcome the powerful hold of Satan upon 'the world' (John 14:17). We shall profess anew our intention to turn away from all that is evil and to turn towards God who is the author of all that is good and the source of all that is holy. As we again make our profession of faith in the triune God – Father, Son and Holy Spirit – we find great hope in the promise of Jesus: 'The Counsellor, the Holy Spirit, whom the

Father will send in my name, he will teach you all things, and bring to your remembrance all that I have said to you' (John 14:26). Christ's promise gives us confidence in the power of this same Holy Spirit to heal the divisions introduced into the Church in the course of the centuries since that first Pentecost day. In this way the renewal of our baptismal vows will become a pledge to do all in our power to co-operate with the grace of the Holy Spirit, who alone can lead us to the day when we will profess the fullness of our faith together.

We can be confident in addressing our prayer for unity to the Holy Spirit today, for according to Christ's promise the Spirit, the Counsellor, will be with us for ever (cf. John 14:16). It was with confidence that Archbishop Fisher made bold to visit Pope John XXIII at the time of the Second Vatican Council, and that Archbishops Ramsey and Coggan came to visit Pope Paul VI. It is with no less confidence that I have responded to the promptings of the Holy Spirit to be with you today at Canterbury.

My dear brothers and sisters of the Anglican Communion, 'whom I love and long for' (Phil. 4:1), how happy I am to be able to speak directly to you today in this great Cathedral! The building itself is an eloquent witness both to our long years of common inheritance and to the sad years of division that followed. Beneath this roof Saint Thomas Becket suffered martyrdom. Here too we recall Augustine and Dunstan and Anselm and all those monks who gave such diligent service in this church. The great events of salvation history are retold in the ancient stained glass windows above us. And we have venerated here the manuscript of the Gospels sent from Rome to Canterbury thirteen hundred years ago. Encouraged by the witness of so many who have professed their faith in Jesus Christ through the centuries – often at the cost of their own lives – a sacrifice which even today is asked of not a few, as the new chapel we shall visit reminds us – I appeal to you in this holy place, all my fellow Christians, and especially the members of the Church of England and the members of the Anglican Communion throughout the world, to accept the commitment to which Archbishop Runcie and I pledge ourselves anew before you today. This commitment is that of praying and working for reconciliation and ecclesial unity according to the mind and heart of our Saviour Jesus Christ.

On this first visit of a Pope to Canterbury, I come to you in love – the love of Peter to whom the Lord said, 'I have prayed for you that your faith may not fail; and when you have turned again, strengthen your brethren' (Luke 22:32). I come to you also in the love of Gregory, who sent Saint Augustine to this place to give the Lord's flock a shepherd's care (cf. 1 Pet. 5:2). Just as every minister of the Gospel must do, so today I echo the words of the Master: 'I am among you as one who serves' (Luke 22:27). With me I bring to you, beloved brothers and sisters of the Anglican Communion, the hopes and the desires, the prayers and good will of all who are united with the Church of Rome, which from earliest times was said to 'preside in love' (Ignatius, *Ad Rom.*, Proem.).

In a few moments Archbishop Runcie will join me in signing a *Common Declaration*, in which we give recognition to the steps we have already taken along the path of unity, and state the plans we propose and the hopes we entertain for the next stage of our common pilgrimage. And yet these hopes and plans will come to nothing if our striving for unity is not rooted in our union with God; for Jesus said, 'In that day you will know that I am in my Father, and you in me, and I in you. He who has my commandments and keeps them, he it is who loves me; and he who loves me will be loved by my Father, and I will love him and manifest myself to him' (John 14:20–1). This love of God is poured out upon us in the person of the Holy Spirit, the Spirit of truth and of unity. Let us open ourselves to his powerful love, as we pray that, speaking the truth in love, we may all grow up in every way into him who is the head, into our Lord Jesus Christ (cf. Eph. 4:15). May the dialogue we have begun lead us to the day of full restoration of unity in faith and love.

On the eve of his Passion, Jesus told his disciples: 'If you love me, you will keep my commandments' (John 14:15). We have felt compelled to come together here today in obedience to the great commandment: the commandment of love. We wish to embrace it in its entirety, to live by it completely, and to experience the power of this commandment in conformity with the words of the Master: 'I pray the Father, and he will give you another Counsellor, to be with you for ever, even the Spirit of truth, whom the world cannot receive, because it neither sees him nor knows him; you know him, for he dwells with you, and will be in you' (John 14:16–17).

Love grows by means of truth, and truth draws near to man by means of love. Mindful of this, I lift up to the Lord this prayer: O Christ, may all that is part of today's encounter be born of the Spirit of truth and be made fruitful through love.

Behold before us: the past and the future!
  Behold before us: the desires of so many hearts!
You, who are the Lord of history and the Lord of human hearts, be with us! Christ Jesus, eternal Son of God, be with us! Amen.

A Pilgrim Church

John Simpson

*The Archbishop of Canterbury, like any diocesan bishop, has his own
Cathedral, but in the case of Canterbury, the Cathedral is both a national
shrine and the Mother Church of the world-wide Anglican Communion.*

*Robert Runcie's love for Canterbury Cathedral – the building, the
community which lives around it, its worship and its traditions – has
been a distinguishing mark of his archiepiscopate. To this Cathedral he
brought Pope John Paul II and also the Patriarchs of Constantinople, Antioch
and Alexandria; only once was it impossible for him to preside at the yearly
commemoration of Canterbury's greatest martyr, Thomas Becket; for
him, the Cathedral was a focus of the 1988 Lambeth Conference; so
frequently, over ten years, was he to be found, unannounced, a
worshipper at the early morning Cathedral Eucharist.*

*Robert Runcie has valued Canterbury. Canterbury has not merely valued
Robert Runcie, but prayed for him each day that he has been Archbishop.*

This sermon was preached on 31 July 1988.

Introduction

For 800 years and more – and even today – Canterbury has been a
place of pilgrimage. People of every class and station, and also of
every country, have made their way here to draw inspiration and
encouragement: from what? A building which is one of the glories
of European Gothic – perhaps. A church which, over the centuries,
has found itself becoming the spiritual centre of a world-wide communion of Christians – perhaps. Or is it a saint who, by his witness
to a principle and his martyrdom, exposes the truth of all martyrdom, that life and victory and resurrection come only by treading
the pathway of suffering and death? – perhaps.

What this Cathedral is

But when these myriads of people come, what do they find? Certainly not a lecture hall, where people sit in serried ranks to be
instructed. Nor yet an arena, where all gather around to watch a
spectacle. No, what is found is a whole complex of separate buildings under one roof. As one medieval writer put it: 'Church seemed

to be piled on Church'; or another writer: 'A new temple was entered as soon as the first was ended.' This church, as it was rebuilt after the great fire of 1174, was not primarily for the monastic community, though the Quire was there for them and their spiritual needs: it was rebuilt as it is in order to house the body of a saint, and a saint who, by his death and martyrdom, was felt to proclaim the priority of the spiritual power over the temporal power.

The Pilgrimage

Within a year or so of his death, pilgrims came flocking to see where Thomas died. They came in their thousands, and this building was rebuilt not just as the goal of their pilgrimage, but, in a real sense, to continue their pilgrimage. They gathered in the Nave to wait – to wait until it was possible for them to be directed through the dark passage that goes beneath the Pulpitum Steps and leads to the place of martyrdom where Thomas fell and where now stands the Altar of the Sword Point. Next, they were taken to the Crypt, to see the relics of the saint. Then, emerging from the South Crypt door, their pilgrimage continued up the Pulpitum Steps, through the Quire, out into the North Presbytery Aisle, to the Pilgrim Steps, which they mounted, most upon their knees, until they came to the holiest place, where first they went to Becket's Crown – our Chapel of Twentieth Saints and Martyrs, where originally Becket's scalp was preserved. And then, to the Shrine itself – great jewel of the Trinity Chapel, raised to house the body of the saint – and standing above the very place where originally, in the Crypt, Thomas had been buried, there to worship or to pray, before being escorted out, inspired and encouraged, to continue on life's pilgrimage.

A Pilgrimage Church and its Values

That is this church: a pilgrimage church. Which is why it is difficult successfully to stage modern worship here, be it the worship of the Prayer Book, or the Alternative Service Book, or any of the modern liturgies we experience today. For Prayer Book worship you must look to the Wren churches of seventeenth-century London, and for the right setting for the Alternative Service Book to St Paul's, Bow Common, London. But Canterbury is one of the great medieval pilgrimage churches, constructed to facilitate pilgrimage and to emphasise the values of pilgrimage. And those values are humility and devotion.

Why humility? Because you cannot think yourself anything when you come face to face with someone who was prepared to let himself be slaughtered, rather than give up the truth of Christ. People came in their hundreds of thousands to Canterbury in the Middle Ages, because here was the body of a man – not a humble man, and perhaps that makes the point more forcibly – a man who, according to his lights, tried to tread the way of Christ, and, by what happened to him, exposed the heart of Christianity itself: that we must all die to ourselves and to evil, so that a new being, a new life may emerge. He made the sacrifice of death, physical death – but the same demand, even though it may not reach the ultimate sacrifice of death itself, is laid on each one of us, as we live our earthly pilgrimage. And facing up to what this means, and all its implications, is creative of humility in us.

The other value or quality or product of pilgrimage, at which I hinted, is devotion: the costly giving of oneself in love. The Shrine of Thomas Becket, Becket's Crown, the Quire, the Crypt, the Martyrdom – for 400 years, these places were laden with costly gifts, the gifts of men and women who perceived the fact that the martyr sacrifice – whether it be the sacrifice of Christ himself in total love for all mankind, or the sacrifice of that select band of his followers who were required to give their own lives – demanded costly gifts of love from those who, though forgiven much, were not required to make the ultimate sacrifice of life itself.

Conclusion

To some, this sermon may have seemed somewhat like a history lesson, recounting pilgrimage in the Middle Ages. I trust not. All I have said of what this building is, and of how it was used, has been meant to ram home two truths from the lessons of this morning's Eucharist. The first from the New Testament lesson: 'If a man imagines himself to be somebody, when he is nothing, he is deluding himself': our need is for HUMILITY. And from the Gospel: 'I tell you that her sins, her many sins, must have been forgiven her, or she would not have shown such great love': DEVOTION.

Continuity and Community

John Witheridge

This sermon was preached at the end of my first year at Eton, in June 1988, and a year after leaving Lambeth, where I had served as Dr Runcie's Chaplain since 1984. Its theme is continuity and community, and their interdependence. Creative history and human harmony are matters close to Dr Runcie's heart and, of course, to this anthology. Reading the sermon again has reminded me of how much these priorities have become my own.

I

If you were to ask me what has impressed me most this year, or what has seemed to me Eton's most distinguishing characteristic, I think I would say the dominating sense of history and tradition which surrounds us here: buildings which span five centuries; a Museum of Eton Life; school dress which ties us to an age of dignity and decorum; names and dates carved or emblazoned in profusion; leavers' portraits and house photographs; the haunting figure of the Founder.

Such an atmosphere of history has a number of effects. Tradition can be a dead weight, a millstone around our necks, which pulls us down and drowns the spirit of progress and reform. A proud history can make us complacent, self-satisfied, blindly conservative. For such people and such institutions one absurd truth is clear: whatever is *old*, is right.

That's the bad side. But a vital sense of the past can be instead an inspiration to the present. The genuinely original politician, poet or painter is the man with a deep consciousness of the policies or culture which he inherits. 'Not only the best, but the most individual parts of the poet's work,' wrote T.S. Eliot, 'may be those in which the dead poets, his ancestors, assert their immortality most vigorously.'

How could the Jews have survived centuries of bitter persecution and exile if it were not for their insistent loyalty to the stories and customs of their forefathers? How can soldiers in battle find the courage and comradeship to fight and survive, if it were not for the proud story of their regiment, and the glories and honours of the past woven into their colours? How could Churchill have found the inspiration and hope to lead this country to victory in the Second

World War, if it hadn't been for his passionate devotion to the History of the English-speaking Peoples?

Above all, a sense of continuity can breed a sense of community. Tradition engenders pride, loyalty and trust – and with these come a feeling of belonging and identity. The strongest societies, those with the greatest sense of common life and purpose, are usually those with the longest and proudest histories.

Eton is a good case in point. The consciousness now and in later life of being an Etonian, of being a part of a distinctive community, of having something special and unique in common – all this depends on a sense of belonging to a stream of history which was flowing before us, and will continue to flow after we have gone. Compare this with the complete lack of community, the anarchy of (say) *Lord of the Flies*. Here there are no past successes to live up to – and the result is Nature, red in tooth and claw.

II

The most powerful example of continuity and community is to be found in the Christian Church. The Church is *literally* rooted in history: in the events of the Old Testament; in the life of Jesus Christ, who suffered under Pontius Pilate, was crucified, and on the third day rose from the dead; and in the examples of the saints and martyrs who have persevered in the faith. This is why the Church can seem old-fashioned. It's bound to be, for it takes its inspiration for the present from what has happened in the past.

At Lambeth Palace there is a priceless collection of portraits of Archbishops of Canterbury. I remember hearing of one occasion when Dr Runcie led a visiting Russian Orthodox Bishop on a tour of the Palace, showing him its treasures with forgivable pride. At the end of the tour he asked the Bishop: 'Well, and what do you think of my London home?' 'It's all very interesting,' came the rather crushing reply. 'You have no religious pictures here.'

In a sense that was true. No doubt in the Bishop's house in the Soviet Union you would not be able to move for icons, crucifixes and statues. But what this Russian Christian failed to appreciate was the way in which these very portraits *are* for us religious pictures. They remind us of English men who have held on to the same Christian faith, often through difficult times, and who link us in a long chain which stretches back even as far as the foundation events in Bethlehem and Jerusalem.

And here too is to be found the Church's strong sense of community, of the communion of saints, past, present and future, united by the bonds of the same faith, hope and love. The Christian Church is first and foremost a community, a brotherhood, a fellowship of believers. 'For just as the body,' says St Paul, 'is one and has many members, and all the members of the body, though many, are one body, so it is with Christ. For by one Spirit we were all baptised into one Body – Jews or Greeks, slaves or free.' This is why disunity in the Church is always so scandalous. 'Though we are many, we are one body, because we all share in one bread' – the bread, that is, of history, the broken body of Christ crucified.

Continuity and community are two distinctive hallmarks of the Church. We see them embodied here in this Chapel. Continuity is in the history of the building, the earliest and most important part of King Henry VI's foundation. The Chapel's perpendicular style and proportions; the stone and wood; the sound of the bell and the choir; even the very smell of the place – all these proclaim our links with medieval Christendom.

And, second, community is symbolised in the furniture: in row upon row of pews and chairs, facing inwards, so that we are always in sight of one another. We don't sit here, as in churches and cathedrals, as individuals, looking east. We face each other – we are never allowed to forget that we come here to worship God not alone, but as the community of faithful people who live and work in this place.

III

Continuity and community: we find them both in abundance at Eton. We find them too at the very heart of the Church. But – and this is my third point – we find them dangerously short in our society.

We are, today, in this country, becoming far less historically-minded, and that's alarming. I don't just mean that history at school is losing ground, though it is. I mean that there is a marked lack of a sense of history and heritage in our public life. Politicians look more to sociology and economics than to history for their ideas and vocabulary. The brutal modern buildings of our cities owe much to the lack of historical sensitivity on the part of architects and planners. Many young people are growing up today with neither interest in nor sense of the past. Instead of reading historical adventures they watch science fiction videos. Model soldiers have been replaced by dungeons and dragons, or intergalactic space stations.

Without a sense of its history, no country, no community, can flourish. Today's rootlessness, today's unawareness and carelessness of our national story is, I believe, much to blame for our fragmented and divided societies – far more so than the popular capitalism of Thatcher's Britain. That may not help. It can certainly give every incentive to individuals to be more competitive, more self-interested, more aggressive. But this very philosophy is itself a product of our loss of feeling for the past.

A knowledge of a nation's history helps to nurture pride in its people, and with it a sense of belonging, loyalty, and concern for rich and poor alike. In a recent book called *The Unprincipled Society*, Professor David Marquand diagnoses our current ills as a loss of any sense of belonging to a community which 'existed before you were born, which will endure after your death, and to the other members of which you have obligations'.

IV

The moral of this sermon should be clear. Through your experience of Eton and through your exposure here to the Christian faith, you have experienced treasures denied today to so many. Without even knowing it, without stopping to think about it, you have breathed in the atmosphere here of continuity, and you have lived in the midst of a vigorous community. These gifts will be with you for the rest of your life.

But it's your responsibility to share them as best you can. Do all in your power to encourage knowledge and reverence for our nation's history. And do all you can to encourage a sense of belonging, one to another. 'We don't live alone,' says the Inspector in J.B. Priestley's *An Inspector Calls*. 'We are members of one body. We are responsible for each other. And I tell you that the time will soon come when, if men will not learn that lesson, then they will be taught it in fire and blood and anguish. Good Night.'

A Priest's Vocation

David Edwards

This sermon, preached in 1982, has two connections with Robert Runcie. It was the last sermon I preached as Dean of Norwich. As my ministry in that Cathedral came to an end I was very sad, but the Archbishop had been one of those who had thought it right to appoint me Provost of Southwark Cathedral in London and I have never ceased to be grateful for his support and encouragement. The sermon was preached in America, at the celebration of the 30th anniversary of a friend's ordination as a priest. For many years Robert Runcie has been active in training, guiding and sustaining priests. As I reflected on the ministry of Dr Frank McClain, and on my own priesthood, I repeated truths which I had learned from the future Archbishop and others at Westcott House, Cambridge, in the far-off 1950s.

'You have not chosen me, but I have chosen you.'

Who is the 'I' who speaks this wonderful, inexhaustible, sentence? He is Jesus, at his last supper with his friends before his death. But this sentence comes from the fourth Gospel, where often the words of Jesus are not played back to us on a tape but are given to us when they have passed through St John's own experience and meditation. In the ancient world an author would think it perfectly proper to put words into the mouth of an historical character, in order to convey something of the impact made by that character on people and events. Moses is said to have made a speech in the wilderness when what is really being said is that Moses under God created the people of Israel. Pericles is said to have made a speech on the Areopagus when what is really being said is that Pericles embodied the glory of Athens. Here, something stupendous is being said about Jesus. The Jesus of the fourth Gospel creates the Church to which St John and his readers belong. He is the vine; they are the branches, if they dwell in him and in the love he has showed them. But more than this, the Jesus of the fourth Gospel is the Word of God, the eternal 'I AM', made flesh and declaring in that flesh the glory of the heavenly Father, a dark world's one true light. The Jesus of the fourth Gospel chooses men and women to follow him, but in that choice is revealed the choice of the God whose light is too dazzling to be seen by mortal creatures. The Jesus of the fourth Gospel humbly washes men's feet; but also, he brings the wine of a life which is abundant and endless, the wine of a joy which is indestructible, for he is to those who hear him and obey him 'my Lord and my God'.

If one is a fundamentalist, one must I suppose insist that Jesus actually said these words one evening in Jerusalem. But many of us have found that it is more profoundly moving and helpful to reflect that these words are given to us by St John. He can bear witness out of his own experience, and out of the experience of the whole first generation of the Christians, that here is truth and here is life and here is the way to God.

The sense of vocation which a person has when he or she says in the heart, 'I want to be a priest', belongs not merely to young ambition or the flicker of idealism which we retain in middle age; it belongs to a realm which ultimately defies psychological analysis, because this sense of vocation is put into the heart by God. The boy says, 'Speak, Lord, for your servant hears.' The man says, 'I will follow you.' The woman says, 'I will listen and I will serve.' That boy may grow up to be involved in many problems and tragedies; he may grow up to do and to be far less than he wanted – but the Lord *did* speak, he is still the Lord's servant; that, he increasingly knows for sure. And because he knows that this call was from God, increasingly he knows that its origin in God matters far more than his response or his failure. God spoke, to that he can hold. When we are young, we are likely to make a great fuss about choosing God – but more and more as the years pass we know that what is important is that God chose us. When we are young, we are likely to be bothered greatly about whether or not we can know that God is real – but more and more we see that what matters is that God knows us. 'He knew me from the womb, He called me before I was conceived'; that was the conviction of the Old Testament prophet, Jeremiah, and it becomes the conviction of every disciple and every minister who has heard of the call of God through Christ. And what a consolation *that* is! The call and the gift of God are not revoked, for God calls from His eternal love and He gives from His Creator's store. 'Through all the changing scenes of life' that call from God, that gift by God of a sense of vocation, can be kept and understood in an ever-increasing depth of wondering adoration. To think that He chose *me* when I was so immature! To think that He has gone on choosing *me* when I have failed Him so often! To think that He chooses *me* for ever although the emotion of being chosen has grown dim! Yes, we marvel at this fact which has come into our little lives. But it *is* a fact, it *is* the most significant fact about our lives, and it *is* the fact that creates 'me'. Each of us is many persons but here is the most real 'me'. 'By the grace of God,' exclaimed St Paul, 'I am what I am.' My friends, may I be personal? I have known many difficulties since (before I was a teenager) I thought I heard the call to be a priest. But I have never been able to escape from this call, and I have found that when other ambitions burn themselves out, and when other happinesses go sour, that call is the rock on which I stood. I am sure that Frank could tell us much the same.

Since this call is from God, since it is a part of the greatest reality there is, it sweeps us into the Creator's invincible purpose. St John wrote for a Christian community which was beginning to find that instead of the world ending dramatically, a terrible battle was beginning with the persecuting power of the Roman empire. But listen to the Jesus of St John's Gospel, with the promise not only that a place in heaven is prepared for Christians but also that here on earth they will do greater things than Jesus did himself, because they will be filled with the power of the Holy Spirit. Jesus lives, Jesus has conquered the world; so they too will live and triumph. God the Father will be glorified as the persecuted disciples of Jesus bear much fruit – fruit which shall remain. God the Father will send His Spirit to guide the perplexed friends of Jesus into all the truth. Their joy will be full. They will find peace, peace amid many storms. I have lived with many people who have cared little about the Church, and I have had to face some hostility or contempt from those who reject the Church. More painful still has been the desolating interior sense of failure. But I live by the promises which I have just repeated to you, and by similar promises in the psalms. I am sure that Frank is similarly upheld.

Having said that, I come to the greatest promise of them all. For what happens when the excitement of being called to be a servant of God has faded almost entirely? What happens when we can achieve nothing more, and when we realise that what we have achieved is very much less than was meant for us? I turn to the last chapter of St John's Gospel. The scholars believe that it was added when St John had thought that his Gospel was finished. It is an epilogue, added to meet a spiritual need which was unsatisfied even by the splendours of the Gospel itself. I believe that the need which this epilogue meets is the need of old age.

You remember the scene. Peter and John are in their old territory, in Galilee beside the lake. How human they are! They are still incapable of grasping the Easter mystery, still bewildered, and they still look into the future with fear. But in the story Jesus comes and they have breakfast together and they talk. Peter is appointed as a pastor, because despite his denials in the past he can say to Jesus: 'Lord, you know everything. You know that I love you.' So the commission, the ordination, comes: 'Feed my lambs. Tend my sheep. Feed my sheep.' And Peter is told that after his impetuously courageous but often foolish youth the time is coming when he will be bound and carried where he would not. That seems to be a reference to the fact that, when this fourth Gospel is written, Peter has been crucified. But still the promise comes. When Peter is carried where he would not, to failure and death, he is still the friend of

Jesus, he is still carried by the love of Jesus, still carried by the love of God, and what awaits him at the end is the glory of Jesus in the glory of God. It always haunts me that in this gospel the last words of Jesus to Peter are the same as the first words: 'Follow me.' Wherever Peter goes, from that Galilean lakeside, into the Mediterranean world of the Greeks, on to Rome itself, on to death, he will find that his friend has gone before, so that he has only to follow. For now the Spirit of Jesus is abroad in all the world and the victory of Jesus has extended even into the terrible mystery of death. The disciple has only to follow, as at the beginning.

A person who hears the call of God to become the servant of God will achieve much and will be richly rewarded. In addition to many of the delights which other men and women know, there will be the special privilege of finding love within the Church as a new family. In the passage I have been quoting, the young and old Christians are pictured as lambs and sheep. Well, that is better than calling them *fish*! But the most profound statement made about the Christians in the gospel is that they are the mother and the twin brothers of Jesus; they are the new family created at the foot of the cross when John and Mary receive each other from Jesus. From that conviction, rooted in his experience, St Paul went on to say that Christians are the living body of Christ, Christ at work in the world. Each Christian is a limb of the Body of Christ! I could tell you many stories about how that has come true in my own experience, but look around at this congregation of Frank's friends. Is there any other profession where an anniversary would be celebrated in such depth?

Greater even than this reward of finding that the Church is a new family is another reward. When our Christian friends love us, we learn that God loves us. The love which we receive from the brethren, wrote St John in one of his letters, shows that we have passed out of death into life. Why? Because that love is so strong because its strength comes from the eternal reality of God's love. Whatever else the future holds, it will hold the greater unfolding, the fuller Advent, of that love. It will bring Christ, the living Christ, and we shall live because he lives, because his life is the life of God. What is the difficulty of life, what is the darkness of death, when this call never ceases to sound in our ears? 'To live is Christ,' wrote St Paul, 'and to die is gain.'

My friends, in this sermon I have spoken about the rewards which come to those who give themselves to the full-time service of God in His Church. Wouldn't it be wonderful if among those in church this evening someone would respond to a vocation to the priesthood, so that in say forty years' time – in the next century – there would be a similar celebration for you? But I hope I have not left the impression that the only thing that matters is a vocation to the full-time ministry. No, full-time ministry is there to be a sign to *all*

Christians about their own callings. Every Christian receives this vocation to be a disciple, whether in the full-time service of the Church or men are supposed to have. No, Christ calls people who are full of doubts, full of self-criticism and self-condemnation. It is as you respond to the call that you learn more and become more.

At the end of his book *The Quest for the Historical Jesus*, Albert Schweitzer turned from his studies to become a medical missionary in Africa. In the last paragraph of his book, he wrote:

> He comes to us as One unknown, without a name, as of old by the lakeside he came to those men who knew him not. He speaks to us the same word: with 'Follow me.' And to those who obey him, whether they be wise or simple, he will reveal himself in the conflicts, the toils, the trials, the sufferings, which they shall undergo in his company, and as a great mystery they shall learn from their own experience who he is.

The English Settlement

Enoch Powell

Archbishop and Pope may have paced the cloisters of Canterbury arm in arm. The president of the General Synod and of the Lambeth Conference may be chafed by the fetters of establishment. The fact remains that the Archbishop of Canterbury cannot cease to be what the Tudors made him – constituted head of the national Church of all the English. Axe and faggot are no longer more than metaphor; but attempted prevarication will still invite the peremptory challenge: 'Friend, how camest thou in hither?' (Matt. 22:12).

This second Keene Lecture was given in Chelmsford Cathedral on 11 October 1988.

'We are nowhere so high in our estate royal,' declared Henry VIII, 'as in this our High Court of Parliament.' It was accordingly the Crown in Parliament which in the sixteenth century became 'on earth the supreme governor of the Church *in* England'. It expressly was the Church *'in'* England, where the all-important preposition 'in' endows the definite article 'the' in front of 'Church' with the implicit assertion of still being part of the church universal. The Church of England – I have deliberately and consciously shifted prepositions – is by definition that part of the universal church of which Crown in Parliament is supreme governor. With two qualifications, it remains territorially limited to the boundaries of England. The two qualifications are, first, that early this century 'England' for this purpose became an England which no longer embraces Wales. The second qualification is the little remembered fact that from 1800 to 1871 it was, under the same, unchanged authority, an integral part of the United Church of England and Ireland.

Acknowledgment of a supreme national authority over the Church of England brought the nation face to face with that division in the universal church, a division arguably corresponding to a deep cleavage in human nature itself, which was rendered overt in the sixteenth century by the mental revolution denoted conventionally as the Renaissance. After violent oscillation, the nation took a typical and uniquely English resolve – to ignore, to compromise, or (to use a favourite term) to settle the whole fundamental issue in a way that would exclude from the Church only those who pertinaciously

adhered to the old external authority and those who equally pertinaciously claimed the independence of their individual judgement
in interpreting the Scriptures and fixing the forms of public worship.
In the Church of England there should be room alike for those who
honoured its continuity with the past (its catholicity) and for those
who honoured its kinship with the new movement stirring men's
minds (its protestantism).

The aloofness of England from the sanguinary persecutions and
the acquisitive conflicts which racked the adjacent European continent confirmed the general affection of her people for the Elizabethan settlement. It was an affection so rooted that, after the alternatives had been devastatingly explored in the middle years of the
seventeenth century, the reinstatement of the settlement virtually
unaltered in 1662 was generally welcomed. That decision was confirmed again after the crisis of 1688, when the supreme governor of
the Church had attempted to use that authority in order to hand it
back to the papacy.

The bloodless revolution of 1688 ensured the continuity not only
of England's parliamentary constitution but of the settlement
embodied in its Church. In an episode which received little attention
even in tercentenary year, William III exerted himself to reopen the
Elizabethan and Stuart settlement with a view to bringing the non-
conformists within its comprehension. His initiative and the new
prayer book which a Royal Commission was induced to put forward
foundered upon the instinctual resistance of the parishes. The heart
of the matter is well taken in a passage where Macaulay imagines a
parish church in which the incumbent introduced the new book:

> A layman might still continue to sit under the accustomed pulpit and to
> kneel at the accustomed altar; but if, just at this juncture his ears and
> eyes had been shocked by changes in the worship to which he was
> fondly attached, if the compositions of the doctors of the Commission
> had taken the place of the old collects, if he had seen clergymen without
> surplices carrying the chalice and the paten up and down the aisle to
> seated communicants, the tie which bound him to the established church
> would have been dissolved.

The historian concluded, somewhat surprisingly for a Whig, that
'it is an indisputable and a most instructive fact that we are in a
great measure indebted for the civil and religious liberty which we
enjoy to the pertinacity with which the High Church party in the
Convocation of 1689 refused even to deliberate on any plan of comprehension.' Macaulay was more right than in 1850 he could possibly
know. It was the Church of an England whose people insisted upon
continuing to kneel in which the great movements, catholic and
evangelical, of the nineteenth and twentieth centuries could take
place without destroying the settlement and the continuity of the
national church – at least until this present time.

While all this was happening, the Crown in Parliament of England was successively merged in the Crown in Parliament of Great Britain, the Crown in Parliament of the United Kingdom of Great Britain and Ireland, and the Crown in Parliament of the United Kingdom of Great Britain and Northern Ireland. It has therefore since 1707 been through a body in which more than England was represented that the Crown governed the Church of England. If this is anomalous, the anomaly is one which has excited no surprise in other contexts. The law of Scotland, protected by the Treaty of Union, is made and amended by the whole Parliament, which also legislates differentially for other specific parts of the kingdom. Indeed, the unity of the legislative authority is inseparable from the unity of the nation itself. The source of authority in the Church of England continues to be equated to the source of all other authority in the nation.

The uniquely territorial nature of the Church of England is marked on another side by its parochial obligations, whereby the principal services of the Church are made available by it as of right to all persons whatsoever, upon the sole condition of their local situation in England. It is the common right and possession of the whole people of England in a sense that no other church is or can be; and the existence of the right, like that of other rights, does not depend on whether or not individuals who possess it choose to exercise it.

The territorial uniqueness of the Church of England was not impaired by that vast colonial, missionary and pastoral activity of its priests and members over more than three centuries which resulted in its forms of worship and particularly its Book of Common Prayer being diffused over large parts of the rest of the inhabited world. Where those territories were or remained under British rule, the ecclesiastical organisation was in effect part of colonial or imperial administration, and the bishops and clergy came frequently from and returned frequently to office in the Church of England; but the Church of England under the Crown as its supreme governor was not thereby enlarged, even though the territories concerned were governed on the ultimate responsibility of the Parliament of the United Kingdom.

In the case of India alone what was called the 'Ecclesiastical Settlement' was covered by British statute law, eventually Part X of the Government of India Act 1915, which was repealed when in 1927 Parliament approved a Church Assembly Measure to dissolve 'the legal union between the Church of England and the Church of England in India'; but even this appears to have been by way of removal of doubt: 'the ecclesiastical law of the Church of England', it declared, '*so far as it exists in India*, shall in India cease to exist as law'.

There consequently occurred no formal termination of the ecclesiastical authority of the Crown in Parliament of the United Kingdom corresponding to that which had to occur when territories formerly under British rule became independent politically. After the First World War, however, there arose a strong predisposition to devise forms and formulae which would conceal the real fact of the termination of Britain's political authority in the former empire. Thereby has hung the long, and not wholly happy, story of the Commonwealth, which claimed to be a continuing political entity despite the effective political independence of the individual parts and which involved the mother country in maintaining obligations to the other territories which they repudiated towards it and towards one another.

The ecclesiastical counterpart of Commonweath, though not geographically coincident, was the so-called Anglican Communion, defined – significantly in 1930, the year before the Statute of Westminster – as 'bound together not by a central legislative and executive authority but by mutual loyalty sustained through the common counsel of the bishops in conference'. It was, once again, the mother church from which the sacrifice necessary to sustain the fiction of continuing unity was required. The Church of England knows no such lawful authority as the common counsel of bishops in conference, whoever those bishops are; but that consent was endowed with persuasive authority, by making it the condition of a unity assumed to be overwhelmingly and self-evidently desirable.

The concept upon which the whole contraption depended was 'communion' with the See of Canterbury. The menace which substitutes the common counsel of certain bishops for the governance of the Crown in Parliament is that, in default of compliance on the part of the Church of England, 'communion' will be at an end. The concept of communion is not so unambiguous as often appears to be taken for granted. It does not apparently in this context mean the admission of a worshipper to the sacraments, and particularly the Eucharist. The definition by the law of England of who may be admitted and who repelled would hardly be challenged by any conceivable measures taken in other churches. They may apply tests or conditions which would exclude a member of the Church of England from *their* sacraments; but that is their business and their right, and none of ours, and does not affect what happens in England.

The meaning of 'communion' which appears to be implied by current debate is interchangeability between those who perform corresponding functions in their respective churches. The law of the Church of England defines what persons, and how qualified, are to perform those functions in it. Nothing but a change in that law can enable other persons or persons differently qualified to do so. It is 'communion' in this sense which would require that definition either to conform to, or to be overriden by, the definitions valid in another church.

The crucial definitions in the current debate are those of 'priest' and 'bishop'. A great commotion has arisen because in certain churches which are deemed on the formula of 1930 to be in communion with the See of Canterbury, persons are made priests and bishops who could not lawfully be made so in the Church of England. In consequence it is proposed that, in order to maintain the status quo of the fiction of continuing ecclesiastical unity, the Crown in Parliament ought so to change the law of the Church of England as either to bring it into line with the rules of those other churches or at least to enable persons qualified in those other churches to perform certain offices to come and perform those offices in the Church of England.

I emphasise that what is at issue is not the undoubted right of those other churches, through their representative duly constituted authorities, to take whatever decisions appear good to them. They may have what priests or bishops they choose. Whether wisely or not, is no business of the Church of England. What is at issue is the presumption that their action creates a corresponding duty on the part of the Church of England to alter its own law with a view to maintaining communion with them. That presumption is offensive to reason and justice. It amounts to claiming that the governance of the Church of England ought henceforward to conform itself to decisions taken by the governing authorities of other churches. If communion with them is to be the overriding obligation, there is no other conclusion that can be drawn. It is a conclusion uniquely insulting to the Church of England because uniquely the Church of England by its *definition* shares the same governing authority as the nation state.

There are great tides in human affairs, tides which from their propensity to affect minds simultaneously in many countries, take on almost the character of epidemics – 'pandemics' should perhaps be the word. Like natural tides however they ebb as well as flow. The reaction to type which is the preservative of all biological species sets in. Signs are accumulating today that one such tide is just upon the turn. For thirty years it has been almost obligatory for public men to affect to regard the independent nation state as an outworn and deplorable institution. Perhaps it was a providential coincidence that the tercentenary year of 1988 has witnessed the official reaffirmation by the Crown's Chief Minister of the supreme value of the independent nation state, which in our case is the independent parliamentary nation state, and rejection of supposed ties and commitments that would be incompatible with that supreme value. In such a changed environment the people of England may with a good conscience and – what a cynic might say is equally important – in keeping with current fashion repudiate any supposed obligations which can only be fulfilled at the price of surrendering national sovereignty. The Church of England is not inhibited by the history of empire from claiming for itself that right of independence which it freely accords to churches both within and without the realm of England which have a different form of government from its own.

Only Connect

Eric James

Few would doubt that Richard Harries' consecration as Bishop of Oxford gave Robert Runcie special pleasure – indeed, it would be surprising if he did not have a particular finger in the pie of Richard's appointment. This sermon was delivered at Richard's consecration in St Paul's Cathedral on Ascension Day, 28 May 1987.

Richard Harries was a student at Cuddesdon when Robert Runcie was its Principal. But they have other 'connections : the Archbishop was Chairman of the BBC and IBA Central Religious Advisory Committee from 1973–9; Richard Harries has made Religious Broadcasting a central concern of his ministry. Both the Archbishop and Richard held university and theological college appointments before their consecration. Both have had a particular concern for relations between the Anglican and Orthodox Churches. Both are known for their recognition of and respect for 'Niebuhrian' 'compromise ethics' and 'moral ambiguity' in being the Church in the world. Both are concerned with Spirituality for Today.

'Only connect . . . '

At your Consecration, Richard, the preacher will surely be forgiven for beginning – and not only beginning – with a literary allusion. 'Only connect . . . ' The power of that epigraph – which Forster set at the front of *Howards End* four years before the beginning of the First World War – is undiminished. Indeed, a book bearing that title, by Robin Green, on 'worship and liturgy from the perspective of pastoral care', has been published this year; and last year Leslie Houlden intentionally echoed it in his book *Connections*. And the more I have thought on the role of a bishop, the more that phrase has seemed to articulate and express it: 'Only connect.'

As an aside, let me say that at Cuddesdon this last Holy Week a student vouchsafed to me – with all the authority of a Cuddesdon ordinand – that the Oxford interregnum had revealed that the *only* task left to a Bishop of Oxford now is to connect: to connect the work of the area bishops.

But Forster's word 'only' did not mean 'only' in that belittling sense. It meant, of course: '*If* you can connect . . . If *only* you can connect . . . all you bring together will be exalted.'

And that word 'connect' – which sounds so deceptively simple, as the phrases of great literature so often do – also needs definition.

Even my 'Scrabble' dictionary relates it to a 'body or society held together by a bond'; and, without realising how near to great theology it is treading, it adds, 'ligaments, membranes, cartileges', and throws in one or two interpretative words for good measure – 'that which gives coherence' – and then treads even holier ground: 'to associate with others in relationship; to enable two or more *disjecta membra* to become one; to unite'.

But if to connect and to unite have so much in common, then we are met here today not simply for some occasion of Church order; we stand within the holy of holies; we draw near to the mystery of the Atonement itself: to the mystery of at-one-ment; and therefore to the mystery of our humanity, of sin and of grace, and to the very Person and Work of Christ.

And that is so; for Forster did not perhaps sufficiently recognise how corrupt and destructive as well as how glorious and exalting our connections can be – in Church as well as State. The Great War, that great slaughter – which began, as I've said, just after *Howards End* was published – occurred, surely, because men had made most terrible and terrifying connections – as they did again a quarter of a century later, and still do now.

The phrase 'well-connected' shows how snobbery and connections are connected; and the religious connection has its own corruption, not least in ecclesiasticism, hierarchy, pietism, prelacy and our own peculiarly Anglican forms of arrogance and snobbery.

My own mentor and friend, Eric Abbott – a revered predecessor, of course, of yours, Richard, as Dean of King's College – used to say to me: 'Boy, if you are to be ordained, you must have almost as high a doctrine of corruption as you have of glory – corruption in Church as well as State.'

When we have 'almost as high a doctrine of corruption as we have of glory', we can face afresh our past, not least our Anglican past: we can face, for instance, the Oxford Anglican connection – 'Soapy Sam', Stubbs, Paget, Gore, Strong – and so on.

Yes. But when we connect 'connecting' with the Atonement itself, we begin to see the pain and the price of connecting: that no bland Anglican sleight of hand will do. At-one-ment is achieved often only at cost and with costly confrontation.

It is of course dangerous to suggest at the consecration of a Bishop of Oxford – Bishop not least of St Aldate's and St Ebbe's – that he has a part to play in the Atonement; but it would only be more dangerous to suggest he has no part to play in it. And perhaps for the avoiding of error we might remember P.T. Forsyth's pithy dictum that 'the real successor to the apostles was not the episcopate but the New Testament'. Most of us are only here today because we believe in the New Testament connection with what we are doing.

'Only connect . . . ' The University of Oxford, they tell me, tends to keep its bishops at arm's length, but Oxford remains one of the great symbols and centres of scholarship and research. It will be no mean achievement, Richard, if you can strengthen the connection between scholarship and the Church – not least in the pulpits and pews of your diocese. But the Gospel has within it truth that is hidden from the wise, and at this time the challenge to a Bishop of Oxford is not least to ensure that those who read and those who teach theology connect with the realities of life, indeed that theology rises out of the realities – the often cruel realities of life – not least the realities of what we have come to call the urban priority areas.

'Only connect . . . ' What resonances of that phrase throb through the Church and the world today! I wonder, Richard, how you will help the rich Oxford commuters to connect with the poor of, say, Cowley; and the decision-makers of the Chilterns connect with those whose destinies they control in the North East and North West; how you will help the employed of Oxford to connect with the unemployed; the white people to worship with the black, and to grow in understanding the Sikhs, Hindus and Muslims in, say, Slough.

'Only connect . . . ' In these last months and years, it has thankfully become abundantly clear that the Church has not lost all its ancient power to connect with and speak to the soul of the nation, and to recall it at such a time as this from an uncaring absorption in sectional avarice to concern for justice and compassion.

'Only connect . . . ' Church and State. Your own appointment, Richard is – for better, for worse – part and parcel with that connection. But in your time as bishop it is urgent that a connection between Church and State be forged and fashioned afresh that better reflects the realities of the religious and social situation of England today – and of the Church of England – and above all the priorities of the Gospel.

'Only connect . . . ' May you never be content, Richard, to be a bishop in the Church of England representing simply that section of Christendom according to whose Use you are being consecrated. A bishop, wherever he is, is called to represent the wholeness of the Catholic Church to its divided parts, to be a creative force of its coming unity. 'Only connect . . . '

Some of those who come from far to take part in your Consecration today, Richard, personify some of the pains – as well as the glories – of our interconnecting. I suppose apartheid, from one point of view, is the very opposite of connecting. But from another it is the very incarnation of connecting based on fear and racial prejudice and self-concern, which is to be found not only in South Africa.

'Only connect . . . ' Richard *Oxon* and Richard Harries – a man, a husband, blessed with a wife and family; and Richard, the private

person, and Richard, the media man. 'Only connect . . . ' the intellectual Richard and the 'feeling' Richard, and 'both will be exalted'.

Harry Williams, in a characteristic preface to Robin Green's *Only
Connect* has written:

> Christian writers have often spoken of our humanity being taken up
> into God. What in fact they have meant is the repression in the sub-
> conscious of a great deal of what we are, so that only half of us – the
> respectable pious half – is offered to God to make His own, while the
> stinking darkness – is left to itself to fester unseen and work its evil spell
> upon us, disguised in this or the other religiously acceptable form.

If our Gospel be true, a Christian bishop should know a lot about
connecting 'the beast and the monk' within – to use Forster's marvellous metaphor – and about helping others, clergy and laity, to make
that connection.

'Only connect . . . ' Recognise the masculinity and femininity in
yourself and you will want to see that masculinity and femininity
in yourself recognised by the Church in the women and the men
who present themselves to you for ministry in Christ's Church.

'Only connect . . . ' Your ministry will often feel lonely and be
lonely, but you will not be alone. Episcope, like priesthood and
ministry, is a function of the whole Church. Every member of the
Church will have a share in your episcope. 'Only connect . . . '

Richard, you will know well that I have a small shelf of books by
you on prayer, signed with your love and good wishes. We are not
here today to speak much about prayer, but to pray with you and
for you. But let me just say this: that last Good Friday, immediately
after I had conducted the Three Hours, a kind Cuddesdon student
drove me into Oxford simply to look at a field of fritillary in bloom
in a water-meadow near Magdalen Bridge. As Housman said:

> to look at things in bloom
> Fifty Springs are little room

But in that half hour, as we wandered along Addison's Walk, I could
not forget that you would be coming to be Bishop of that place –
that City, that University, that Diocese – but secondly, that the God
who would empower you had revealed Himself both in a Man who
hung on a Cross the first Good Friday and cried 'My God my
God, why?' and in that field of frail and vulnerable fritillary. 'Only
connect . . . ' He will be alongside you as you pay the price and
bear the pain of at-one-ment and connecting.

'The head that once was crowned with thorns is crowned with
glory now.' Ascension Day is a feast of glory, and a most marvellous
day for your Consecration, Richard. The hands that will soon be
laid upon you – 'only connect' – will say in what we now call 'body
language' that: 'He who ascended is the same also as He who
descended – that He might fill all things' – which He does still. Still.

'Christ our God to earth descendeth
Our full *homage*' – (a word with peculiarly English episcopal
Establishment resonances) –
'Our *full homage* to demand.'

'Only connect . . . '

A Strange Land

Owen Chadwick

*Robert Runcie was Principal of Cuddesdon College near Oxford 1960–70.
It was and is a place for training clergy, and each June held (and holds)
an annual festival for its old members, with a service of thanksgiving in
one of the most beautiful country churches in the land, and afterwards a
sort of speech day with no prizes. The festival of June 1966 coincided with
the opening of the Graham Room, which was designed in memory of Runcie's
predecessor but two as Principal and bore Graham's portrait on the north
wall. (The Graham Room was opened by the Bishop of Peterborough,
Cyril Eastaugh, who had been Vice-Principal of the College during part
of Graham's time.) In the nave of the church were 320 clergymen who,
when ordinands, were at Cuddesdon, and in the chancel, where they could
not hear, were several bishops.*

*This then was the commemoration sermon at the Cuddesdon festival of
1966 and was directed towards those who are Christian ministers and
among them those who were grateful for Eric Graham.*

How shall we sing the Lord's song in a strange land? (Psalm 137:4)

The traveller, returning to this place, has a feeling that he comes
home. The heart lifts in gratitude at what once was. The memory
discards the moments of pettiness and retains the moments of
beauty. Many years ago you knelt in this church at the presence of
God in the sacrament of the altar, and you knew that you glimpsed
the vision of truth. You were at home. No strange land.

But now as you walk the churchyard and perambulate the bishop's
garden, you experience a twinge of melancholy. They were high
ideals that then possessed you. They possessed you the more readily
because putting them into practice lay in the future. You were not
then troubling yourselves about coming down into the dust. The
aspiration had nobility. But it was noble like the idealism of a boy
who does not know how ideals become corrupt as they seek to
express themselves in society. We were idealists partly because we
were immature, partly because we were ignorant. But whether
immature or ignorant, still we were idealists. And now? Your twinge
of melancholy may pass into a stab of penitence.

For it is a strange land in which God's people live. I must retain my ideals among people who do not share them. I must demand moral principle where voices question the axioms on which my principle rests. I must retain simplicity where the economic structure demolishes an old-fashioned virtue like thrift. I must sing though some tell me that it is the song of a dreamer. I must pursue a Christian policy though I know that any or every practicable policy means compromise with non-Christian men. I am no longer so immature. I am no longer quite so ignorant; and I know that I am a stranger in the land.

History has this utility; the student knows that however bad things seem at the moment, there were times when they were worse. If you have a sense of the past, you are not likely to be so elevated by the momentary victory of today, nor so downcast at the momentary defeat of tomorrow. The Catholic Church is a tree with deep roots, which hold fast whether the upper branches shine in the sunlight or bend in a gale. The mind goes back to the evening when from this hill the eastern sky was livid with the light of London burning, and here young men longed to help, and felt helpless, and were half-relieved that they were out of the fire, and then ashamed that they felt relieved. The mind goes further back to the days when quaint old Golightly, decaying at last in his mind, issued his penultimate pamphlet among so many pamphlets, *A Solemn Warning against Cuddesdon College*. The mind goes further back to him who in his simple person reflected the best in the high Anglican tradition of pastoral care, John Keble; who advised our founders, and composed us a hymn (though we dare not use its words unaltered), and wrote letters so precious to Liddon that Liddon took special care that they be preserved. Religion, taught Keble, if it be true religion, is never popular. If it is popular, it is not true religion. God and the world are sundered far. Face it that the Christians are a protest against the society in which they live. Face it that their kingdom is not of this world – 'Jerusalem my happy home, when shall I come to thee? Ye are strangers and pilgrims,' you can hear St Peter's (1 Pet. 2:2) word. You have no long time to stay. The hooves of the galloping horses can already be heard as distant thunder. The sacrament of this altar, which to us is peace, and rest, and comfort, was founded in a sacrifice of pain and loneliness. Will the man wholly at home in the world ever be wholly at home in God? 'What doth it profit a man if he shall gain the whole world, and lose his own soul?'

There is the first division of this text: 'How shall we sing the Lord's song in a strange land?' If we would sing to the Lord's tune, the land ought to be strange.

The second division of the text is the Lord's *song*. A song, a hymn. How shall I sing? How shall I reason the Lord's philosophy? How shall I practise the Lord's Commandments? How shall I organise the Lord's company? Go before television and pretend that religion

is only an argument. Go into a church meeting and pretend that we
only need efficient administration. Go into the Women's Institute
and pretend that religion is only social reform. Despise not an argument, despise not efficiency, despise not social reform, three neces-
saries of Christian endeavour. But when we were young, and Cuddesdon forced us for a few terms to neglect social reform, and be
more silent in argument than usual, and know nothing of ecclesiastical efficiency, then it was as plain to us as it has ever been, that the
multi-coloured work of the Church is taken up into worship; that
we end not merely in philosophy, not merely in the Church Commissioners, not (I dare not say 'not merely') in the Commandments,
but in the Lord's song –

> O fons puritatis, Jesu Domine,
> Me immundum munda tuo sanguine
> Cujus una stilla . . .

Cleanse us, unclean, with thy most cleansing blood – it was a hymn
which they had, unforgettably, at a Eucharist when the nave altar
was first here. I know a member of the College who has never since
been able to sing *Adoro te devote* without a vivid image of Cuddesdon
church.

The third division of the text: *How* shall we sing the Lord's song?
Of course in penitence and in faith. This psalmist was only melancholy. He thought that Palestine was the Lord's land, and that
Babylon far from home was not. So he was over-defensive. It was
an excess. He built a Chinese wall; a wall of the Law to keep out
the world. He clung to his orthodoxy not because it was truth but
because it was orthodoxy. It is a spirit which can afflict Christians;
strangers in the world, build high the bastions against the world.
Fortify the sacred trenches with barbed wire. Be so passionate in
your love for Jerusalem that you end by blessing those who bash in
the heads of its enemies' children. Russian persecution bred a touch
of this in Eastern Orthodoxy; African persecution bred a touch of it
in Tertullian; Garibaldi bred it, calamitously for all Christendom, in
the Italian Ultramontanes of the last century. Liddon had a flavour
of this spirit in his youthful early days at Cuddesdon; as though
this place was a fortress, a barricade against the passing life of man.
Liddon was one of the greatest of Victorian Christians. Yet, more
than Liddon, his colleague here Edward King knew that this world
was God's world, that His purpose for the world is to be trusted,
that change, even a change that looks menacing, may be brought
within the scope of providence.

We had a touch of the fortress-mentality in my generation. The
future historian of the College may look back upon the end of the
1930s to see a touch of excess. That excess was not ignoble. In the
days of Munich, and Prague, and the rape of Poland, and friends
being killed, and our hands seeming idle, it would have been ignoble

if there had not been a touch of excess. What, when friends and companions are settling the fate of humanity, nothing but say prayers, and study the old Fathers dusty on the shelves, and work for a future Church when there might be no future Church to work for? Sometimes we silence our inward questionings by excess of zeal. We were not always wise. Our Principal, Eric Graham, was teaching us the serene Christian philosophy of Gore and Temple. But the books which we liked to read were not serene. They were the fiercest of theologies; *credo quia absurdum*, terror-divinity. We preferred authors who dipped their pens in blood. We talked much of remnant theory. We thought much of 'little flock' texts. We had more of Liddon than of Edward King in our make-up.

None of this was due to our Principal. He was like a rock. When we could switch on our radio and listen to the baying of *Sieg Heil* from a hundred thousand throats at a Nuremberg rally, it was not easy to see that God rules over the earth; that He is still King, be the people never so impatient. But Graham knew with his whole being that the world is still God's.

His mind was not sufficiently sceptical in its questionings to make a first-rank philosopher, and was far too charitable in its judgements to make an historian, but it had system, clarity, coherence. He had the happiest of homes. He had a dry, delicate, penetrating sense of humour. He had a deep sense of the tradition and authority of the Catholic Church and yet he was deeply Biblical, Scriptural in his religious outlook. He gave devotional addresses which not seldom we failed to understand. He never pressed us. No emotionalism, no excess of fervour, no hurry, no suggestion that we must be saints by tomorrow. As a director of souls he was immensely gentle; so gentle that stern old Jansenist critics might even have charged him with too little severity in his direction. In words there was no pressure whatever. Yet there was a pressure upon us. This pressure came from his rule of life. He disciplined his personal conduct to an extraordinary degree.

He knew of the 'little flock' texts. He knew of the theology of the sanctuary, none better. But he also knew of God's providence for the world. Never for one moment did he encourage us to read authors with gall in their ink. Never for a moment did he waver in his faith in the divine governance of the world.

You are strangers and pilgrims in the land. The land ought to be, in some way, strange. But let us get the reason right. Because we live amidst easy clamour, and brash publicity, and argument more for the sake of noise than for the sake of truth, we retreat and find our sanctuary in the stillness before the altar of God; somewhat as in this church, during the weeks of Dunkirk, men found in Cuddesdon church a seal of eternal peace as they knelt near the sacrament reserved at the east end of the chancel. A blessed sanctuary. But a sanctuary to reach outwards. Not a hiding-place from the shrapnel of the world. Let us not hedge our shrine against a world that we presume to be hostile. Let us not begin to be Pharisees; defending our purity with the obsolete muskets of vanished campaigns; buttressed by a holiness which at last is not the holiness of faith but of Leviticus. Let us get the reason right. You are strangers not because this earth is given over to the powers of darkness. The earth is still the Lord's. You are not fully at home here because your eyes are fixed upon a city whose foundations are eternal and not of earth. Perhaps my people reject my gospel; they are God's created beings still; of kindness and courage and sometimes thirst for truth; a people to whom we must go, whether they will hear or forbear. The world is not demonic but sacramental. 'Turn the stone and thou shalt find me, cleave the wood and there am I.'

How shall we sing the Lord's song in a strange land? Why not? The Psalmist hung up his harp upon the willows by the water's edge and would not sing. He knew Palestine was holy, and that was all he did know. The land, though strange, is not the land of Baal, nor of Moloch, nor of Dagon, nor of Thor, nor of Wotan, nor of mammon, nor of Stalin. It is still the land of the Lord, the Creator, the Almighty, Maker of heaven and earth, and of all things visible and invisible.

Here then are three divisions of this text: how shall we sing?

the first, the land ought to be strange; for what shall
it profit a man if he gain the whole world and lose
his own soul;

the second, it is a song; for religion ends in the
worship of the whole man;

the third, it is a strange land because we look for
another country; not because it is a land of savages
and devils.

When, a few years ago or many years ago, you knelt before God in the sacrament of this altar, it was not possible to doubt his reality and his power. We came to this College questioning, hesitant, sceptical; and the questioning of my generation was multiplied tenfold by the onset of war. But here in the quietness of worship we found a reality unmistakable. We have all moved far from this retreat. We are still hesitant, still questioning; and now we know that truth is less tidy, and that words are more impotent even than we then thought them. We have soiled ourselves in a heap of the world's soot. But we do not forget what we once have seen. Despite all that has happened to us since those Cuddesdon days, it is still impossible to doubt God's reality and God's power; the Lord is King though the people be impatient; he sitteth between the cherubim, be the earth never so unquiet. *God of God, Light of Light, Very God of Very God, begotten not made, being of one substance with the Father,* the great Nicene words are as powerful now as those years ago. The truths by which we then learnt to live are truths still; and when we are faithful to ourselves we know them still to be living truths.

How then shall we sing the Lord's song in the modern world? How shall we not?

Ministry and Vision

Stuart Blanch

One of my more agreeable tasks as Archbishop of York was to preach at the celebration of John Habgood's tenth anniversary at Durham in May 1983, and the sermon, slightly abbreviated, is reprinted in this volume to celebrate Robert Runcie's ten years as Archbishop of Canterbury. So for John read Robert, for Durham read the Anglican Communion – and for ten years read ten years!

Samuel may be seen as a model for both. He was an influential figure, much respected in the Church and State of Israel. He regularly travelled the length and breadth of the land, untiring in his efforts for the people. And in a nation in which vision seemed to have been lost, he cherished a vision which survived the accidents and disappointments of a long ministry. Like him Robert has cherished a vision of a renewed Anglican Communion, prepared to live creatively with its dissonances. He has kept alive the vision of one Church, transcending its differences for the common good, and in public and in private he has consistently stood for the vision of a humane society, founded on the Word of God as made known to us in Holy Scripture. It is a pleasure to have this sermon reprinted in his honour.

The Word of the Lord was precious (rare) in those days and there was no open (frequent) vision (1 Sam. 3:1)

As the text makes clear, Samuel was born into a world unfamiliar with the word of God and short of vision. His vocation therefore was to be a hearer of God's word (signified by his experience in the Temple as a child) and to represent that word of God in the community at large. He was to be a man to call the people back to their original allegiance to the law of God and to call them forward to the kingdom which he saw from afar. So it was that 'Samuel told the people the manner of the kingdom and wrote it in a book and laid it up before the Lord' (1 Sam. 10:25).

Could it be that these are the characteristics of Church and Nation now in our own country – unfamiliar with the word of God and short of vision?

Dr Alan Shapiro, a lawyer by training, and now a senior member of the oldest kibbutz in Israel and a regular correspondent for the *Jerusalem Post*, wrote in an article last year [1982] of the two essential elements that go to make up a Nation: 'shared experience and shared vision'. He made the point that Israel was rich in shared experience (3,000 years of it), and poor in shared vision. If he had known England as well as he knows Israel, he could have said the same of us. We have plenty of shared experience. We have a long history and precious traditions which make us one of the greatest tourist attractions in the world. We are enthusiastic conservers of the past, unrivalled at keeping our ancient ruins in repair. But a shared past will not serve us unless we have also a shared vision. And there is little evidence of shared vision in our political and social manifestos. We live by political confrontation, assiduously cultivated by the mass media, and set one system over against another, making them, so it would seem, incompatible with each other. On the one hand there is the vision of a managed economy and the abolition of all social and class differentiation. On the other hand we have a vision of well-motivated individuals encouraged to pursue wealth, efficiency and new styles. Put crudely, it is the values of the high-rise block of corporation flats over against the values of a successful supermarket – not much shared vision there.

The Church is rich in shared experience, well supplied with ancient monuments (of which undoubtedly Durham Cathedral is one) and outworn intellectual categories. We are still trapped in old allegiances, looking back to a golden age of evangelical revival or to the tractarian movement, or perhaps nowadays to Pentecost itself. We are suspicious of 'messages from the Lord and too frequent visions'. We have no vision of the Promised Land. We do not aspire to Caanan and are content to wander in our desert. We do not positively seek that Kingdom which Christ has promised and for which we pray with unthinking regularity every day of our lives – 'Thy kingdom come'.

Samuel was a busy man. He went on endless circuits of Israel just as John no doubt goes on endless circuits of the Diocese of Durham – and that without the benefit of the official car. But in the Bible it says of Samuel (1 Sam. 7:16–17) that 'He went from year to year in circuit to Bethel and Gilgal and Mizpah, and he judged Israel in all those places. But he always returned to Ramah, for there was his home and there he judged Israel and he built there an altar unto the Lord.'

If there are two characteristics of a bishop which are enjoined upon him not only by the words of the Consecration Service but by the exigencies of our own time, they would be:

1. *Attention to the word of God.*
   Bishops are flooded with innumerable messages from men – incessant correspondence, limitless memoranda from Diocesan and Central sources, many powerful pleas for their support and advocacy, and among them all the occasional plaintive cry

of those who feel lost and bewildered in a world they no longer understand. If he is to keep sane, much less minister effectively, he needs, as Samuel did, to return often to Ramah, to his home, where he has built an altar to the Lord. There is no substitute for attention to the word of God, not just for guidance or 'messages', but for that renewing of the mind so easily distracted by much serving. He needs more often than most to sit at the Lord's feet and to hear His word.

2. *The application of the word of God.*
(a) *To the Church.*
   The Bishop always needs to be summoning people back to the basics, helping them to transcend their party differences, and their petty bigotries, their ancient prejudices and their new-found convictions, inviting them to share a vision of the future, not just a devotion to the past. For example, with no union scheme within sight, we ought perhaps to lift our eyes beyond the inshore anchorage and the harbour buildings and look to the more distant horizon for signs and portents of salvation, open to what the Lord will say to us.
(b) *To the Nation.*
   In a world of confrontation politics, we need a vision which transcends these inescapable but transient controversies, to discover the vision so rare and the message so infrequent of the Kingdom of God – of a society which at least honours, if it does not wholly understand or obey, the basic principles upon which the universe is built. We weary ourselves in vain, bruising ourselves on immovable obstacles, when perhaps there is already a way in this wilderness by which we are being summoned to the promised land. 'This is the way, walk in it.' Far beyond its responsibilities for espousing the cause of the needy and involving ourselves in the politics of social change, we need ourselves to have a vision from God which could perhaps become the shared vision of our people. It remains true, although I have to acknowledge that it is not the exact meaning of the text that 'where there is no vision, people perish', however well housed, however well fed, however satisfied with their lot on earth, however successful in business, however diligent in their service of mankind.

I have to congratulate John on having survived ten years in the episcopate and, what is more, survived with humour and dignity in an office which can undermine the strongest constitution and cloud the clearest mind. But I hope you will look after him and not make impossible and unnecessary demands upon him. He stands in the Samuel tradition, wise in his perception of the dangerous currents at work in society, more aware than most of the effects of our unhappy divisions upon the life and witness of the Church. I hope therefore you will give him regular opportunities amidst his circuits of Israel, to return to his home at Ramah, there to kneel before the altar he has built and hear for himself the word of God – in a society where the word of God is rare and visions of the Lord unusual.

Promise, Presence and Parousia

Michael Nazir-Ali

Robert Runcie's thinking is characterised by a profound awareness of God's presence in the world. This is held together with the belief that God is preparing different groups of people in diverse and wonderful ways for the good news of His Kingdom. At the same time, he is conscious of the darkness which encroaches on the divine light and the state of rebellion which is endemic in humanity.

Humanity needs not only revelation, so that its ignorance may be dispelled, but salvation from corporate and individual evil. For him, both revelation and salvation are brought together in the person of Jesus Christ who not only reveals the Father but charts a way out for humanity from the 'solidarity of sin' to a restoration of 'fellowship with the Father'. As he has said, 'Jesus Christ is for me the definitive apprehension of the divine'. It is on a basis such as this that the Church mission to the contemporary world needs to be based.

The sermon which follows was preached by Bishop Michael Nazir-Ali at his installation as General Secretary of the Church Missionary Society in 1990. It draws out some of the themes mentioned above and develops them towards a theology of mission.

The national poet of Pakistan, Muhammad Iqbal – who was, of course, a Muslim – has said about Jesus, 'Son of Mary, Lamp of the Universe, Infinite and yet Incarnate Light!' St Paul, in the second letter to the Corinthians, expresses much the same sentiment, because he tries to hold together the Word responsible for Creation and revealed in Creation with the Word revealed in the face of Jesus Christ (2 Cor. 4:6). Creation and redemption are held together. The Word is revealed in the natural world and the Word is revealed in Jesus Christ as a declaration – a communication of God's purposes and, at the same time, a way of obedience that is set out for human beings – a way of obedience that leads to reconciliation.

The Word present and revealed

But this Word also comes to us in whatever it is that makes us distinctively human. He comes to us, therefore, in our moral awareness. He comes to us in our power of rational thought. He comes to us in our aesthetic sense and our power of creativity.

George Steiner, in his new book *Real Presences*, tells us that every act of human communication, especially every act of human communication that has also to do with human creativity, is art, whether painting or sculpture or dance or music. Every human act of communication in this way is a wager on the transcendent – a wager on God. According to Steiner, human creativity cannot be understood without reference to transcendence.

But what is it in the end that enables us to discern where the Eternal Word reveals himself in Creation, whether natural or human? How do we discern the coming and the presence of that Word? The natural world, as we know, is full of imperfection and, indeed, corruption – corruption for which, I suppose, human beings are partly responsible. Where there is design, there is also an absence of design. To use theological words, where there is teleology there is also dysteleology. But what is it that enables us to discern the Eternal Word in the order and the beauty of Creation? And what is it that enables us to discern the presence of the Eternal Word in human endeavour and human achievement?

For St Paul, the Word is revealed in the face of Jesus Christ, that is, in the person and the work and the teaching and the dying and the living of Jesus Christ. In other words, to know where to look for the presence of the Eternal Word, to discern that coming and that presence, we have to use the Jesus Christ of the Gospels, of the New Testament– preached and worshipped in the Church and celebrated in the sacraments – as a definitive, normative criterion.

It is not only in discerning the presence of the Word in art or literature or in the natural world that this definitiveness is necessary; but also in discerning the presence of the Word in *us*. St John tells us at the very beginning of his Gospel that the Eternal Word which becomes flesh is that same Word who illumines all human beings who come into the world (John 1:9).

The evangelisation of the world – and that must mean the evangelisation of human beings: men, women, children – must be by the light of the Eternal Word, seen in the face of Jesus Christ, probing the depths of the human person.

In the fourth chapter of the Epistle to the Hebrews, the writer tells us how the Word of God probes and cuts through the sinews and the joints to get to what is authentic about humanity. The Word in Christ meets the illumination of the Word in us. So, in a very real sense, evangelisation is truly educative. It is bringing out what God has graciously given to humanity in Creation. But, of course, we know also that the coming of the Eternal Word in Christ, God's declaration of His purposes for us in Christ, the setting out of the way of obedience, of reconciliation in Christ, is a tragedy, because human beings turn away from this declaration, from this setting out of the way of obedience.

Sin, suffering and the Saviour

Before the Word in Christ can discover the Word in us, a great deal of sin and corruption has to be cleared away. The medieval mystics, both Christian and Muslim, used the image of a metal mirror that had rust on it and had to be polished. There is then the coming of the Word as suffering love. On the human side it is bound up with, of course, rejection; but on the Godward side, if you like, this suffering of the Incarnate Word is part of the revelation in Christ that is given to us. It discloses something to us of the very nature of God Himself and, at the same time, by the radical obedience of Jesus, it deals with human rebelliousness and sin.

But then the Word comes to us as the risen Christ – the Resurrection is a vindication of the suffering and a verification of the Incarnation. The risen Christ is not the same as the earthly Jesus, of course. The risen Christ incorporates the humanity of Jesus, but in a totally new and transformed way – not simply the earthly Jesus, but not divorced totally from the earthly Jesus either.

Krister Stendahl, the famous Lutheran New Testament scholar who is now Bishop Emeritus of the Church of Sweden and Chaplain of Harvard Divinity School, remarks that the Resurrection tradition in the Gospels has its nucleus not in visions and revelations but in the experience of an empty tomb. The fashion of speaking of the risen Christ without reference to the earthly Jesus, as it has developed, particularly in European theology since the Second World War, has led to a great deal of unprincipled manipulation. If you separate the risen Christ totally from what is given in the earthly Jesus, then you can say anything of the risen Christ. It is interesting, in this regard, to observe the very high value placed by liberation theologians on a recovery of the historical Jesus. For them, all authentic *praxis* depends on such a recovery.

I am interested to note how often, in Chapter 28 of St Matthew's Gospel, the risen Christ is described as *Jesus*. He comes to us as the risen Christ as he came to those women. They had been loyal – they had stayed by the foot of the Cross, they had watched his burial, and perhaps participated in it, and they had come again – loyal, but, I suspect, hopeless and sorrowful. When he comes to them, he brings them faith and hope and, yes, even a little fear. It is interesting that the text tells us that they were afraid, but the joy is described as great. The fear is not described as great, it is the joy that is great.

He comes also to the disciples; those who had run away, those who had not proved strong in the test. He does not come to them where they are, at least in the traditions that we find in Matthew and

Mark, but he charges the women (who become the first preachers of the Gospel, the apostles to the apostles, as it were) to go and tell these disciples to meet him in Galilee. As my children would say, 'Back to the Future!'

The Galilean Option

The risen Christ comes to us from the future. But he comes to us in a familiar place. Galilee – that word is loaded with significance. The other day I travelled with two very senior Christian friends on the train to London and, just to pass the time, I asked them, 'When I say the word Galilee, what images are evoked in your minds?' The woman said, 'lakes', and the man said, 'barren hills'. No doubt this is true. But Galilee for the first three Gospels, for the synoptics, is the place that Jesus chose for most of his ministry. It is where he was affirmed. It is where he was also persecuted. It is where he carried on with his healing and his teaching.

The liberation theologians of Latin America call this the Galilean Option of Jesus. He deliberately did not choose Jerusalem or even Judah, but Galilee; poor, rural and neglected. 'The people who walked in darkness have seen a great light' and, of course, the prophet is speaking of Galilee (Isa. 9:2).

Galilee was the first bit of territory of the land given to the people of Israel to be colonised by the Assyrians. When the Assyrians took it, in the eighth century BC, they exiled many of the people – the inhabitants of Galilee – and brought in and settled other people from different parts of their empire which stretched to southern Iran and what is now Afghanistan.

Galilee stands for oppression and being oppressed. It is poor. Can any good come out of Nazareth? When Peter is seen at the trial of Jesus, he is accused of being a Galilean and is recognised by his accent (Matt. 26:69–75). Well, many parts of the Diocese of Raiwind where I was Bishop were very poor and very rural. And when these people came to the city of Lahore, which was very urban and comparatively rich, they were recognised instantly, by their dress, by the way they walked and, most of all, by their language.

Oppressed and poor. But then it was also Galilee of the Nations. It was multi-racial and multi-cultural. Most of those encounters of Jesus which I believe alerted him to the significance of his mission, the universality of his mission, took place in Galilee. The Roman centurion and the Syro-Phoenician woman symbolise Galilee of the Nations. And of course these people represented not only different races but also different faiths. And yet Jesus could say of the centurion, 'I have not found such faith in Israel' (Matt. 8:10).

The disciples are being sent home by Jesus, rather as he sent back the demoniac he had healed. The demoniac wanted to follow Jesus, and Jesus said, 'No, go back to your relatives' (Mark 5:18–20). They are being sent home, back to Galilee. Yet in this sending them home there are the seeds of universal mission.

It is tremendously significant to me that I should have been commissioned at St Andrew's-tide which is also the eve of Advent.

St Andrew, tradition tells us, went on to be a great cross-cultural missionary in the direction of Iran, Central Asia, and of Patras in the Peloponnese. But before he did that, he went home and brought his brother Simon to the Lord.

We find here a challenge, I think, to the Church Missionary Society at this time, as we are about to begin the Decade of Evangelism. In a very real way, any mission to the world remains inauthentic if it is not concerned with mission at home. It is in our engagement with mission at home that we find the possibilities of a universal mission at all.

Finally, Jesus in this passage ends with a promise. 'Lo!' he says, 'I am with you always.' There were very few people in the Churches of the Reformation in the sixteenth century who thought much about world mission, but one of them was a Dutchman called Adrian Saravia. Adrian Saravia became convinced of the need for an Episcopal Church. He came to England and wrote a tract on the need for bishops in the Church, as a focus of unity and as the principal agents for mission in the areas entrusted to their care.

Unusually for his age Saravia, in his exegesis of Matthew 28, points out that the promise, 'I am with you always to the close of the age', is inextricably related to the Great Commission. The presence of Jesus is assured for the Church so long as the Church is faithful in her mission; pointing always to the Promised One who came, is now present with the Church, and will come again in great glory.

Maranatha! Come, Lord Jesus!

A Gift of the Holy Spirit

Derek Worlock

Each year there are few days in the Week of Prayer for Unity when I do not find myself called on to preach in some part of the country on the promotion of the unity for which Christ prayed the night before he died. Despite what is often alleged, my experience is that there is mounting enthusiasm for this, even though there is growing appreciation of the doctrinal issues which still divide Christians.

No one of my generation can doubt the changes in attitudes and relationships which have developed in the last 25 years since the end of the Second Vatican Council. There is much for which we thank God, but it remains plain that the fullness of Christian Unity must surely be a gift of the Holy Spirit. There is no way in which it can be achieved merely by some academic treaty or armistice.

It was for this reason that I disagreed with Archbishop Runcie when, in his early months at Canterbury, he set AD 2000 as the deadline for the achievement of Christian Unity. On the other hand his own patient and humble approach to this all-important subject has been a major contribution to the advances which have been made. This particular sermon in an Anglican church in Liverpool, at Pentecost in June 1987, testifies to our need for the grace of the Spirit.

There is something exciting and challenging about the phrase 'on the road to Jerusalem', and the picture of the disciples, following after Jesus, lacks nothing of that challenge. In the city ahead of them, the Council had made their decision to take action against Jesus. They saw his action in raising Lazarus as fuel to the fire of the revolution they feared from his words. The apostles had warning of this and the sensible thing was to lie low. But the Pasch was near and when Jesus went forward, his friends and disciples followed, even if in a bit of a daze.

At a certain point, Jesus called the apostles up with him and began to prepare them for his betrayal and arrest. He would be delivered to the Gentiles, mocked, spat upon and scourged. He would be put to death and on the third day he would rise again. Oh, it's easy enough for us. We know and we understand. But not those puzzled men, still dazzled by the power of their Master. Two of them, James and John, evidently appreciating that the crunch had come, could only think in terms of victory and the establishment of the Kingdom.

They mention the matter to their mother and Mrs Zebedee was not slow in pressing her son's claims. 'You don't know what you are asking,' the Lord replies. But that was nothing to the indignation of the others, who were clearly jealous of the impetuous ambition of the Sons of Thunder.

It is not difficult to imagine the scene and the senseless rivalries until Our Lord calls a halt to it all by saying quite simply that that was not his way. He could not be likened to an earthly ruler. He had come to serve, not to be served. If they wished to be with him, they must be marked by humility, service and sacrifice. The leadership asked of the disciples, and the discipleship asked of us, lies in humility, service and sacrifice. On the road to Jerusalem we approach the Easter Garden via Gethsemane and Golgotha.

It is good, therefore, that as we look to unity among Christians we should focus on the risen life of Jesus and begin to think of his presence among us through the Holy Spirit. Although we do so much together throughout the year nowadays, increasingly at Pentecost Christians are coming together to pray for the fullness of Christian Unity. Doubtless there will be some who excuse themselves this opportunity on the score that 'things are so much better nowadays', that it is better to build the general intentions of ecumenism into the living relationships among Christians the year round. It is almost the same as saying that we do not really need that sort of thing nowadays. We can be content to say 'Stand' to the divine dealer and not risk the unknown. Indeed there are undoubtedly those who are prepared to write off the remaining differences and, in this age of détente and deterrence, to settle for co-existence in non-belligerence.

Those of us with long memories will understand all this, thankful for what has with God's grace been achieved in the last 25 or 30 years. Less understandable, even more dangerous, are the views of those who, either with burned-out enthusiasm or frustrated because they have not succeeded in forcing the pace to their own chosen pattern, have thrown in the towel rather than thrown down the ecumenical gauntlet, and have informed others within their hearing that the 'steam' has gone out of ecumenism. My diary and the many engagements I share with Bishop Sheppard do not support this theory.

Perhaps I sound almost a little too optimistic, even among fellow pilgrims, not strangers. Knowing the quite serious social problems we face in the North West, journalists often ask me what grounds I can have for optimism in our situation. I can only reply that, quite apart from the uncrushable spirit of our people, I believe in the Resurrection.

Simplistic or snide, that is the only viewpoint of the Christian in facing the challenges of his daily life, the problems of the world's contradiction of the Beatitudes, the frustration of man-made obstacles on the way which is the truth and the life, the crushing sense of guilt and defeat when one's best-laid plans for the implementation of Christ's will for us meet with the failure which we do not recognise as Gethsemane.

It would not be original for me to claim that the criteria for success for the worldly-wise are in large measure a contradiction of the Gospel. But in saying that, I am thinking not just of the breakdown of public morality but also of the use and distribution of this world's goods, of the wealth – actual or relative – of a small part of our world and the really dreadful poverty and hunger of so many. But however we may regard these things or the injustices and tragedies which fill the pages of our newspapers, there is no viewpoint for a Christian to adopt save within the shadow of the Cross, no answer or meaning save within the light of the Resurrection.

So, my dear brothers and sisters in Christ, whatever differences may yet divide us, we to whom has been given this work of reconciliation are one in a risen Christ. If we are to seek a way forward in the world which presents so many problems at this time that way must be his way. The fullness of unity for which he prayed the night before he died, and for which we too pray amidst all our difficulties and conscientiously-held differences, can only be through him, with him and in him. And in the reconciliation of the world with God and of ourselves one with another, we may have supreme hope in him who has called us to follow him and to walk his way together.

The danger of course is if we are content to leave it there: to spend our time together reminding one another of the bad old days and to find comfort in all the progress of recent years; to compliment one another on our joint hymn-singing, without facing up to the theological differences and doctrinal distinctions which we make mentally as we recite common formulae. Certainly there is much for which to thank God, much to which we may look forward in hope, much to pray for as we recognise true unity among Christians as a gift from God, not an administrative arrangement. But there is also much which can and must be done together now because of the bond of baptism which leads us in partnership – even if in some matters still divided – in common witness to proclaim together by example and word the good news that Jesus, our Lord, has risen from the dead, has promised to return and to take us to the Father; and in the meantime has called us to share in his work of redeeming the world.

Through baptism the Holy Spirit incorporates all Christians into Christ, into a single body. We recognise one another as partners in the mission-field in which we have been placed: not a reluctant partnership made expedient by the size of the opposition, but a loving acceptance of God's will for us as we work together towards the fullness of that unity which, as the Second Vatican Council says, we 'almost all desire, though in different ways'.

This partnership calls for faith and it calls for hope. It is a great mystery. We pray for something which is outside our experience and which, in its precise form, defies our understanding. We do not know in what form the fullness of unity can be achieved. In the past we have known only varying degrees of division which, with all our pain and sorrow, are to be associated with the broken and wounded body of Christ: a sorrow to us and a stumbling block to others.

Our pilgrimage in pursuit of Christian Unity implies the healing of those wounds and calls for hope as well as faith, hope in spite of the obvious difficulties of our progress. Christian hope begins when human hope is challenged, when all human means have broken down and everything appears to be in ruins. Hope is not for the feeble or for superficially optimistic hearts. It is essentially for the strong of heart accustomed to suffering and to death. It is this which lifts our hope for Christian Unity within the shadow of the Cross and the light of the Resurrection.

When we say that as Christians we meet at the foot of the Cross, it can only be as one body, already reconciled in charity and forgiveness, even though some of those differences remain, some of those wounds are still not healed. But we cannot look up at Christ upon the Cross and believe that the broken members of His body are not to be made whole again in the glorious risen life of Christ into whom we are incorporated by our baptism. He wills us to be one and, even if we have to accept this in faith, because we do not know precisely how, we must be united in desire that his will be done. It is that reconciliation in charity and unity of desire that brings us together in common worship tonight.

My emphasis of the word 'reconciliation' is deliberate. In some ways it is easier to contemplate a conversion of heart than it is to think in terms of total comprehensive theological agreement and uniformity of worship. We have differences in tradition and in loyalties. But the essential loyalty is to Christ. We know that we shall not achieve unity by a patched up amalgam of Churches, pledged for administrative purposes to keep the peace. We accept that within the Church of Christ, in which we pray we may one day be united, there may be room for legitimate diversity: indeed that very diversity may lead to our mutal enrichment.

That is the beauty of this work for the fullness of unity. It calls forth from us the Christian virtue of unquenchable hope, as well as faith and humility. How else can we approach unity, when we recall that Jesus Christ described it as being like his unity with the Father, 'That they may be one, Father, as we are one: so completely one that the world may believe that it was you who sent me' (John, 17:22–3).

That is the picture of unity we seek and hope for. It does not mean conquest or capitulation. We shall meet in Christ who is our reconciliation. We must reach forward in faith, without fear or mistrust, undeterred by the past failures, resolute in our belief that in so far as we reflect in our lives the love and forgiveness of Christ, share in his compassion for the multitude who are suffering, in so far as we are humble and not self-righteous in our service of the community, then we are sharing in the work of reconciling and healing.

We must never lose heart. Before the glory of his resurrection from the tomb, Christ suffered the mockery of those who feared the consequences of his championing the powerless; he bore upon his face the spittle of man's contempt for his apparent ineffectualness; he knew the sorrow of abandonment under pressure by those to whom he had given his friendship; his broken heart was pierced by the lance of those who could not wait to see him die. This is the Christ who on Calvary is our meeting point, who calls us to share with him these 'garments of salvation'. This is the Christ who is our hope. This is the Christ of unity.

Becoming Free Men

Robert Hardy

One of the privileges of my time as Bishop of Maidstone was to be able to sit alongside the Archbishop and St Augustine's Throne on Maundy Thursday each year. On that day, the Archbishop called together the clergy of the Canterbury Diocese. He Blessed the Oils and we renewed our Ordination Vows. Since coming to Lincoln, I have initiated this practice and the sermon below is the one I delivered to the clergy in 1990. Because of the distances in the Diocese of Lincoln, we have separated the Blessing of the Oils on Maundy Thursday from the Renewal of Ordination Vows on St Peter's Day. The occasion is much valued by the clergy, and I have come to value it greatly as an important occasion in the life of this diocese.

I owe the Archbishop a very great deal personally, as he was my Theological College Principal. He had therefore a very real hand in my own formation and was always supportive to me at different stages of my ministry. In 1980 he invited me to become Bishop of Maidstone and to be a part of his own diocese. Then followed six exciting years when I began to learn something about what it means to be a bishop. The Archbishop was always supportive to me personally and was marvellous in going round to different parishes in my part of the Canterbury Diocese. I would usually prepare a brief for him giving details of the parish and the incumbent's family, etc. He would always use the brief with great imagination and skill – so much so that he managed to convey a deep sense of personal knowledge and concern for individuals and their situation. Not infrequently when I asked him to focus on a particular aspect or pastoral difficulty in the life of a parish, he would do so with enormous skill and deftness, usually extending what I said, putting his own gloss upon it and handling it with both insight and sensitivity. Few people realise what a very personal ministry Robert Runcie has carried on as Archbishop. This is deeply treasured by those who have had the privilege of knowing him. It remains an inspiration to me and to many others.

John 8:30–6

The passage I have just read comes from that controversial section at the heart of St John's Gospel which begins to explore the meaning of such fundamental themes as authority and status, security and freedom. Jesus is addressing 'the Jews who believed in him', that is to say, he is speaking to the people already deeply grounded in religious tradition; those who had come to put their trust in him. If you like, they knew where they stood, or thought they did. So you can imagine their incredulity at what they heard. No wonder they asked, 'What do you mean by saying, "You will *become* free men"?' They thought they were secure and free already!

Well, it's in some such similar context that I suggest Christ addresses us today in this service. Ordination revolves around those same themes of authority and status, security and freedom. There is an inescapable grandeur and solemnity about it; those of us who reflect on our own ordination are conscious of a rich and valued heritage. Nowhere, perhaps, is the Church of England more subtly rooted in tradition, nowhere is it somehow more itself than in the ordinations at Petertide in a Cathedral city like this. It's easy therefore on such an occasion to fall back on certainties that seem proof against change and decay. Indeed, I could discourse upon them with genuine confidence and conviction. For it is a fact that there have been dykes and buttresses by which the ordained mystery has been surrounded, and they *have* afforded us real authority and status, security and freedom. No one is saying they are wrong, any more than Jesus was decrying the Jews' descent from Abraham. And yet there comes a moment – and in Christ it has come – when we must face the truth that we cannot rest upon them. For many of those traditional confidences are in fact dissolving fast. Let me simply mention three:

First, there's been that line which has subtly but firmly divided clergy and laity. In our tradition the line has been drawn below the diaconate, despite the fact that in function deacons and readers, not to mention local ministers, have almost everything in common. It's a line, of course, of which the New Testament knows little. But it is now being blurred, not by obliterating real distinction of ministerial function, but by liberating them from the stranglehold of what we have been pleased to call 'the threefold ministry'. To many of us, that's threatening. It makes us question our distinctive role.

Dissolving, too, is the security that has been afforded by holy orders as a profession. No longer is ordination necessarily a job for life. No longer is it the exclusive preserve of men. New patterns and new pressures have already subtly shifted the balance.

Third, and much more intangible, is the magic circle, that spiritual 'ring of confidence', that has been thrown round holy orders since the Middle Ages. Like the 'divinity that doth hedge a king' or the mystical sense of 'degree' upon which Shakespeare commented, the mystique of orders has often given us marvellous protection as a clerical caste. But it has sometimes done this to the detriment of other ministries; and to most of the world around us it now begins to mean increasingly less and less.

I've spoken of these securities by which in the past the ordained ministry has been defined and protected – the line between those in the clergy and those not, the line marking off this profession from 'worldly' occupations, and the line which puts it on the other side of ordinary job-changes. All these have served a real purpose, and most people in the Church would say, like St Paul of the Law, that they were 'holy and righteous and good'. And they will ask, as the Jews did of Jesus, 'What do you mean by saying, "You will *become* free men"?'

Yet the truth is we dare not *rest* on these securities, any more than on Abrahamic pedigree or circumcision. We are part of ordained ministry at a time when in many ways its future is in the melting pot. This is something that I believe we should welcome. But it means, of course, that true freedom, as opposed to sloppiness and indecision, is a desperately valuable commodity.

So how, in our situation, are we to become *free*, as men and women?

First, we must recognise the need for it. And this, for those of us who are in the position of the 'Jews who believe' is almost the most difficult thing of all. Only last February, the Houses of Convocation debated the freehold and the rights of the clergy: not a very edifying exercise, perhaps, but at least a straw in the wind.

Second, we must really believe that it is the *truth* that sets us free and not some man-made contrivance or convenience. Most of us don't like facing up to this. We don't mind it so long as we can choose the bits that fit, but we're not too good with the rest. Yet only a passionate facing of truth will ever make us free.

And, third, it's not just a facing of common human facts of which Jesus speaks. Rather, he says, 'if you dwell within the revelation I have brought, if you continue in my word . . . you shall know the truth, and the truth will set you free . . . If, then, the Son sets you free, you will be free indeed.' Real and deep freedom is the freedom of sons and daughters of men and women come of age, in contrast with the relationship of minors and of slaves. And we shall know this freedom only if we are prepared to rest our ministry on no other security than that of our being-in-Christ. If we continue in his word. This is what St Paul's battle for justification was about. It is what the Gospel is about. And it is to bring ourselves and others back to this, that we must be prepared to sit light to any other foundation, and not to get too fussed if it appears to be shaken or undermined. Let it go if necessary, even if it's precious. For if the Son sets us free, then we shall be free, free to reckon anything else as refuse or as dung.

My prayer, then, for our Church is that as Ministers of Christ we shall be truly free; men and women who rely on no adventitious supports, hate nothing but evil, fear no one but God, and have the love of Christ richly in our hearts. For with that, as John Wesley once said, we can change the world.

Guard the Deposit

Stephen Sykes

In this sermon I have tried to tackle the problem with which Archbishop Robert Runcie wrestled in practice throughout his episcopate, that of tradition and innovation. I do so with gratitude to God for his uprightness, goodness, fidelity, love, fortitude and gentleness of which the letter to Timothy speaks.

But you, man of God, must shun all that, and pursue justice, piety, integrity, love, fortitude and gentleness. Run the great race of faith and take hold of eternal life, for to this you were called, when you confessed your faith nobly before many witnesses. Now in the presence of God, who gives life to all things, and of Jesus Christ, who himself made that noble confession in his testimony before Pontius Pilate, I charge you to obey your orders without fault or failure until the appearance of our Lord Jesus Christ which God will bring about in his own good time. He is the blessed and only Sovereign, King of kings and Lord of lords; he alone possesses immortality, dwelling in unapproachable light; him no one has ever seen or can ever see; to him be honour and dominion for ever! Amen.

Instruct those who are rich in this world's goods not to be proud, and to fix their hopes not on so uncertain a thing as money, but on God, who richly provides all things for us to enjoy. They are to do good and to be rich in well-doing, to be ready to give generously and to share with others, and so acquire a treasure which will form a good foundation for the future. Then they will grasp the life that is life indeed.

Timothy, keep safe what has been entrusted to you. Turn a deaf ear to empty and irreligious chatter, and the contradictions of 'knowledge' so-called, for by laying claim to it some have strayed far from the faith.

Grace be with you all!

(1 Tim. 6:11–16)

Timothy, keep safe what has been entrusted to you, or, *Timothy, guard the deposit;* and the reason why this blunter, more literal translation would be appropriate is the fact that the metaphor is financial and legal. Something has been placed on trust, and now must be kept safe, like a will or money, or title deeds.

And yet, of course, the metaphor can mislead, as well as guide. Are we not, by its very financial connotations, reminded of the parable of the talents, where the one who precisely and literally guarded what was given was blamed for failing to trade with it, and profit from it?

It seems, also, to be a rule of human culture that if something is preserved unchanged over centuries, the mere passage of time, with its inevitable cultural shifts, guarantees that it will not signify the same thing. This struck me with especial force while attending a recent Royal Maundy Service. The royal procession was like something out of Gilbert and Sullivan. The Yeoman of the Guard, preceding the yeomen carrying the silver alms dishes – on their heads – bore felt-tipped staffs which they clattered on the ground with every step, combining with their spurred boots to produce a sound for all the world like that of a man with three wooden legs. Their magnificent beauty, their pompous bewhiskerment, was such as to make one doubt whether late-twentieth-century British genes would any longer carry the capacity for such physical specimens!

But then I reflected, such treasonable thoughts are certainly in the idiom of the late twentieth century. The preservation of the Royal Maundy Service as 'a great tradition', is something which, while *symbolising* continuity, certainly *signifies* something different to those who see it. Can you imagine a Radio 1 disc jockey describing a ceremony like the Royal Maundy for his or her audience? Those whose everyday life is wrapped in wall-to-wall joky banality spiced with innuendo simply could not *see* the Royal Maundy ceremony as their mothers and grandmothers and great grandmothers would have done.

If a tradition is literally kept like a deposit in a bank vault and cannot or does not interact with the fresh air of a culture, its ritual manifestation comes imperceptibly to signify something different. But at the same time, of course, part of what it symbolises is a determination to preserve continuity; and that determination is itself significant.

The first and second letters to Timothy have about them the strong flavour of coming from a time later than St Paul. They reek of 'routinisation'. This rude-sounding word is a sociological term for the process by which an originally charismatic movement (charismatic in the non-theological sense) attempts to cope with the problem of succession or leadership. Who is going to be the new leader, how is the new leader going to be chosen, what authority will this leader have, how will this leader be supported financially? These are practical questions which every new religious movement (and many political ones) have to solve, down to and including the pentecostal and house church movements of our own day.

And routinisation is there on the page of the Pastoral epistles, in their concern for the ministry, specifically for the authority of Timothy, as Paul's own 'son' in the Lord, how he was going to be paid and supported, and what his relation to Paul's Gospel was to be. Part of his authority, indeed, is precisely the fact that he is only going to preach *what has been entrusted to him*.

But in numerous other ways we see, especially in 1 Timothy, a

Church which is coming to terms with the culture of which it is part. Women are to keep in their place, not to be teachers in the Church. Slaves are not to respect their masters the less for being Christian brothers. All Christians should commend themselves as good citizens, not as lawless and unruly persons. The rich have got to be generous, and the poor have got to give up wanting to be rich. The Christian religion, in short, is depicted as promoting domestic and civil concord and harmony.

There are other signs too of a post-Pauline situation. There is a quotation of apparently liturgical formulae. God is:

> King of kings and Lord of lords; he alone possesses immortality, dwelling in unapproachable light; him no one has ever seen or can ever see; to him be honour and dominion for ever. Amen!
>
> (1 Tim. 6:15–16)

And in these writings a characteristic Pauline word like righteousness means not 'justification', as in Romans or Galatians, but one of a list of virtues. 'But you, man of God, must pursue *justice*, piety, fidelity, love, fortitude and gentleness' (1 Tim. 6:11).

All this makes tough reading for restless, contemporary Christian radicalism. But the fact that the New Testament records this process of routinisation and reflects its trials and tensions is, I believe, instructive of us today, living as we do in the midst of another '-isation', not so much routine as secular. How they, the congregations mirrored in the Pastorals, coped with inevitable change has some marvellously instructive lessons for us too.

For there was no alternative for the post-Pauline Churches. When St Paul died there *had* to be other leaders. Routinisation does not mean, as it is so often painted, decline and disintegration. It is a process of change which is simply inevitable – as inevitable, I am tempted to say, as having to put up with a successor to a great professor.

Routinisation is a mode of detaching the impact of the Christian Gospel from the person of a particularly gifted leader, like St Paul. It is, precisely, a way of providing for the continuation of the Church, even if a person of the inherent moral and spiritual authority of St Paul does not appear.

Embedded in our passage for this evening are a whole series of evidences of the process I have been describing:

- A reference to a baptismal or ordination confession ('in the presence of Jesus Christ who himself made the same noble confession and gave his testimony to it before Pontius Pilate');
- The quotation of a liturgical formula (a doxology in praise of 'the blessed and only Potentate');
- The incapsulation of the faith in a single, comprehensive 'commandment' or 'deposit', the special concern of a designated and authoritative leader called 'Timothy';

- The promotion of civic virtues to seek to guarantee those conditions conducive to the orderly growth of the Church by open preaching, and the deflection of gossip and hostile criticism.

Each of these is a sign of the community adapting itself to the long-term process of providing for the continuation of the Christian Gospel in a largely indifferent or actively hostile culture. And I have chosen to focus on the complex relation between the *deposit* of which the writer speaks and other aspects of his message.

For the deposit is that *symbol* of continuity, which certainly, if guarded and preserved in precisely the manner which the writer recommends would, in the course of time, come to mean something different. The Pastoral epistles do not cite anything absolutely corresponding to our credal summaries, but we can well imagine that something describable as a 'commandment' or a 'deposit' would be delivered at baptism in a single memorable formula; a formula, of course, of which our liturgical creeds are a later outgrowth. And it is these very creeds, the symbols *par excellence* of the continuity of the Christian faith over the centuries, which absolutely guarantee changing signification. The same is true of all the other symbols of continuity, the Bible itself, the sacraments, the special ministry of the Church – all of these signify new things with changing times.

And yet that could only be a part of the truth. The *fact* that the same creed, Bible, sacrament or ministerial office is retained itself manifests an intention to be faithful to an original time of special authority. The act of guarding the deposit, in a period of cultural change, is a determinate act of great importance; and the more rapid the cultural change, the greater the value of the fixed (or apparently fixed) points of reference.

It now appears that we have backed the Church into an inescapable dilemma. By retaining its symbols of continuity it guarantes discontinuity. What is it to do to preserve the *reality*, rather than the *appearance* of its basic identity? The corollary of my argument is that the Church must be apparently innovative if it proposes to be and do the same thing over time; but it must submit to the requirement that it be innovative 'in character'.

We have to admit that the endorsement of innovation appeals to the neophiliac strain in our make-up. Most of us have been severely over-exposed to the habit of rapid changes of habit, and in some the damage has been severe. Neophilia, the love of novelty, must, in Christian circles, be subject to very severe scrutiny. Innovation in the Church, which is a necessity, can only ever be 'in character'. The analogy here is a precise one, in so far as the Church itself is a *community of character*, an environment in which certain human traits are preserved and encouraged, and others discouraged or disallowed.

And it is a community of that kind that our writer has in mind when he urges that the people of God should shun the love of money and the envy that goes with it, and pursue justice, uprightness, piety (godliness of life), faith or fidelity, love, fortitude and gentleness. I called these earlier 'civic virtues', and it may be thought that I was dismissing them. Not at all. This is the new commonwealth, in the midst of the world, but not of it; requiring for its normal maintenance public peace and order, but not resourceless in the face of breakdown; it was these tiny communities which so took root in the ancient world that they revolutionised its corporate morality.

Now we today are living through another period of social change which sociologists call secularisation. Looked at from a Christian point of view, secularisation, like routinisation, cannot seriously be deplored. If human rational processes are the way they are, and the structures of the world the way they are, then sooner or later a certain way of seeing the world will come to predominate. And this will have severe consequences for the religious life we have hitherto known.

What, under these circumstances, is the Christian strategy? If my analogy is right, it will have three aspects:

(a) First, Christians will guard the deposit. They will retain their grip upon what they know and what has been handed down.
(b) Second, they will realise that the very act of holding on to what is traditional in new circumstances alters the significance of these entities, and they will recognise the need for innovation.
(c) Third, they will be open to proposals for innovation 'in character', precisely in order to preserve the identity of the faith.

The *sources* of the deposit are the same as they always have been: the creeds, the Bible itself, the sacraments, the special ministry. To hold firm by these is of especial importance in an era of rapid social change. To renew our grasp upon them in depth, to eschew all superficiality in their interpretation, to defend them with dignity is to enable them to continue to do their mysterious work of transformation of the human conscience.

But we must resist the package offered us by traditionalists, who assert that their mere preservation guarantees the continuous identity of the Church. On the contrary, it is only when the deposit is supported by inventiveness within the parameters of uprightness, godliness, fidelity, love, fortitude and gentleness, that the Christian faith will be represented with the wholeness it requires in our present age.

We frankly do not know what will become of the Church in a secularising culture. No one has been this way before. It is equally pointless to be elated by apparent success, as to be down-cast by apparent failure. What is required of us is – unsurprisingly – fidelity, faithfulness. And, of course, since proposals for innovation will inevitably bring with them conflict and controversy, we are required – again without surprise – to practise gentleness.

The lesson of 1 Timothy for us today is that guarding the deposit and being a community of character is the way for a Church to live through social change. And it is for God himself to prepare His own future for the Church of Jesus Christ.

On a Huge Hill

Michael Mayne

*In February 1985 Great St Mary's, Cambridge (where I was Vicar), and
the Roman Catholic Chaplaincy were the centre for an ecumenical
Teaching Week called Encounters. We aimed at a presentation of Christian
belief which was thought-provoking and honest, an interpretation of life
which took account of its mystery and its daunting mixture of good and
evil.*

*Not least we wanted students to understand better the legitimate breadth
and space of faith and discipleship and the need for diverse and
complementary insights in our encounters with God.*

*The main speaker was Archbishop Robert Runcie. He was not chosen
because he was Primate: he was chosen for his ability to engage both
mind and heart and communicate with wit and conviction the faith that
sustains him; for his sense of the mystery of things; for his own infectious
humanity.*

*This is a sermon I preached in Great St Mary's on the previous Sunday,
and I dare to hope that it is true to the spirit of that type of Anglicanism
which the Archbishop best represents.*

Last Monday *The Times* published a thoughtful first leader on the
subject of doctrine and belief in the Church of England. 'In recent
times,' it said, 'no slur against the Church has been more damaging
than the charge that an Anglican may believe anything or everything
– or nothing. And nothing would be more bracing to the Church
than to regain the sense that there are truths worth living by and
even dying for, and that the Church of England rests on a solid
bedrock of sure faith.'

This morning, on the eve of the Teaching Week which is about
to begin, I want to reflect on the nature of such truths. Looking to
the future, Jesus said to his disciples that 'the Spirit of truth will
guide you into all truth', and 'you will know the truth and the truth
shall set you free'.

In one of the sermons he preached in Trinity College Chapel,
Harry Williams makes the distinction between two kinds of truth:
what he calls the 'outside' kind and the 'inside' kind. The first kind
is what universities are concerned to teach. They train people to
observe objects and encounter ideas with accuracy and imagination
and see how they relate to each other, and the mastery of a subject

by one who has become expert in at least some aspect of it may be publicly recognised by conferring the degree Master of Arts or Master of Science.

But there is another sort of truth which is less easily defined and which can't be mastered in this way. The 'inside' sort. Truth which can't be kept at a distance and which has little to do with the marshalling of factual information. This kind of truth comes from outside us and claims us, and at its core there is a heart of mystery. It may be described as a kind of visitation to which we are invited to respond.

Think of something of great beauty: a painting or a poem or a concerto. You can master the outside of it, analyse its content and structure, the way the notes of music or the words lie on the page or the paint on the canvas, but having done all that there remains a quality, a beauty, a truth which claims you and which may even judge you; and you can only respond to this mystery with a kind of wonder.

Now the truth of God is like that: the 'inside' sort of truth. For the mysterious truth of God is that He is self-giving Love, and the response to love, like the response to beauty, is a matter for the heart, for an inner response of our whole being. 'I do not know the truth', wrote Kierkegaard, 'except when it becomes part of me.'

But where do we find the truth of God which we are to make part of ourselves and which we are judged by? In the Church? If so, in what tradition of the Church, speaking as it does with such diverse and confusing voices? In the Bible? If so, in what parts of the Bible, for it gives us no consistent answers? And so the deeper question we must ask is: 'What is this truth which has created both the Bible and the Church?' And the answer is quite clear. Truth is not what *we* think or say about God. Truth is what God has done and is doing.

The truth is Jesus Christ. God discloses himself in a life which, writes St John, 'is full of grace and truth'. 'I am the truth,' says Jesus. 'He,' writes St Paul, 'is the image of the invisible God.' So the truth of God centres on this life, this death and Resurrection; and it is learned in the common life of the community which sprang from those events. And the Christian life is a pilgrimage where, as we learn to be open to the Spirit at work within and among us, this truth is slowly apprehended and made part of us.

Today we recognise that the creeds, those attempts in the early centuries to capture what Christians most deeply believe about God, are expressed in fallible, shifting, limited human language drawn from the Bible and the early Christian councils. They contain different kinds of statements – some historical, some symbolic or poetic. For the New Testament writers and the Church fathers were well aware of the paradox Christians always have to face: the more we come to understand God, the more we become aware of the ultimate mystery of His Being.

For the present, all our insights into the truth are partial ones. Yet sadly, such is the nature of our insecurity, each one of us behaves as if *my* insight, *my* experience, *my* understanding is more valid than yours. In social or political terms truth becomes the way *I* see it; and unhappily, when it comes to religion, truth tends to mean 'my Catholic understanding of the nature of the male priesthood' or 'my Conservative Evangelical understanding of salvation', with scores of little minor fortresses in between. So, for example, we have the recent passionate demand that all bishops should be asked to subscribe to the truth of the Virgin Birth; or we have some hardline members of the Christian Union in Cambridge circularising all other members and urging them not to take part in next week's Teaching Week as Roman Catholics are involved and 'the true Gospel will not be preached'.

Now I take my stand on what that *Times* leader calls 'the solid bedrock of sure faith': the belief that God was in Christ, reconciling us to Himself, that His nature is love, that I am created in His likeness, that my sins are forgiven, that God (in a new creative act) raised Jesus from the dead and invites me to work for His Kingdom. But I also believe that the truth of God is infinitely greater than all our individual perceptions of it and that we only begin to apprehend what it is by looking at what are the insights of *this* Tradition and what are the insights of *that* Tradition and saying, 'Yes, you are right; and yes, *you* are right, too!' I am an Anglican because it gives me room to breathe in the tolerant air of a Church which in its pursuit of truth allows its members a wide liberty of theological speculation, and because it believes that no one person or Party or Church has a monopoly of the truth; and this comprehensiveness is not the weakness of the Church of England but its strength.

How could one feel anything else standing in this pulpit? I cannot think there is a parish church in England which was so closely involved in the events of the Reformation, and the hammering out of the Church of England ethos under the Elizabethan Settlement and in the succeeding centuries. This university played a critical role in the development of the English Church, and all its most influential theologians preached within these walls. Cranmer, Latimer, Ridley, Whitgift, Matthew Parker, Lancelot Andrewes – all were Masters or Fellows of Cambridge colleges. What we call Anglicanism is a deeply scriptural faith, with equal emphasis on the Word and the sacraments. Its form was greatly influenced by the intellectual collision between the Bible-loving Puritans and the High Church Sacramentalists in Cambridge in the sixteenth and seventeenth centuries. Later, Charles Simeon, Vicar of our neighbouring parish of Holy Trinity for nearly 50 years, was one of the leaders of the Evangelical Revival; and Westcott, Lightfoot and Hort, all Cambridge men,

between them worked to establish those principles of biblical scholarship which have had such a profound and liberating effect on the
whole Church of God.

Those groups of Christians who look for a kind of authoritarian,
absolute, bullet-proof, cast-iron certainty about everything are therefore not typical of the spirit of the Church of England, with its long
history of freedom of scholarship and its appeal to reason. No other
Church allows its members so much spiritual freedom, and at its
best shows the strength of toleration and comprehensiveness.

By toleration I mean a willingness to suffer for the time being
what may appear to be error. And a refusal to be partisan (which is
so much easier), preferring to allow wide interpretation of doctrine.
'Comprehensiveness,' said the report of the 1968 Lambeth Conference, 'is an attitude of mind we have learned from the controversies
of our history. It demands agreement on fundamentals, while tolera-
ting disagreement in matters on which Christians may differ without
feeling the necessity of breaking communion . . . It implies that the
apprehension of truth is a growing thing . . . and there must be a
continuing search for the whole truth in which the Protestant and
Catholic elements will find complete reconciliation.' As Charles
Simeon wisely said: 'The truth does not lie between two extremes,
but in both extremes.' And throughout its history various parties and
traditions have made their contribution to our Church: Evangelical,
Catholic, Liberal. They still do, and we are the richer for it.

Let me give you just one example of what it means for there to
be what has been called, by William Temple, 'the utmost liberty of
thought that is compatible with the maintenance of spiritual fellowship'. In the Doctrine Commission Report published 50 years ago,
a Committee under the chairmanship of Archbishop Temple published a note on different views of the Virgin Birth in the Church of
England. They said that, for many, the Virgin Birth speaks of an act
of sheer graciousness on the part of God, the fact that in Jesus
humanity makes a new beginning: here is God breaking into history
and inaugurating a new age. 'Many of us hold the belief that the
Word made flesh is integrally bound up with belief in the Virgin
Birth, that this will increasingly be recognised.'

But others, believing that a child inherits his or her genes and
chromosomes jointly from both father and mother, and believing
that Jesus was a true human being like us, think that our Lord's
birth took place under the normal conditions of human generation.
'In their minds,' said the Report, 'the notion of a Virgin Birth tends
to mar the completeness of the belief that in the Incarnation God
revealed Himself at every point in and through human nature.' And
they go on (and these are important words for us to remember
in our present angry disputes): 'We recognize that both
these views . . . are held by members of the Church, as of this

Commission, who fully accept the reality of our Lord's Incarnation, which is the central truth of the Christian faith.'

I chose to call this sermon 'On a Huge Hill'. The words come from a poem of John Donne:

> On a huge hill,
> Craggy and steep, Truth stands, and he who will
> Seek him about must, and about must go.

Many people want a kind of certainty, and you can buy it in various fundamentalist or other authoritarian stores. But that kind of certainty does not seem to me what the New Testament means by 'faith' or 'truth'. It is not that kind of openness to new apprehensions of truth of which St Paul speaks when he says, 'Now I see through a glass darkly, now I know in part, but (one day) I shall know even as I am known.'

There is a nice story of Bishop Westcott, who so valued speculation as an approach to truth, being met in Cambridge by one of his pupils, who said to him: 'Thank you. Thank you, Dr Westcott! You have made everything perfectly clear to me.' 'Oh!' replied Westcott. 'I hope not! I hope not!'

What we have tried to do, in setting up this Teaching Week in Great St Mary's, is to enable those who are searching for God at all kinds of levels to hear men and women of different traditions – Roman Catholic, Anglican, Methodist, Baptist – speak of how God in Christ has encountered them. The speakers will not attempt to thrust down others' throats their own understanding of truth: all they can hope for is that others will discern in them an authentic experience of God and then, in their different ways, seek to make it their own.

Faithful under Pressure

Michael Turnbull

One of the most admirable things about Robert Runcie is his ability to cope with pressure and, at the same time, to remain faithful to his God, his colleagues and himself. As a new Bishop I have been fortunate to have experienced the Archbishop's pastoral patience. He gave me quality time when he was under the pressure of the Lambeth Conference. As a neighbour, I have caught glimpses of his concern for local issues when national and international matters crowded in. The inevitable assumption is that Robert Runcie draws deeply from spiritual imperatives. He deciphers the dangers among the opportunities which pressure creates. Hence I offer the following address, unedited from its context of the Intercon Conference, High Leigh, May 1990, as an all too shallow tribute to a counsellor, leader and friend of profound depths.

When I was given this title I wondered, at first, whether it was an advertisement for tyres. That is not a bad starting point because a tyre is no good without pressure, but it is dangerous when it has too much pressure, and it can send you off the road. Let's look at good pressures and then dangerous pressures, and then see what it means to be faithful.

Good pressures

1. *The pressure of the Gospel*
Paul writes to the Corinthians that he feels this kind of pressure. In 2 Cor. 5:14, 'The love of Christ constrains us when we have reached the conclusion that one man died for all.' The Gospel leaves us no choice. The same word is used by Paul in Phil. 1:23, when he says he would like to go and be with Christ, but he feels this pressure, constraint to stay with them. Drawn like a magnet to Christ and his Cross, we live lives continually under the pressure of having no choice but to follow him, love him and proclaim him. It is a pressure we do not want to be without. It keeps us on the road, and is the very reason for our being on the road.

2. *The pressure of the Holy Spirit*
The disciples in the early Church were *compelled* to speak by the

Holy Spirit. Such was the pressure they could do no other (Acts 4:31). Stephen, under pressure of stones and death, found a greater pressure (Acts 7:55). The Church, upheld by the pressure of the Holy Spirit, held its way and grew (Acts 9:31). Barnabas and Saul were sent on their mission by the pressure of the Holy Spirit (Acts 13:4). The decisions in the Synod in Acts 15 are described as the decisions of the Holy Spirit (verse 28). The pressure here is of clear guidance. How I wish that our modern-day synods would experience this kind of pressure which comes to a group of people waiting upon God for His will. We sadly have to contrast that with our procedures of contention. I met a young person recently who, when I asked him how he had known the guidance of God, said, 'You know in your knower.' He knew the pressure of the Holy Spirit and I think that many of us could echo that experience.

3.   *The pressure of the fellowship of believers*
Acts 2:42 and following show us a sense of the pressure of a joyful fellowship which met regularly for worship. It was not a limiting pressure, but a freeing pressure. If you have ever tried to ride a bicycle without tyres – without pressure – you will know the feeling of how limiting that is. So is the Christian life without fellowship. I remember a physics master at school beginning a lesson on the Archimedes principle by saying, 'When lying in a bath of water, you sense the water buoying you up.' The pressure of a fellowship of believers is the spiritual parallel to that. In the early Church they had a sense of awe, of faith drawing them together, they were of one mind, and they grew in numbers. This came from the pressure of collective worship, collective action and collective discipline. The Church was on the road – riding on the pressure of the fellowship.

4.   *The pressure of our vocation*
Timothy knew this when Paul wrote to him in 2 Tim. 1:6,7, 'Stir into flame your gift.' The spirit is not a dissipated pressure which causes chaos, but love, strength, soundness of mind and judgement. That is the pressure which produces self-awareness and a sense of uniqueness. The scientific developments which have produced genetic fingerprinting mean that from a hair or a trace of any part of our body we can be identified and distinguished from any other human being. That is a confirmation of our uniqueness in God's creation. That being true, our development and growth is a particular and unique one and this contains the seeds of a particular vocation within us. That is the pressure of our personal vocation.

5.   *The pressure of holiness, love and suffering*
Perhaps this is better described as the *attractiveness* of holiness, rather than the pressure. The things which mark the Christian life become our chief desire as we move on in it. We are drawn to holiness, love

and suffering. I think that that can be described as pressure. In 1 Pet. 1:22, there is described a progression from obedience to purity, to feeling sincere affection. That is the pressure to love, even at the cost of suffering. There are no short cuts to this kind of affection. It is not superficial, it is not laid on, but it is an inevitable pressure of love, following obedience and purity.

6. *The pressure of opportunity*

There is no doubt the early Church felt this. The Acts of the Apostles is a story of grasping opportunities among the religious and super-stitious fervour of the first-century Middle East. They were taking the opportunities special to a persecuted people. Now I believe that those of us who have a special concern for Europe in this decade are sensing the pressure of a new opportunity. The new Europe contains new politics, new economics, new mobility. In Kent we are conscious of the opportunities afforded by the prospect of the open-ing of the Channel Tunnel. We have made a plea for it to be a Tunnel not just of commerce and competition, but a Tunnel of love and sharing. There are strong signs that God is opening up new opportunities in Europe, perhaps on a scale to match those of the early Church. There is the backcloth of secularisation, humanism and materialism, but the signs are that the tide is turning. Intercon is in a superb position to feel the pressure of opportunity. The signs are that there is a spiritual hunger, and though there is little comfort for institutional religion, many small new Churches are evolving and growing. The numbers of Protestant pastors are increasing, for instance in France, while the Roman Catholic Church experiences a crisis of vocation. A recent survey in France has shown a strong belief in the supernatural, a growth in Islam and a growth in Christ-ian Pentecostalists. The renewal movement is touching all Churches including the Roman Catholic Church – which is, perhaps, more ready to co-operate than its English counterpart. I am glad to read that Operation Mobilisation France has declared a strategy to make the local Church both a point of departure and arrival of its evangel-ism. I know that the clergy and congregations of the Diocese of Europe welcome this new phase of opportunity, and Intercon is an integral part of that.

Those are the good pressures: the Gospel, the Holy Spirit, fellow-ship, vocation, holiness and opportunity. Now we must be warned about the dangerous pressures.

Dangerous Pressures

1. *The pressure of a secularised world*

There is a strong temptation to think that if we had a great deal of money, we could convert the world. It is a temptation of mission agencies, of PCCs and of individuals. We all have our dreams which begin, 'if only I had the money . . . ' Money is important, but we should not be deluded into thinking that it is the most important thing. Indeed, the Churches growing fastest in the world are the poorest ones. There is strong evidence that where there is personal commitment, the money looks after itself. There is little evidence that Churches and organisations with the greatest resources are the most successful. We have only to contrast East Europe, China and Africa with America and the United Kingdom to see the truth of this. There is a pressure of conformity to the world to suggest that money is the key to everything. The striving after money, comfort, ease, avoidance of sacrifice and suffering, can be a pressure that ultimately lets the tyres down and takes us off the road.

2.   *The pressure of the media*
Communication is necessary and potentially good, but half-truths or untruths in headlines are dangerous pressures. It is easy to capture the headlines with quick answers and trivial pursuits. There is a strong seduction to think that popular media provide the quickest answer to proclamation. We know, of course, that it is patient, slow demonstration of the Gospel which is effective in the long term. This can come in the best kind of religious broadcasting and writing, but it is not a short cut.

3.   *The pressure of institutionalisation*
We look around our Churches and discover the pressure to get things right in structure, organisation and pseudo-legality. But we note that an overemphasis on the institution is the mark of a failing Church. It produces strife, contention and bureaucracy. There is a proper untidiness of the Holy Spirit which cannot be institutionalised. There is, at the heart of the Gospel, a waste of resources. Look again at the parable of the sower, generously throwing seed knowing that much of it will be wasted. Part of this is a temptation to think that mission is in our hands, but it is, in fact, God's mission. The scriptural unfolding of God's evangelism begins in Genesis and ends in Revelation. Our participation is seeing where and how He is working, and trying to do it with Him. Someone has described mission imaginatively as 'loitering with intent'. That response needs to be ready to take unreasonable risks, to be flexible, to be surprised by the ways of God. The pressure of the institution is to minimise risk, to be inflexible and to comform to expectations.

4.   *The pressure of the ego*
In our ministries and witness, we have to beware of the dangerous pressure to work only to fulfil our own satisfactions. This is a subtle pressure and part of the armoury of the Devil. Programmes,

policies and strategies are important, but need to be kept in their place. We need to watch lest we succumb to diary domination, the love of popularity (stroking people rather than witnessing their conversion). The command to us is not to go out into the world and please everybody, but to go out into the world and preach the Gospel. We shall find our own affirmation in inverse proportion to the effort we give to achieving it.

Those are some of the dangerous pressures. Now we must ask how do we remain faithful under the good pressures and the dangerous ones? There are two clues in the teachings of Jesus and the experience of Paul. Both run contrary to organisational or psychological advice we may turn to.

The first is from Jesus and it is that *actively* we can do nothing. We are required *passively* to abide. In John 15:4–8, we are taught to abide passively in Christ and that leads to fruitful activity. Frenetic activity leads to uselessness. This is as much true of missionary organisations as it is of individuals. Abiding in Jesus means abiding in his words so that we see him as the creative Word of God. The Bible is not the Word of God. Jesus is the Word of God, but we discover the Word by reading his words. The whole passage in John 15 is in the context of love and obedience. Without this faithful abiding (and the *cost* of evangelism), we are fruitless and worthy only to be cast aside. A doctor, or a lawyer or a carpenter may get by in achieving useful things, even if they are bad people. The Christian minister can achieve *nothing* worthwhile without this faithful abiding. If you take one thing away from this conference, I hope it may be: 'where do my priorities lie, and am I abiding in him?'

The second aspect of *faith* under pressure is the experience of Paul. In 2 Cor. 12:8–10, strength for a Christian has a paradox at its heart. It was when Paul knew he was weak that he was at his strongest. Someone asked me the other day what was the greatest change about me becoming a bishop. I thought a little bit about that and replied that in my spirituality I was driven more often to my knees. Any Christian minister knows the helplessness among the pressures. It may be the pressures of the world, the media, our ethical decisions, our personal judgement, and the expectations of others. It is when we *don't* know and are driven in our weakness to his strength, that we have the greatest potential. And at the heart of this is the Cross. That was Jesus's way of achievement: to produce strength out of weakness, and to acknowledge the pressure both good and dangerous. In the end we have to say, 'I have no strength of my own to handle this.' It is then that we discover that temptations become opportunities; that weaknesses become strengths; and that pressure is turned into power.

A Case for Christian Schools

Edward Norman

The continued involvement of the Churches in the conduct of educational establishments has been questioned by many Christians during the last 20 years. The problem, so often viewed from the perspectives of one nation, is actually international, and it has been one of the characteristics of Dr Runcie's primacy that he has persisted in encouraging Christian educational work throughout the wider context of the whole Anglican Communion. What follows is part of an address delivered in 1984 at a school in Zimbabwe.

What is the continuing justification of separate Christian education? I think there are very compelling reasons, but none which should in any way express hostility to the secular schools. The days are past when Christians anywhere should look to the State to protect their teachings and to embody their moral principles in civil constitutions. The old ideals of Christendom have simply fallen away, and the Church of the present day must recognise itself as existing in societies which will not necessarily correspond to former Christian notions of government. The history of the Church shows that it can exist within very many different types of governmental and social systems, and Church leaders have, as a matter of record, managed to identify the Church's teaching with large numbers of them. It is perhaps the most useful of modern insights to recognise that this was always mistaken, and that the modern secular world is doing the Church the great service of showing it what was always in reality the case: that in the world it has no abiding habitation. The duty of Christians to obey the State, and to recognise its positive qualities as the guardian of the principles of order and justice, ordained by God, still survives. The duty of the State to educate its citizens into its own values must also be acknowledged by Christians.

From this sort of perspective one thing seems clear. Christians will claim from the start, as a right, freedom of religious expression. Part of that freedom must be the ability to educate their children in Christianity. That principle, so simply stated, is fraught with complications. Sometimes the State will deny it. Sometimes this is because the State and the Churches cannot arrive at agreed formulae to demarcate the things of Caesar from the things of God. But where conditions are favourable, a strong case can still be made for separate Church schools. Let me outline the reason why I think this is so.

Traditional Christian involvement with education emphasised the inseparability of sacred and secular learning. That was true in the centuries before the rise of modern secularism, and before intellectual disciplines themselves had shed their religious garments; and it was true in the nineteenth century, when the distinction was becoming almost painfully evident. Christianity claimed, as it still should, that it discloses a universal view of things, sealed in the revelation of God Himself. This did not mean, of course, that religious information was the appropriate source for explaining the physical laws of the Creation, which were, as modern science has shown, open to natural knowledge. It was a past mistake of religious men to confuse a knowledge of the Creator with actual cosmology; they should have settled, as Christians now do, for the truth that the mechanics of the Creation must be explored by methods which are appropriate to the data. But Christianity does claim that it has the essential criterion of all knowledge: that for sense to be made of all the mechanics of things there has to be a resort to Revealed Truth. It therefore supposes that so-called 'secular' subjects, though in themselves tending to be value-free in idea, are in reality moulded and received according to existing values in the individual or the society. Christianity thus seeks to associate the acquisition of secular knowledge with religious knowledge, to bring them together, not in some grand incorporative philosophical scheme of things, but in the classroom, laying them sympathetically side by side, so that children are brought up to see that the works of God can be examined with intellectual integrity combined with faith. Grand philosophical designs are laid up with God Himself. Christianity is not a 'system' or a 'philosophical' position: it is the Revelation of a Person, of Christ himself, calling to each one of us to desert the world of material preoccupations so that we may re-enter it from the perspective of eternity. The Kingdom of God starts now, here in life, and it is addressed to men and women as they are, not as they ought to be in some well-ordered Utopia imagined by the political sensibilities of the secular world. How, then, can it be right for Christian people not to want to educate their children with the association of the sacred and the secular as a daily practice – for the sacred and the secular are not, in reality, two distinct realms at all, but the single order of the creation? Modern Christians who are prepared, on the evidence of seemingly shared material values between Christianity and the world of contemporary political idealism, to allow the State complete control of their children's education should look at their own understanding of the faith. They have probably lost sight of its spiritual genius and origin; and the State, for its part, can give no realistic guarantees that it may not, at some future point, propagate educational ideals which are positively antipathetic to a

Christian understanding of the world. A balance is required. Many children will inevitably have to attend State schools, since the resources of the Churches cannot always provide alternatives, and in some cases, in some countries, the law may not allow them to do so. In that situation it is plainly the duty of the parent to see that he or she acquires, from the State teachers, a full programme of so-called 'secular' knowledge for their child, and also a loyalty to the values of the society which established the school – where those values are not directly hostile to religion. The children are to use the experience to become good citizens. Parents and the clergy, in that situation, then have the additional duty to instruct the child in religion, and, at the same time, they must do so in a way that recognises the legitimate sphere of the State as the embodiment of God's order. Where conditions are favourable, however, the reasons which led to that enormous expansion of Church schools in the nineteenth century are still – perhaps more than ever – compelling. Christianity comprises a sort of 'counter-culture' to the world. It has its own view of man and his fallen condition, its own vocabulary of spirituality, and its own means of conveying truth. The last is the most important: Christian truth is conveyed through worship. It is the association of learning with prayer which is the key element in authentic Christian scholarship – alas, so little practised in these days, even in Christian seminaries. Too many who speak today of 'Christian' education really refer only to religious ethicism. They reduce the whole faith to a small component of itself, its moral dimension. Christianity, however, is mostly concerned with the need of men for redemption, with seeing the world as an expression of the creative will of God, and with regarding the non-material perceptions through which the Divine interposes in the affairs of men. It is witness to the great truth, so little esteemed in the modern world, that the most important and personal values are not political ones. It is quite false to suppose, as so many contemporary Christians appear to do, that religious phenomena can somehow be picked up from the surrounding secular culture without any specialist training or preparation. These religious phenomena are, of course, implicit in the culture of the world, as the whole of human affairs are in the providence of God; but the criteria for recognising religious truths are definitely not lying around waiting to be employed. It is wrong to believe that children can be left to be brought up in the secular culture, and that when they are old enough to 'think for themselves' they will then make an educated choice one way or the other. The world discloses a conflict and competition of ideologies, and it is clearly disadvantageous to Christianity that the tenets of its rivals should be inculcated from an early age when its own insights are not. All education is a matter of preferences and values, and a man who really believes his religion will not leave to chance the eternal future of his children, but will seek to pass on the one great dimension of life that he himself should prize above all others. Church schools ought to be founded with that purpose in mind: it is their sole reason for existence. They are a way of declaring that the systems of the world cannot be trusted with ultimate truth; that one of the errors of the secularised modern mind is the elevation of the political order as a substitute church; that the value of a man is not exhausted in his civic capacity; and that true religion has unique insights into the most basic aspects of all life. The Christian teacher is one who is, in the proper sense, prophetic. His duty is to distinguish within Christianity itself those things which are essentially part of Revelation, and those things which are merely reflections of the culture of each place through which the Church passes on its earthly pilgrimage. That is a very difficult thing to do, and the greatest minds of Christianity have been engaged in it for two thousand years. But not to make the effort, or to see the need for it, is to fail as witnesses to the Lord who placed men and women to be in the world but not of it. The illumination of Christian learning was never more needed than at the present time.

Moses and Aaron

Christopher Lewis

*The most obvious connection between this sermon and Robert Runcie is
that it was preached in Cuddesdon, where he was Vicar and Principal
for ten years. The occasion was the tenth anniversary on 20 June 1985 of
the new college – Ripon College, Cuddesdon – born of a marriage between
Cuddesdon College and Ripon Hall. Yet mere geographical or historical
relatedness are less important than that of ideas. The attempt here is to
preach on that delicate (and Anglican) combination of pastor and theologian
which has characterised the theological colleges mentioned and also the
Archbishop's ministry. Neither Aaron's comforting idol nor Moses'
merciless law are appropriate symbols for his time as Archbishop, for he
has shown himself to have, in admirable alliance, the qualities of leader,
pastor and theologian. Those are qualities about which it is hard to
theorise; it is better to see them worked out in practice, with each giving
shape and depth to the others.*

Exodus 32:24 (and Acts 17:22–34)

I am not going to sum up the last ten years of this College, let alone
the lives of its parents, although it is worth saying that the child
has become a being of independent judgement, to the horror of
some and to the joy of most. The only piece of summary necessary
is to recognise and praise those who have helped the College to
have a mind and soul of its own.

I hope that I have not returned here from nostalgia. Nostalgia is
usually a sad thing, especially in its religious mode. Around theological colleges, it feeds on the belief that some privileged individuals
are allowed a kind of idyllic interlude, kindly paid for by others,
before plunging into the gritty real world of life in a parish. Yet it
would be just as accurate to see colleges as two or three years of
real life, facing the pressing issues of the world, before retreating
into the ivory tower of parish life. Actually, searches for the real
world are usually fruitless. Perhaps the real world is that ivory tower
in the sky, that great firmament where cherubim and seraphim
engage in endless in-service training.

Which brings me to my text. Moses and Joshua were a long time
up the mountain collecting all that weight of truth. You know what
theologians are! In the meantime, the people had pastoral needs

which they expressed to Aaron in a direct way. He met their felt needs, and so the golden calf followed and a feast as well.

Then Moses and Joshua came down with all the Commandments, right in the middle of the party. Moses was angry; he smashed tablets, calf and all. So he turned to Aaron who swiftly passed on the blame – shades of Adam and Eve. Aaron told of the collection of gold and the melting down and he ended with those marvellous, immortal words: 'I threw it in the fire; and out came this calf.' Or, as a modern translation has it: 'There was nothing I could do, mate; it fell off the back of a lorry.'

Where was the real world then? Moses was right and Aaron was wrong. Mind you, it is not quite as easy as that, for the next piece of Exodus is terrible. The vengeance of Moses was spectacular in its viciousness and about 3,000 died at the hands of the Levites. Where was the real world then?

The answer is that it is hard to tell. Indeed to talk of real worlds and ivory towers is a lazy way of avoiding issues of truth. And for truth you need faith and experience of the Gospel in action, and you need to be able to apply the mind.

The search for truth and the practice of it are alternatives to nostalgia, to idolatry and to the kind of pastoral practice of which the golden calf is an enduring symbol. Not that the search is easy; it requires all those difficult things like training and prayer and the guidance of the Holy Spirit.

In the part of Lincolnshire which I come from, there are tulips, daffodils and much of being nearer to God in your garden. It is easy to engage in gentle golden calf theology. After all, our hands are tied; what else can we do? For it is often what people want, both within the congregation and outside it; and we should always remember that 'people' includes ourselves. Pastoral practice panders to the needs.

In other parts of the world, the agenda is different. Each place has its golden calves. In one place it is war, in another it is peace. In one place it is the Bible, in another it is the mind. In Jerusalem, the golden calf is Jerusalem and in Cuddesdon it can be Cuddesdon.

The only protection against golden calves which fall off the backs of lorries is faith, and good pastoral practice mixed with good theology. It is as easy as that!

Dare I say it, however, such protection requires long, good training, through the grace of God. For then the poise necessary to stand up to all the golden calves may be gained. It may be clerical or it may be lay, but it must certainly be trained. Indigenous lay (or indeed clerical) theology is seldom enough. To say that is to voice a heresy in today's Church where the ordinary layman is told to hold the key. Yet indigenous lay theology, thoroughly contextualised, was what Aaron ministered with and to. In one place it is paperbacks on prayer, in another it is idolatry of a building, in another it may suddenly have the ring of truth. Yet untrained theology is much less reliable than trained theology; that needs, now and again, to be said.

For the apostles, the apprenticeship was long and still they found it hard to get the point. The track record of other followers of Jesus has also been patchy. That is an argument not for less training but for more: reflection and experience married together. Although, by the way, it is right to beware the golden calf of experience, destroyed in that splendid remark: 'He's not had thirty years of experience; he's had one year of experience thirty times.'

It can be the great skill and character of Anglicanism to be faithful to the Gospel, yet sensitive to people's needs, keeping the theologian and the pastor together, Moses and Aaron. For Moses that means greater understanding of what is going on in the camp, and then neither producing a golden calf nor throwing tablets around. The Gospel is not to be compromised, yet people are met where they are. It is the supreme challenge of ministry. Aaron got it wrong; Moses got it wrong.

It is the tension met by St Paul in Athens. He does not write off the beliefs of the Athenians. The altar of the unknown god is a point of contact. Nor does he leave things there, for it is after Jesus Christ that the Athenians are groping. He leads some on, losing others on the way. There is a meeting and good theology, for which Paul has had training both in the schools and in his experience. He is not only chosen for the task but also fitted for it.

Experiments on human embryos; the Bishop of Durham's understanding of the resurrection; the proportion of the church fête money which should go to Ethiopia, wedding sermons when you have four on a Saturday afternoon; whether to have a Masonic hymn at a funeral – or indeed how to spend the precious time which God gives to us. In trying to live with and meet all these questions, there is no substitute for good theology married to pastoral practice. Only then we may come to a true simplicity: not naïve, but experienced and reflective.

'Out came this calf' theology will not do, however much money must be saved and however much we feel the urgency of getting on with real jobs in a real world. There is no substitute for asking God to help us to seek the truth, clearly and calmly.

There are places, of which this theological college is one, which hold the delicate balance, neither flinging tablets around, nor being midwives to golden calves. It is a hard task, especially in today's Church where there are many pressures to take short cuts, whether from fear or from the mood of the age.

There remains a great ideal. Not to be seduced either into the pastoring of Aaron or into the theology of Moses. St Paul's example in Athens is a good one. The pastoral theologian; the theological pastor. Amen.

The Coronation Mass

Christopher Hill

As a member of Dr Robert Runcie's personal staff for almost ten years, I learnt much from his preaching and addresses, as well as doing staff spade work on some of them. He was acutely aware of the debased value of the coinage of religious language in a secular age. His answer to unbelief, or the more common half-belief, was never 'turn the volume up louder'. I do not think Schleiermacher was regular bedside preaching, but Robert Runcie instinctively wished to present religion to its 'cultural despisers' without shrill sectarianism or anti-intellectual fundamentalism. So he occasionally preached on historical and cultural themes rather than 'directly on the Gospel'. My St Paul's sermon of July 1990 on Mozart's Coronation Mass is similary oblique.

On the Sundays in July it is now traditional at St Paul's for the choir to be augmented by an orchestra, the City of London Sinfonia, for one of the great orchestral Masses to be performed liturgically. These great Eucharists are awe-inspiring occasions of worship. They are more than concerts. Many people on the fringes of faith come with musical motives as much as faith. And music can speak to us all in a way which words cannot.

I would also like to think that this sermon might appeal to Mrs Rosalind Runcie, the professional musician in the Runcie household, remembering that Robert Runcie also has the highest respect for 'professionals' in any field of life – not least his wife.

In a recently published book, Mozart is decribed as a 'Professional Music-maker beloved of God'. Today's Coronation Mass surely illustrates this. The argument of the book is that we must replace much of the romantic legend about Mozart's life with the less exciting story of a man who was quintessentially a professional musician.

Many of you will have seen the play or film about Mozart's life and death, *Amadeus*. Excellent as they were as play or film, they portrayed the legend not the history. In particular, Mozart was not poisoned by a jealous rival composer. Nor did he die a pauper, in declining popularity, with a mysterious visitor commissioning Mozart's own Requiem Mass. All myth. But with the Gothic clutter gone, we may be able to see Mozart, on the eve of his bicentennial, in a clearer light.

It is sometimes suggested that Mozart's Church music did not occupy a central position in his output. It would be truer to say that, as a professional, his output depended upon what he had been commissioned to compose. While Mozart was in Salzburg he was employed by the Archbishop as Court Organist and Director of Music. In the employment of the Church he composed most of his great Church music, including today's Coronation Mass.

Mozart's relation with his ecclesiastical patron does not seem to have been smooth. As a boy prodigy he had toured Europe playing with his sister and father in the households of royalty. In Salzburg, under the Church, he found himself dining at the servants' table. In the end the Archbishop sacked him.

The relationship between the Church and its musicians has always had its ups and downs. But the hapless Archbishop may also have inadvertently helped Mozart to create some of the greatest sacred music ever composed. Church music is less personal than other composition. It is inserted into a liturgical order and is more resistant to subjective treatment. In Salzburg, Mozart found himself more strictly regimented than was congenial. In 1776 he wrote to an Italian musician:

> Our Church music is different from that of Italy, since a mass . . . must not last longer than ¾ of an hour – even on the most solemn occasions when the Lord Archbishop reads the mass. And that goes for a mass with full orchestra, including trumpet and drums. This style of writing demands special study.

When the Archbishop asked for shorter masses he was probably reacting against Italian Church music of the day which had really become a continuation of the pleasures of the opera house.

Mozart was instructed to produce something more dignified and fitting for the services of the Church. And if this seemed to constrain Mozart, we must remember that the Archbishop's demands have made Mozart's Salzburg Masses liturgically usable to this day. This cannot be said for much Italian Church music of the same period. Having to write strictly in the confines of the liturgy gave Mozart's sacred music a formal conciseness which is now recognised as part of its greatness. 'This style of writing demands special study,' wrote Mozart, and he gave it special study because he was a professional who, in the end, did what was asked of him. For the musicians present, it may give you some comfort that Mozart must have received some posthumous comfort in his disputes with the Archbishop of Salzburg: for that prelate died in 1812 in Vienna (where Mozart had become famous), driven out of his Archbishopric by secularisation.

Now, you may wonder whether this sermon has slipped rather badly into a mere programme note. But I have talked about Mozart the professional and his difficulty with the Church as his patron because the performing of the Coronation Mass seems the right occasion to say something about the Church and its musicians.

To this day in the Eastern Orthodox Church, vocal ability is one of the qualifications of priesthood. In the West since the late Middle Ages the clerical and musical professions have been divided. But the ancient custom of our choir boys and gentlemen vicars choral robing in cassock and surplice shows we have the same origins. The cathedral tradition of English Church music has always been strong in patronage of professional musicians. I hope this is a tradition which can be renewed and strengthened. It was good that last Sunday here at St Paul's a new psalm by John Tavener was performed for the first time, commissioned by the City of London Festival.

But the idea of professional music in the service of the Church has its critics. In the seventeenth century the Puritans abolished it – as they abolished both the Church of England and the monarchy. And there have been critics since.

Let me remind you of Barchester a century and a half ago. Dr Proudie has just become Bishop, together with Mrs Proudie. On his first Sunday in his Cathedral Church the Bishop has invited his Chaplain, the oleaginous Mr Slope, to preach.

> The Dean was there, and so was the Archdeacon. So also were the Chancellor, the Treasurer, the Precentor, sundry Canons, and Minor Canons, and every lay member of the choir, prepared to sing the new Bishop in with due melody and harmonious expression of sacred welcome . . . The service was certainly very well performed. Such was always the case at Barchester, as the musical education of the choir had been good and the voices had been carefully selected. The psalms were beautifully chanted: the Te Deum was magnificently sung and the litany was given in the manner peculiar to Barchester. And at last Mr Slope got into the Pulpit – only to denounce the undue preponderance which, he asserted, music had over meaning in the beautiful service which they had just heard. The words of our moving service, how beautiful, how apposite, how intelligible they were, when read with simple and distinct decorum! But how much the meaning of the service was lost when they were produced with all the meretricious charms of melody!

You can read more of Slope's denunciation of Cathedral music in the Chapter of *Barchester Towers* entitled: 'War'.

Though a fictional denunciation, there are still those in the Church who constrict meaning to words, and worship to utility. But life is more than verbiage, and worship is more than usefulness. This is why men and women in every age and of every religion have enlisted music in the praise of their Creator. And this is why cathedrals and churches and monasteries, such as St Paul's, offer up to God the daily sacrifice of praise in music as well as words with all the professional excellence we can muster. And this is why we offer for God's consecration the Coronation Mass here in St

Paul's this morning with full choir and the orchestra of the City of London Sinfonia.

I will end with a twentieth-century reference from a person who does not claim to be a Christian but who was once deeply moved by the offering of professional cathedral music – something Barchester, Mozart and St Paul's well understand – even if Mr Slope did not. The travel and historical writer Jan Morris once visited an English cathedral on a dark winter's afternoon. In her book, *Journeys*, she has a chapter entitled: 'A Visit to Barchester':

> Like nearly everybody else in sight, I loitered about the interior of the cathedral while evensong proceeded beyond the narrow entrance of the choir, allowing me, from the dimmer recesses of the nave, suggestive glimpses of surplices, shaded lamps, anthem sheets and musical motions within. It was magical. The rest of the great building lay in hush, and encapsulated there in their bright-lit chamber, as though in heavenly orbit, the musicians and a handful of devoted worshippers performed their evening ritual.
>
> The anthem was S.S. Wesley's 'Thou Wilt Keep Him', among the most lyrical in the repertoire, and it was touching to see how many of the tourists leant in silence against pillars, or paused thoughtfully in their decipherment of epitaphs, as the sweet melody sounded through the half-light.
>
> The music of the Cathedral . . . is intensely professional. I much enjoyed this feeling of disinterested technique, so remote from commercial competition or union claim. I saw something truly noble in the spectacle of that daily choral celebration performed to the last degree of excellence attended by almost nobody but the celebrants themselves . . .

Here at St Paul's this morning, as we experience the glory of Mozart's Coronation Mass, we can share something of that magic. The Cathedral is packed. It is a glorious sunny Sunday morning – quite different from a winter's afternoon in Barchester – it was Wells, actually. But the offering of excellence to God is the same: in Salzburg, Wells or St Paul's, in Mozart's day, in our own, and, I hope and pray, as long as churches and cathedrals remain.

Listening to One Another

Metropolitan Anthony of Sourozh

Dr Robert Runcie said that he wished to be remembered as 'Robert the Reconciler', the man who would keep together the different trends of the Anglican Communion, foster the dialogue between the various Churches of Christendom, involve the Church in the secular and political spheres, attempt to reconcile conflicting views in the realm of faith and theology – which to an Orthodox cannot be harmonised. He has been active and sincere in his endeavour and will be remembered above all for his openness. He has been sowing seeds and whether they will grow or not, time alone will show. Whether the way he chose to foster rapprochement was right is a matter of personal appreciation; but as it is Unity that has been his main concern, it is a sermon on Unity that I offer him on his leaving the See of Canterbury. My views differ from his greatly, but they are held as sincerely as his and in this we are at one.

> The Body of Christ is broken and distributed, which being ever broken, never is divided . . . but halloweth them that partake thereof (a prayer from the Orthodox Liturgy).

Since the Orthodox Church has joined the Ecumenical Movement, many of her members are offended by the term, currently used, of 'the Undivided Church'. Does such an expression postulate that the Church is, or can be, divided? Can the Body be severed from the Head? 'Is Christ divided?' Do we not proclaim in the Creed that the Church is one? Do not St John's words, 'They who went out from us were not with us', exclude radically from the saving mystery of the Church – one as God is One – those who have fallen into schism or heresy? Can one be in Christ yet outside the Church?

Such statements awake in me both a measure of sympathy and a deep feeling of worry: a measure of sympathy shared with the great majority of Orthodox on reading the eirenic declarations of the various ecumenical committees – fanciful statements concerning the degree of unity in the faith that allegedly exists between the heterodox and us; disturbing propositions which make too many Christians delight in the delusion that unity is close at hand while it is still out of reach, as it can be won by nothing less than an uncompromising, heroic, sacrificial acceptance of God's own truth, a true conversion of us all to the integrity of the Gospel. I have a sense of worry also because the perplexity of the 'integrists' is, to a great extent, founded on a narrow vision of the ways of God and of the human response. The Lord who has said, 'I have not brought peace but a sword', has also said, 'I have not come to judge the world but to save the world', and at the moment of his Passion, prayed his supreme prayer, 'Forgive them, Father, they know not what they are doing'.

The Early Councils defined with total clarity and definitiveness our faith in God, in our Lord Jesus Christ, in the Mother of God. But, while proclaiming the essential nature of the Church, they have assigned no boundaries to her. This body, simultaneously and equally human and divine, the place, the mode and the mystery of the union between God and His Creation, is the eschatological body *par excellence*, in which all things are already fulfilled while they are still becoming. God is already in our midst; He has already united all things to Himself through His Incarnation, yet each person must enter freely into the mystery of the world already in the process of becoming the Kingdom, in which, as Metropolitan Philaret of Moscow wrote in the nineteenth century, 'our human divisions do not reach the heavens'. God is at work in the whole creation as leaven, as eternity poured into time, until God be 'all in all', until we have become partakers of the Divine Nature, until, in the daring words of St Ireneus of Lyon, 'we have all become in the Only-Begotten Son, the Only-Begotten Son of God'.

No Orthodox doubts that it is the Orthodox Church which is *The Church* one and undivided. But what does it say about the heterodox? Can they possibly confess Jesus Christ as their Lord otherwise than through a revelation of the Holy Spirit? Is it possible to be guided by him, give one's life to Christ, die for him and yet remain a stranger in his Kingdom? Can a personal error of judgement, an individual lack of experience, or the chances of history determining the place of our birth in a non-Orthodox surrounding alienate us from Christ? The Lord himself forbade his disciples to reject a man who was not of their company, yet preached him as the Saviour and worked miracles in his name. One cannot be even a heretic without relating in some way to Christ and the Church. We do not call a Buddhist or a Muslim a heretic. To be one, one must be a Christian! Did not a spiritual writer of the past say that at the moment he reads the Gospel to his congregation even the most objectionable heretic is no heretic, as he allows God Himself to speak the truth to His people?

Metropolitan Anthony (Khrapovtisky), one who would have gloried in the appellation of 'integrist', wrote in the 1920s, before the birth of the ecumenical movement, an article in which he analysed the change in attitude of the Church to its opponents throughout the centuries. The first heresies were condemned without mercy and those who held them excommunicated. But as time went on the judgement of the Church on the successive heresies became less radical – the teachings were condemned, their adherents were debarred from the sacraments, but a measure of mutual recognition grew from generation to generation. A simple, cynical explanation would aver that, as the Orthodox were becoming less sensitive both to truth and error, they became more lenient to schism and heresy. To accept such a reason would be tantamount to saying that the spirit of truth had departed from the Church. The Metropolitan accounts for this change of attitude in a different way: namely, that as time passed, every new heresy preserved within it a greater amount of the original faith, distorting the truth in lesser and lesser ways, and remaining, therefore, nearer to its roots. Concentrating her attention primarily on what remained of the genuine faith, the Church recognises in those who had fallen away from her, the lost sheep who were to be found and redeemed. It is obvious that to deny the divinity of Christ, his humanity, i.e. the Incarnation, his birth from the Virgin, the union of his two natures in the unity of One Person, are graver departures from the truth than later errors like the primacy and infallibility of the Pope, the *Filioque* clause, the branch-theory, predestination, salvation through faith alone and other ancient or modern false doctrines.

But the Orthodox themselves must realise and remember always that they carry the Holy Things in earthen vessels and that, now, as in St Paul's days, it is because of us that the message we bring is reviled; that we may well proclaim the truth but unless we live by it, we are ourselves 'heretics in life', to use a phrase of Dr Visser t'Hooft. We are 'in patria' only to the extent to which we are in Christ at a given moment, 'in via' all the time, and St Ephraim of Syria could say that 'the Church is not an assembly of saints but a crowd of repentant sinners' – repentant meaning 'turned God-wards'.

How, then, can the Orthodox believe that it is our Church which is at the heart of Christendom? Because she sees herself as the keeper of the 'faith once delivered to the saints' – unadulterated by false doctrines, free from man-made interpretations, destined to adjust it to the tastes or the intellectual searchings of the moment, uncompromisingly stable in the essentials, yet neither static nor fossilised, but sensitive to the 'becoming' of the world, its new problems, and the necessity of confronting them, not only together with the rest of Christendom but also with the whole of mankind. The Feast of the Triumph of Orthodoxy does not speak to us of the triumph of the Orthodox over other Christians, but of God's victory over us, of the Divine Light piercing through our human darkness. We want to give back to the rest of Christendom their own inheritance, recognisable to them in spite of the confusion, distortion and impoverishment brought about by the centuries of dividedness; we are their past, their own past, although they are not our present or our future. But we also want to receive from them what the spirit of God has taught them during our long estrangement. May the whole of Christendom enter again into possession of this treasure and bring forth with new vitality the fruit that we have proved unable to bear! Let us therefore listen to one another with the determination to understand one another, hearing beyond the words that divide, the beating of sincere hearts, aglow with faith and hope and an awakening sense of love, so that we may, with one mind and one heart, acknowledge Him who is all truth, the only way to the fullness of life and unity to which we are called! Amen.

Begotten from Above

Alec Graham

This sermon was preached on Tuesday 27 March 1990 at the institution of the Rev. Richard Hill as Vicar of All Saints' Gosforth, Newcastle-upon-Tyne, the parish in which the Archbishop served as a curate from 1950 to 1952, and in which he is still remembered with affection. Reference is made in the sermon to two of the parish's clergy: Andrew Shipton, who is at present Curate there; and Reg West, who was serving as Curate in another parish in the city of Newcastle at the same time as the Archbishop was working here. The subject of the sermon touches on the renewal of parochial life, a theme which throughout his ministry has been very close to the Archbishop's heart.

Our service this evening marks a notable occasion in the life of this diocese and deanery, in the life of this parish and in the life of the new parish priest and of his family. In their life because today a new chapter begins in the new Vicar's ministry, a new home, too, to which his family will move before long. Inevitably the life of the parish will be affected – there's an understatement – for though it has prospered marvellously without a Vicar for almost a year, capably served by Andrew Shipton, helped by Reg West, a new Vicar here is bound to make a difference, and he will make a difference, too, to the life of this diocese and deanery, for over the years clergy and people of All Saints' have made important contributions to the life of the wider Church – and there's another understatement!

That has been so in the past. No doubt it will be so in the future. This evening we look to the future, and to help us with our thoughts and prayers we turn to this evening's second lesson: Jesus and Nicodemus. At first sight perhaps a surprising lesson, surprising at this season, surprising on this occasion. Surprising at this season, for this lesson is often associated with Christmas and with Whitsun: with Christmas, for 'Ye must be born again' is very close to 'Except ye . . . become as little children', itself a Christmas theme; with Whitsun, because of the theme of our being born from the Spirit; and the wind, which blows where it will, reminds us of the rushing mighty wind of the first Whit Sunday. Yet our lesson belongs as much to Passiontide and Easter, very appropriate for this stage in the Church's year. Its climax was in the lifting up of the Son of man, his lifting up on the Cross and his lifting up to heaven: in both his lifting up to glory. As Moses lifted up the serpent in the wilderness, so too was the Son of man to be lifted up.

Nor does this lesson turn out to be surprising on this occasion. This passage, it is true, is often used by those who have had some powerful experience of conversion or of spiritual renewal in their lives. No doubt it can be used by both groups. 'Ye must be born again': in common speech, we refer to those who have had some dramatic conversion as 'twice born' or as 'born again Christians'. And the theme of renewal throughout this passage can fit in with movements and moments of vivid spiritual awareness.

But there is no need for this passage to be monopolised in the interest of those two groups, for it speaks about the Christian faith and life of us all. Jesus was speaking to Nicodemus, a Pharisee, and to the Jewish people. 'Ye must be born again.' Better, 'You must all be begotten from above and thus be born again, born anew.' Jesus said that to the Pharisee. For Christian people, the remarkable truth is that we have been; we have been both begotten again and born again, of water and the Spirit, by faith and baptism. Do not let us try to go into their precise relationship this evening. It is enough to say that nearly everyone here has, I reckon, been made in baptism, as the catechism puts it, 'the child of God, a member of Christ, an inheritor of the kingdom of heaven'. Enough to say that nearly everyone here has, to some extent, made that his own by faith. Already, by faith and baptism, we have been begotten from above and born again; and if we have been born again, we are not to remain as babes, as infants. We are to grow up in the Christian life, grow in understanding, faith, devotion, grow into our responsibilities. We grow up in these respects as we fasten on to the truth that we have our origin as Christian people for eternity from above. In this Gospel, disciples are those who are of the Spirit, of God, of the truth, from above. Our point of origin is from above. We derive from above. 'Seeing the kingdom of God' is not some sort of natural development here below, some sort of process which just happens, nor one for which we can work. It is purely the gift of God. It goes with our drinking of that well of water which springs up unto eternal life; and that life is His Spirit. It runs clean contrary to ordinary, natural human processes by which, as we grow older, we decline, degenerate, decay and die. Rather, those who have been begotten again from above, of the Spirit, are renewed for eternal life. This is not far from St Paul's assertion that, 'though our outward man perish, yet the inward man is renewed day by day'.

The Gospels contain many such reversals of expectation. Not only as we grow older are we renewed, but also, 'Many that are first shall be last and the last first', 'Whosoever shall exalt himself shall be abased, and he that shall humble himself shall be exalted' (just like the Magnificat), or, from St Paul, 'When I am weak, then I am strong'. All these reversals of expectation draw their meaning from the greatest reversal of all, the death and Resurrection of Christ. A religion which has the Cross as its distinctive mark or badge must contain some pretty startling reversals of general expectation, even among the religious.

And what reversals of expectation in our day may it be that the Church in general, this parish in particular, may have to take on board, live with and make its own? Well, here are a few suggestions, and I reckon that, if pursued, they will result in the life of our Church being not so much turned upside down, as in those quotations from the Gospels just now, but rather, in the life of our parishes being turned inside out, inside out – no less. Let us think of some respects in which this may be so.

Over generations, we have been taught, and rightly taught, to concentrate on finding God in our midst, in our worship and in our fellowship. We need perhaps to redress the balance and not to forget to look for Him outside as well. Over generations, we have been taught, and rightly taught, to find the truth in our Scriptures and in our Church's understanding of them. We need as well, now, to look for God in the world outside the Church. The Scriptures and the Church's teaching from the past become creative and fruitful as they are brought into interplay with the problems of people and of the world in the present. Over generations we have been taught, and rightly taught, that people will find the truth in Church, and that Church people will tell, tell the outside world the saving message. Equally, we need to listen, to listen to what is being said and to what is not being said, in the outside world, that is if we are to communicate with it at all fruitfully. Over generations we have been taught, and rightly taught, that we exist to serve the outside world, taking initiatives there being taken by no other agency, say in education or in care for delinquents or for the sick. Equally, we need to discover what is already going on in the outside world, seek to co-operate with it, lending whatever help we can to whatever is good and wholesome there. Those are but some of the ways in which the lives of our parishes may perhaps need to be turned inside out.

What now about our clergy, about our attitude to them, and theirs to us? Well, there are many among both the clergy and the laity who expect the parish priest to do all the ministering and to do it to the people, particularly to the congregation. He to visit them, he to provide for them, he to teach them, he to inspire them, he to meet their needs, he to be endlessly adaptable in cosseting and pastoring them – in a sense, he to provide a chaplaincy service for them, even to be their personal friend. He to minister, he to do it, he to be the giver; they to be ministered unto, they to be on the receiving end of his personal service, a uniquely favoured group. They, the congregation, to be ministered unto, he to minister, and as for those in the outside world, they hardly get a look in. After all, it is all provided for them here, isn't it, if they want it? That is often an unspoken assumption.

If you think I exaggerate, I can assure you that I do not. Too often I hear from the lips both of clergy and of lay people remarks which make it clear that they use the term 'parishioners' to refer only to members of the congregation. And if there is one thing made clear by this service this evening, then I hope it is the truth that we have just instituted a new Vicar, a new Vicar for the entire parish here, and not merely a chaplain to Church families. All this really is a question of our being turned inside out: many parishes and many clergy in their expectations; the congregation not so much to be ministered unto, as to minister; clergy and people, as they minister, to stop, look and listen, as it used to say at level crossings; stop, look, listen and learn at the intersection of Church and world, and in any case to look outward in interest, in affection and in embrace. Not so much to be Church-centred as to be Christ-centred. Having found him particularly in Church to discern him in the world, to make him explicit there, to articulate there his demands and his promise, and to promote his cause there.

As Nicodemus asked, 'How can these things be?'; how can this reversal of expectations take effect? How can our Church, our Church of England in this diocese, be turned inside out? 'How can a man be born when he is old? Can he enter the second time into his mother's womb, and be born?' No, of course not. Nicodemus only half understood. We return where we began. The necessity is to return to the truth that we have been begotten from above, deepest truth of all in the Christian life of each of us; we have been already. Passiontide, Holy Week, Easter, all are soon upon us; all provide us with God-given opportunities to grasp hold more deeply and sincerely of this simple basic truth and to reflect on its implications. 'As Moses lifted up the serpent in the wilderness, even so must the Son of man be lifted up.' This Son of man descended from heaven; He was to ascend to heaven, his ascent by way of the Cross. For those who have been begotten again from above, the secret of our origin, of our destiny and of our present life in Christ is all there. 'He that hath ears to hear, let him hear.'

A Deacon in the Church of God

Donald Coggan

*One of the most awesome tasks to which any bishop or archbishop is called
is that of the ordination of deacons and priests in the Church of God.
For 20 years, at St Albans and at Canterbury, Robert Runcie has done
this work with his usual dedication and dignity. Many of his 'sons and
daughters' will look back with gratitude to their ordination at his hands
and to the retreats which preceded them.*

*This sermon was preached in Dorchester Abbey on 1 October 1989, at
the Ordination of Deacons in the Diocese of Oxford.*

Let me tell you of an addition which I would like to see made to
our services of Ordination, to be used not on every occasion, but
from time to time. When the main service is over, I would like to
have the bishop withdraw, divest himself of his robes, return with
a towel tied round him, pour water into a basin, and wash the feet
of the men and women whom he has ordained, and wipe them with
the towel.

That silent act would be a most eloquent sermon. It would say to
all who observed it: 'The Son of man came not to be ministered to
but to minister . . . I am among you as one who serves . . . Once a
deacon, always a deacon, whatever may be the rank to which you
attain in the ministry of the Church.'

To that office in the Church of God you will be ordained today.
For that office you will be empowered – you will hear the Bishop
pray: 'Send down the Holy Spirit upon your servant . . . for the
office and work of a deacon in your Church.'

You are joining a goodly company – Anselm and Chad, Patrick
and Cuthbert, Augustine and Alban, Lancelot Andrewes and
Charles Simeon, martyrs like James Hannington and Janani Luwum,
scholars like William Temple, parish priests like George Herbert
working away in obscurity – deacons all, like you.

Does not that make you feel very small? That is as it should be.
The Epistle reminds us: 'I bid everyone among you not to think of
himself more highly than he ought to think . . . ' Because your collar
is inverted, it should not follow that your ego is inflated. Covet the
title which St Paul loved so much: 'a slave of Jesus Christ'.

Now let me tell you something which will give you confidence.
Let me tell it to you in story fashion:

You are in Rome, not Dorchester. The year is 65 or thereabouts, not 1989. On the throne is Nero, not Elizabeth II. The Eucharist is being celebrated in a humble living-room, not in a lovely Abbey. The Gospel is read from a book just out, the Gospel of Jesus Christ according to Mark who, who if Papias's Elder is right, 'wrote down accurately all that Peter remembered of the things said or done by Christ'. You are half listening, and half wondering whether *you* may be the next to be called out to martyrdom when the crowds scream: 'The Christians to the lions!' But listen! What is Mark saying? In 'the wilderness . . . he remained for forty days tempted by Satan. He was among the wild beasts; and angels attended to his needs.' It was a battle royal. *He* had beasts to wrestle with. Yes, but he had angels too. They *deaconed* him – so the Greek. They *ministered* to him – so the Latin.

Wouldn't you like to have been one of those angels, deaconing Jesus? Helping him through the agony in the wilderness? You can be just that, for inasmuch as you do it to the least of his brethren, you do it to him. That applies to us all, but especially to those who have been made deacons at this service today.

Yours is angelic work. Go to it humbly. Go to it proudly, remembering whose you are and whom you serve; remembering who it is who empowers you, and who it is to whom one day you will report.

Remember, too, and above all else, that the greatest service you can render the people to whom you minister, is the service of pointing them to your Lord. Make little of yourself. Make much of him.

Be content, like John the Baptist, to be a pointer: 'Look, there is God's Lamb who takes away the sin of the world.' He must increase; you must decrease.

In that process, you will enter into the glory of your diaconate to which you are committed until the day of your death and of your glory.

One Body, One Spirit

Mark Santer

As Archbishop of Canterbury, Robert Runcie has put the search for reconciliation and unity between divided Christians at the centre of his concerns. To it he has brought his incomparable gifts of friendship and personal understanding.

No Archbishop of Canterbury can forget that his See was founded by St Augustine, a monk sent to pagan England as a missionary from Rome. So the visit of Pope John Paul II to Canterbury at Pentecost 1982, and the Archbishop's to Rome at Michaelmas 1989 were of particular symbolic importance.

The following sermon, preached before the University of Birmingham in October 1989, arose out of this visit to Rome.

A fortnight ago I was in Rome, standing in the sun at the Papal Mass in front of St Peter's. For the Pope it was in most ways an ordinary Sunday morning, Mass for the 26th Ordinary Sunday of the year, with 29 beatifications. But in one way it was a quite extraordinary Sunday. The Archbishop of Canterbury was there as chief and honoured guest – the successor both of Thomas Cranmer and of Reginald Pole; and both names matter, if one is to grasp the symbolic force of the occasion.

The Pope and the Archbishop did not share eucharistic communion. Yet their meeting was an expression and demonstration of 'that certain yet imperfect communion' which Roman Catholics and Anglicans already share, and of which Pope and Archbishop spoke in their Common Declaration. During that Mass, as the Sacrament of the Lord's Body and Blood lay on the altar, they exchanged the sign of Christ's peace before that very altar. During the weekend of which that Mass was a part, they prayed together, privately and publicly, in silence and aloud. Together they made pilgrimage to the Church of St Gregory, to the very place from which that great Bishop of Rome sent St Augustine to baptise the English. During the liturgy of Vespers there, prayer was offered for both Pope and Archbishop. They ate together, an act which, as the Pope himself said to us, represents 'a very high degree of communion'. For when Christians eat together, that is itself a true foretaste of Christ's heavenly banquet.

All these things done together were living evidence of a trust and an acceptance and a commitment to one another in the Lord, which these two pastors were expressing on behalf of their people. They were acting as spokesmen, leaders and examples to their fellow-pastors and to their flocks.

Such an experience is hard to communicate. But it must be shared and communicated, if what happened in Rome that weekend is to bear its fruit in our two communities, and not in ours only, throughout the world. For without love, and trust, and perseverance, and without a will and desire for reconciliation, shared between pastors and pastors, and people and people, all the talks and dialogues of theologians and churchmen will be no more than sand in the mouth. Unless those for whom our leaders and representatives speak share their longing for unity, their work will produce only paper, and not deeds.

In our churches, there are people who do share this longing for reconciliation. Two days after I returned from Rome I was in a small 'Inner City' church of the evangelical tradition. No Cross, no candles. Not a place, you might think, where a meeting of Pope and Archbishop would make much of a sympathetic echo. But one of the churchwardens was married to a Catholic. She knew what it was about. And so did many others: Asian, Afro-Caribbean and white Christians. They were glad and proud that I, as their Bishop, had been there. They felt encouraged; and I felt encouraged by them.

But by no means everyone sees it that way. I know from the press, from the radio, and from my postbag, that there are very many people who distrust the Archbishop for going to Rome, and do not feel that he was speaking or acting for them. There are many who mistrust the Pope and the whole apparatus of the Roman Catholic Church. There are many who mistrust, and simply do not believe in, the quest for sacramental, ecclesial unity between our separated communities.

It is of course tempting simply to dismiss the dafter or more hysterical objections. What has it got to do with a Baptist minister from Margate who phoned in to tell me that the Archbishop was betraying his oath to uphold the Protestant religion? What has it got to do with the British constitution, or the evils of the Common Market? What does one say to a lady who says that she believes in spiritual unity, and that no Pope, Archbishop or any other clergyman is going to put himself between her and her God?

Cries of this kind come out of a deep well of fear and anxiety. Fear above all of a threat to identity. People don't want to be swallowed up in what they perceive as a wholly alien culture, machinating and totalitarian. It is a potent mix, with its respectable as well as its less respectable elements: the atavistic fear of Popery, the drum-beating of Protestantism (both openly conservative and ostensibly liberal), anxiety about freedom, and sheer dislike of change. The strength of these fears is not to be underestimated.

Faced with all of that, we naturally ask ourselves: is it all worth it? Why fiddle with the Church while the world is burning? The quest for communion within a visible, sacramental order – is it a hopeless will-o'-the-wisp? Or is it in fact the essence of the Christian faith, and therefore something we cannot abandon?

There are those who remind us that Christians have always been divided. Look at the New Testament, they say, look at the Church of the Fathers. Christianity never was any more than a loose federation at best.

But look again at the evidence. We see two things. First, the apostles and the Fathers never accepted disunity as normal. 'Strive,' says St Paul, 'to maintain the unity of the Spirit in the bond of peace. There is one body and one Spirit . . . ; one Lord, one faith, one baptism . . . ' (Eph. 4:4f). The embodiment of the reconciliation wrought by the Lord through the Cross – that is the heart of the Church's vocation.

Second, we see that the forms and structures which have held Christians together, when they *have* stayed together, have varied from age to age. There are some constant and necessary elements – we shall come back to that later – but there is no one model of Christian unity. Modern Papal government is almost as novel as the Anglican Communion.

The forms may change, but the substance is indispensable. The unity of Christians is a matter of faith, as integral to the Creed as our confession of faith in Father, Son and Holy Spirit. 'We believe in one, holy, catholic and apostolic Church.' Our striving for unity is a prayer that we may be true to our confession and our calling. We pray that God's will may be done on earth as it is in heaven; that as Father, Son and Holy Spirit are one in heaven, so we on earth may be one. Because we are corporeal beings, our unity must be corporeal, visible, sacramental. We can't love each other without using our bodies.

In the Apostles' Creed we say that we believe in the Communion of Saints. That helps us to get nearer to the heart of the matter. The Latin phrase *Communio Sanctorum* is notoriously ambiguous. Is it a communion of holy things, or is it a communion of holy people? It is both. There is a sharing of holy things, of those holy realities which we confess together and of which St Paul speaks: 'one body and one Spirit; one hope . . . ; one Lord, one faith, one baptism; one God and Father of all'. The sharing of the same holy things makes us a holy community.

Just like a marriage or any other living bond between people, this is a relationship, a communion, which does not look after itself. It has to be maintained and nourished and renewed. There will have to be rules and conventions; maintaining communion will have a canonical or juridical aspect. But the heart of it lies in the humility, the gentleness, the patience, of which St Paul speaks; in forbearance, and love, and forgiveness; in the sharing of one Spirit. These things are the soul of communion. But they have to be visibly embodied; they have to be visibly and sacramentally expressed.

If Christians on earth are to be recognisably one, recognisably to each other and recognisably to the rest of the world, there are certain things they will publicly share, certain visible marks of unity.

They will confess a common faith; and the more deeply they trust one another, the more ready they will be to live with diversity in the expression of that faith. They will pray together, and the sacraments celebrated in one community will be acknowledged as the sacraments of the whole Christian community. Each person baptised as a member of Christ will be acknowledged as a member of the whole Christ. Everyone called by ordination to be a minister of Christ will be acknowledged as a minister of the whole Christ. They will share their material resources.

Also – and this is the hard bit, but it is inescapable if the Church is to remain in communion with itself – there must be persons acknowledged by all as charged by the Lord, and not merely by the community, with authority to speak for all and to all. For if the Church is called to be a fellowship on earth, not only local but also universal, there must be means, instantiated in persons, for maintaining the fellowship and holding it to its identity in good times and bad. This ministry of unity is no imposition; it is a gift from the Spirit of unity.

The Archbishop was pointing to the need for this ministry when in Rome he renewed the plea he made at the Lambeth Conference: 'Could not all Christians come to reconsider the kind of Primacy the Bishop of Rome exercised within the early Church, a "presiding in love" for the sake of the unity of the Churches in the diversity of their mission?' It is of course evidently the case that such a position of leadership is open to abuse. But it is equally evident that those Christian bodies which have no effective personal focus of unity seem doomed either to fissiparousness or to fossilisation.

For Christians on earth there can be no such thing as a merely invisible or merely spiritual unity. That would be to deny our corporeality. For us the Spirit always comes in flesh.

But precisely because the Church on earth must be visible, it is also of necessity imperfect. Imperfect in its members, imperfect in its ministers. This has an important consequence, too easily forgotten. If we insist that we shall assent to reconciliation with some other body of Christians only when they or their structures are perfect, we shall never be reconciled. If perfection is required, we too shall be an obstacle; for we ourselves and our own structures are as problematical as anyone else's.

There must come the point when we trust one another to

surrender, not our faith, but ourselves to each other in the Lord. Of course we shall be changed, and so will they, just as a husband and wife are both changed by sharing their life together. One does not swallow up the other. They remain themselves, but indelibly marked by the fact that they belong together.

To reach this point of trust, the meetings, the meals, and the prayer together are indispensable. That is our experience in ARCIC. The fact that we meet, we eat and we pray together, profoundly affects the work that we do together. This is something we need to repeat and replicate everywhere with our Christian brothers and sisters if we are indeed to share a common life.

Let me give you an example. A friend of mine, who is a priest in the country, meets every Monday morning for prayers and breakfast with his ministerial neighbours – Methodist, United Reformed, and Roman Catholic, and the Vicar of the next parish. When preparing some adults for Confirmation, he found them asking questions about Roman Catholicism. So instead of giving them an Anglican view of Roman Catholicism, he asked his Catholic neighbour to come and tell them himself. Because of their meeting, eating and praying together, they trusted each other's integrity. That way lies progress.

'I implore you then,' says the apostle, 'I, a prisoner for the Lord's sake: as God has called you, live up to your calling. Be humble always and gentle, and patient too, putting up with each other's failings in the spirit of love . . . There is one body and one Spirit, just as there is one hope held out in God's call to you; one Lord, one faith, one baptism; one God and Father of all, who is over all and through all and in all' (Eph. 4:1–6).

To whom, through the Son, and with the Holy Spirit, be all glory, praise and honour, in earth as in heaven, now and for ever. Amen.

Part III
ONE WORLD

A Voice and Inspiration in the Land

Mary Whitehouse

I am delighted and honoured by this opportunity to pay tribute to Dr Robert Runcie on the occasion of his retirement. As his willingness to accept our invitation to present our Award to 'Songs of Praise' indicated, Dr Runcie has been willing to be counted publicly among those who have shown sympathy with our work.

This address was given to the congregation of St Anselm's Church, Harrow Weald, on 18 May 1986.

My belief as a Christian is that certain aspects of contemporary life despoil not only God's purpose for man but violate also the highest human aspirations. There are also, it seems to me, certain aspects of this violation with which the Church, by and large, does not wish to become entangled.

The truth is that there are elements of destruction in today's society which belie its claim to be civilised, and which result in self-afflicted wounds of the most grievous kind. They create a legacy of suffering, both personal and collective, which should have no place in a compassionate, let alone a Christian country – and the Church is strangely silent.

Yet we have witnessed, in the last three decades a massive attack upon the quality of personal and collective character, upon those values, rooted in the Christian faith, which are the hallmark of a truly caring society.

In one's thinking about such matters one is always conscious of what is happening to the young. It seems to me that perhaps never before in our history have they been better cared for in material terms, but it is also surely true that never before have they been so much at risk from emotional exploiters on the one hand and libertarian freethinkers on the other.

Jesus said, 'Suffer the little children to come unto me' – not into the prostitute's car, as witness the recent case of the eight-year-old girl in the Midlands who was offered a lift and taken to a brothel.

Jesus also said, 'Better a millstone be hung round your neck and you be cast into the sea, than that you cause one of these my little ones to stumble' – to stumble – let alone to suffer indescribably, as so many do in the society we have all created.

All very dramatic, no doubt, but I find it impossible to speak otherwise. Our hearts should burn within us. We should indeed, in the midst of the common anger we so rightly feel, ask ourselves why and how we have come to where we find ourselves – and where are we? Is there really a problem or is it all media-hype?

Well let's look, for example, at the Metropolitan Police figures for rape over the last, say, fifty years. We find that in the twenty years between 1938 and 1958 they increased only from ten cases to twenty-seven. Now I am not going to blame what has happened in the years since wholly on the passing of the present Obscene Publications Act in 1959, or even on television. But the fact remains that since the arrival of that Act on the Statute Book those figures have dramatically risen year by year until they reached 365 in 1984, and Home Office figures for 1985 show a 40 per cent increase on that figure for reported rape in the Metropolitan area for that one year alone – and every case carries with it the suffering of individuals.

But will you allow me also to say that there really is no place for any 'holier-than-thou' attitude in any of us in all this. Jesus said, 'Judge not that ye be not judged' – and indeed we should all be judged and carry the burden not only, for instance, for what has happened to those rape victims but for the criminal too. He, also, could well be the victim of the sex-obsessed, indulgent, 'I have a right to see, to hear, to do what I want because I want to' philosophy, to which so many of us, and indeed the Church itself, have subscribed, or which we have been unwilling to challenge effectively.

How many of us remember a Thames TV Eye programme last summer which looked into the appalling scandal of child sex abuse in one area of Leeds? It was stated that an estimated one in ten children are involved and that what is happening there is almost certainly happening elsewhere. It was reported that a child as young as twelve months old had been sexually assaulted until its tiny genitals were bruised and swollen beyond recognition. Another little one of two years old had contracted gonorrhea. There is a madness abroad which makes the unbelievable a reality.

You are all aware, I feel sure, of the filibustering which killed Mr Winston Churchill's Bill of an amendment to the Obscene Publications Act which had successfully passed through its Committee Stage. It would, if it had become law, have brought broadcasting under the control of the Act, into line with the rest of the media. It would also have made it illegal to sell pornography to anyone under the age of eighteen.

The hysteria of those who saw the possibility of their own financial and professional interests being limited by this Bill has, to say the least, been illuminating.

Their self-interest, which won the day, had a hard metallic quality which allowed of no compassion or understanding of the purpose of the Bill, which carries in its title the words 'protection of children'.

Again the Church was silent. I do not think a single Church leader gave Mr Churchill any encouragement. I understand the natural reluctance to get involved, to soil one's mind, with issues as dark and evil as is the issue of pornography and violence. But when I am tempted – as I sometimes am – to say, 'I've had enough of such things', I recall the challenge of the story of the Good Samaritan. The victim in that story, too, was stripped of his clothes, beaten and left to die, but the Samaritan took pity on him and it is those who, with tragic certainty, if not this day then certainly this week, will be stripped and beaten somewhere in this lovely land of ours.

It is this exploitation of the love between men and women, even between men and children which lies at the heart of the corruption which characterises our day and age and against which we are committed to fight.

There is much rightful concern about our physical environment – that people shall enjoy the countryside and conserve it. There is much rightful concern that people shall be free to enjoy full employment and the benefits of civilised life; that they shall be free from any kind of racial discrimination; that exploitation in all its forms should not exist; that we shall have peace. In other words, that the Kingdom of Heaven should come on earth.

The trouble is that we have forgotten the ground of our peace. St Paul, in his letter to the Philippians, was in no doubt about it. Put into practice, he said, 'whatsoever is true, whatsoever is noble, whatsoever is right, whatsoever is pure, whatsoever is lovely, whatsoever is admirable, whatsoever is excellent or praiseworthy.' It is about *these* things, said St Paul, that we are to think. Then, and only then, shall we have peace – peace of heart, of mind, social and international peace.

These are great and challenging, indeed haunting, words. The question is, how are we to interpret them, in the age in which we live? Some of the stories, particularly of the abuse of children, which have followed one another in such horrible succession over recent weeks, underline for us how very far we are from being a civilised, let alone a Christian, country.

God has given us a very beautiful world, certainly in this part of it. He has given to many of us the gift of a happy home, healthy children, a job which gives us satisfaction, and good friends. The temptation is bound to be one of self-sufficiency: how to protect what we have without becoming too involved with the evils we see all around us.

The truth is that there is no place today for apathy or complacency. The days when we could say, 'It is all a matter of personal taste', or, 'You can always switch off', are long gone, and the cost in human suffering of such complacency is clear for all to see. So is the fact that all of us, however secure our background and sound our faith may be, are at risk.

Conscious as I am of the beauty of this holy place I find myself tempted to apologise for the crudity and horror of the stories I have told. But then I ask myself, where better? And then I think what right have we to our comfort when these children – and without doubt countless more – have suffered, at our hands, psychological and physical damage from which they may never recover?

One is concerned not only with pornography and physical violence, but with the verbally obscene and blasphemous language which characterises so much of our culture and about which again the Church is so silent. Our desire to live and enjoy our lives as we would choose is increasingly put at risk by the way in which violence is made to appear commonplace, even desirable – the easiest and most immediate solution to problems both great and small.

There is no longer any secret or question about the link between televised and social violence. There now exist 700 pieces of scientific study internationally which confirm this link, while to the best of our knowledge no research exists to support the opinion, fashionable in certain quarters, that no such link exists.

But there must be answers to these challenges. There must be hope for ourselves, our children and those who follow after. You will be well aware of the quotation from Edmund Burke: 'All that is needed for evil to triumph is that good men do nothing.'

If we are to enjoy the gifts the Lord has blessed us with then we are surely called to play what is a unique role in this day and generation.

Generalisations, however, are not enough for me to leave you with. You will each have your own particular commitments, your own ideas as to how best to meet the needs of the day, I do not doubt. But so far as the matters I have been talking about this evening are concerned, there are practical steps which can be taken to ensure that the tide of moral corruption and exploitation which so disturbs us all is reversed.

We can for instance call on our Government – and letters to the Prime Minister on these matters would not, I think, fall on deaf ears – to make, for example, our obscenity law more effective – and a Bill to do just that has now been prepared by us. We can ask that broadcasting, at present exempt from such controls, is included in it. We can put pressure on the BBC and IBA to decrease the amount of violence on our television screens. That is one cause of social violence which can be quickly and effectively dealt with at source. All our experience leads us to believe that only continuing public pressure backed up by adequate legislation will have effect. And we can call upon the Church. It is the *Church*'s role to give moral leadership, and I believe it is its failure to speak out, or indeed to be uncertain when it does, that lies at the heart of the disillusion with the Church which characterises our day as it sometimes has in the past.

Outspoken, fearless, much maligned . . . very much 'A Voice Crying in the Wilderness'. In fact that's how I see that marvellous Old Testament prophet Jeremiah, whose powerful words are as relevant now as they were when he uttered them. Indeed to hear him speak is to realise how little has changed through the history of unredeemed mankind: When we, as individuals or as nations, turn our back on God, there is *always* an inevitable and immeasurable price to pay.

And we have much to learn from Jeremiah. He was of course a great communicator. The children of Israel may not have obeyed his message, but they certainly couldn't ignore it. He compelled them to make choices. His use of words was masterly. I could read them over and over again for their own sake:

> Stand ye in the ways, and see, and ask for the old paths, where is the good way, and walk therein, and ye shall find rest for your souls.

Jeremiah was such an expert at cutting through humbug, pride and self-interest, and revealing forgotten but fundamental truths.

The sins which Jeremiah identified in his generation – theft, murder, adultery, the worship of other gods (Baal in his day, money in ours) – are no less characteristic of our own. He was determined, it seems to me, to shake the Israelites into the knowledge of just how far they had fallen from grace as God's chosen people. And they had to be made to understand the fearful consequences of turning away from Him. So confident was Jeremiah of being on the side of the angels that he always spoke in God's name, never in his own:

> Hear now this, O foolish people, and without understanding; which have eyes, and see not; which have ears, and hear not: Fear ye not me? saith the Lord . . . Your iniquities have turned away these things, and your sins have withholden good things from you . . . A wonderful and horrible thing is committed in the land . . . and my people love to have it so.

It is the eternal relevance of his words which makes Jeremiah so much a man for our own day. 'Foolish and senseless people' – he doesn't call us progressive or liberated, but foolish and senseless. I know for myself that his words offer an immense challenge. It is so easy to be committed to God's will in principle; it is quite another matter to interpret that will into the daily round of personal exchanges and activities.

But what kind of man was this Jeremiah? In many ways, I imagine, very much like the rest of us, thank goodness. When the Lord appointed him as 'a prophet to the nations' Jeremiah ran the metaphorical mile . . .

> I, Ah, Lord God! behold, I cannot speak: for I am a child.

I suspect that his pleading with God, as he played hopefully on the

Lord's sympathy, went something like this: 'I'm not clever, I've had no experience of public speaking, I shall only let you down, and truth to tell, I'm frightened to death – couldn't you please find someone else?' That I suspect applies to us all! We are *all* called to be prophets in this needy generation. How many bells that rings! How often have I thought, 'I can't do it; I don't have the experience; in any case what about the family, not to mention my beloved garden?' Then I remember Jeremiah, the humble, inexperienced priest who simply said 'yes' to the Lord. He didn't, of course, know the suffering that would come his way; that sense of isolation that Jeremiah came to feel among other prophets and priests was something he had not anticipated. He challenged their ineffectiveness, and they didn't welcome it. Perhaps it is only as each of us, as individuals, accept that challenge that the Church itself, and its leadership, will be the voice and inspiration in the land that the Lord intends it to be.

A Cry of Pain

David Sheppard

The Archbishop of Canterbury's Commission on Urban Priority Areas was set up in 1983. Serving on that Commission gave me insight into what was happening in all our major cities. After serving in the 'Inner City' in East and South London for twenty years, I moved to Liverpool in 1975.

This sermon was a lunch-time address during Lent 1984 at Liverpool Parish Church early in the life of the Commission. The whole Commission had recently visited Merseyside so that I had the unusual experience of being part of a visit to my own 'patch'. The sermon was preached during dark days for Liverpool, when militants led the City Council on a confrontation course with the Government.

Faith in the City, the Report of the Commisson, brought great encouragement to Christians living and serving in the Urban Priority Areas: when the Report came under fire, it meant much that the Archbishop stood firmly by it. He consistently made it clear that the Church must give greater priority to tackling what Faith in the City *called a fundamental injustice in our country. He gave a strong lead, too, to putting greater Church resources into Urban Prority Areas.*

I feel I should congratulate you all for coming to hear the Bishop speak on Urban Priority Areas again. I hope I can persuade you that it's right to stay with this subject, though I know clergy are tempted to repeat themselves. Sometimes a simple word makes us realise when we are repeating ourselves unnecessarily. I recently confirmed a mentally handicapped young man, well-known and well-liked in his parish. The Vicar told me that when he came to the parish he questioned a practice at the end of the Service: the Choir went out to the vestry and the Reader said a concluding prayer for all to hear. The Vicar went down to the door and was expected to follow it with a second concluding prayer. He thought it was a curious idea, but didn't want to make immediate changes. But change came quicker than he expected. The Reader had said his concluding prayer: the Vicar started out on his. And young David said in a loud voice, 'O God, not another one!'

I claim justification for 'another one' on Urban Priority Areas. I want to say that *there is a cry of pain* and that it should be *the concern of the whole body.* And I will describe some signs of hope for 1984 in that I see a growing concern of the whole body.

A major sign of hope is that the Archbishop of Canterbury has appointed a two-year Commission on Urban Priority Areas. He sees the needs of these areas as being an urgent priority in Church and nation. The task of the Commission is to listen to Church people and others in Urban Priority Areas and understand the strengths and weaknesses of Church life. The phrase 'Urban Priority Area' is used rather than 'Inner City' because people on the great Corporation Housing Estates feel that there is so much talk about the Inner City and that they are being left out of the concern and out of the provision of fresh resources.

The Commission is also to raise questions about what helps and what hinders urban people from believing and from practising what they believe. And it is charged with raising public policy questions.

Last month the Archbishop's Commission made a two-day visit to Merseyside. I'm a member of the Commission and had the unusual experience of paying a visit to my own patch. We saw real signs of hope for 1984. Commission members said they were impressed at many clergy and lay people in Priority Areas who were not looking inwards all the time at Church life, but were deeply involved in the life of the whole community. I am very thankful as Bishop at the quality of the clergy who want to come to Liverpool and to stay in the areas of which we speak.

We met one Roman Catholic priest in Scotland Road whose attitude would be matched by a number of our clergy: he said that if the Archbishop asked him to go to Southport, he was not sure if his ordination stretched that far.

I wish you could have been with me for one particular part of the Commission's visit. We invited people to come to an Open Forum on the Friday evening and Saturday morning: we divided up into three groups in three places. I was at the Forum in Kirkby. I found that evening almost overwhelming. In a sense I had heard it all before, but there was a cry of pain.

Unemployment filled the foregound – very long-term unemployment. We were told that large-scale unemployment hit Kirkby first when the Labour Government introduced Selective Employment Tax in the 1960s. – Lately-come firms immediately shed labour which wasn't absolutely necessary and hundreds of young people were unemployed.

One woman told us she had lived with unemployment for ten years. 'My husband's pride is at the bottom. He's forty-two and on the scrapheap. He's a very talented man, but he can't use most of his talents, because they cost money. My children are embarrassed to ask him for anything. I'm desperate as a mother of five to sustain our family. One child wants to study archaeology. One is thoroughly anti-social.'

Her husband had said a bit earlier, 'Indignity is put on us by the *Sun* newspaper with its talk about scroungers. Christmas comes and you've got to starve yourself to give your kids a present. Give us our dignity.'

I told the Rector of Kirkby next morning how impressed I was by what these two said. He told me they would never have been able to speak up in a group like that a year ago. I asked what had changed for them. He said it was to do with their experience in coming to St Andrew's, Tower Hill in Kirkby. The way they were treated made them feel that they mattered, that people wanted to hear their story. Their self-confidence grew and soon they were surprising themselves by how articulate they were.

That's a flicker of hope for 1984.

In a good many priority areas I meet people who've been given their dignity by belonging to the Christian company: as self-confidence grows so their ability becomes plain and they dare to start accepting responsibility. No one will persuade me that there is not the intelligence and ability for leadership in such areas.

People at Kirkby said, 'We need reduction of working hours and of the retiring age. Trade Unions have not got to be so greedy for overtime.' But they also said, 'Industry no longer needs manpower.' The chairman of a major company who is a member of the Commission had just said that they had invested £17 million in a new plant but that this was making only 150 jobs.

One person said, 'We hope your Commission will dream a little – look at ways of using man's creativity outside industry. Find a way in which people can contribute to society and receive a reasonable wage for it.'

It was indeed a cry of pain, and it should bring the concern of the whole body. If someone goes to hospital with a serious pain, the hospital will not just attend to the part of the body where the pain is. They will start a series of tests, for the cause may be in another part of the body, and the whole body will be affected.

'If one organ suffers, they all suffer together' that's how St Paul puts it, when he says that the Church is the body of Christ. 'God has combined the various parts of the body, giving special honour to the humbler parts so that there might be no sense of division in the body, but that all its organs might feel the same concern for one another.'

So it was following a right instinct when Church people at Kirkby forum said to us, 'Tell Chichester about this'. In the Archbishop's Commission we have said to each other that if we really want to get things changed in Urban Priority Areas, we must find ways of talking to St Alban's, Winchester, Chester, and the business City of London: the cause of the pain may be in other parts of the body. This concern is not just the Bishop of Liverpool's hobby horse or the priority of a radical fringe: it springs from mainstream, historic Christianity and is the concern of the whole body.

Some Christians want to say that St Paul's language about the body is only about the Church and we shouldn't be concerned with secular needs and groups. For example, at that very painful moment following the riots, when the British Council of Churches made a small grant to the Liverpool 8 Defence Committee, I received a letter from a suburban parish in Liverpool asking me please to make sure that in future any Church money was given to Churches, not to secular bodies.

Such a theological view would go right back to the early days of the Old Testament, when the Jews believed they were only to be concerned with needs among their own people. That attitude was sharply challenged in the years of Exile.

The mood among the exiles is reflected in that Psalm, 'By the waters of Babylon we sat down and wept . . . As for our harps, we hung them up . . . For they that led us away captive required of us then a song – sing us one of the songs of Zion. How shall we sing the Lord's song in a strange land? If I forget thee O Jerusalem, let my right hand forget her cunning.'

That was the mood among the exiles. Then a letter arrived from the prophet Jeremiah, who was still living with the little remnant left in Jerusalem. The letter told the exiles to settle in Babylon and to seek its welfare and pray to the Lord for it 'On its welfare your welfare will depend.'

On the welfare of Babylon! With all the evil which that name carried for the Jews. That shook the old theology. And it says to us that there is no welfare for the Church unless we too seek the welfare of the whole community in which God has set us. We are not just to concern ourselves with the needs of Christians.

There is hope in 1984 in those who do concern themselves with the pain. One employer in another part of the country told my wife that he was giving substantial money to a voluntary body in Merseyside because 'my welfare and the welfare of my work force is bound up with their welfare.'

I find hope for 1984, too, in meeting a number of employers who have determined to break the vicious circle of black unemployment in this city and who refuse to give up in the face of repeated disappointments.

These are most anxious days for Liverpool. What will happen in the City Council Chamber on 29 March? There is talk of a 60 per cent rate increase for a standstill budget; of a 175 per cent rate increase for some growth in jobs and housing renewal; also of making 4,000 Council employees redundant; and of refusing to make a legal rate with the highly uncertain consequences which might follow.

I do not believe that the good of the poor in Liverpool will be achieved through physical threats or disorder on the streets. But that cry of anguish is born of alienation and despair. My Christian comment is that this cry of pain should be the concern of the whole body.

Some of us are trying to persuade people not to abandon the rule of law and peaceful processes of change. But, if we are successful in such law-abiding persuasion, and they pull back from the brink, what will happen then? Will prosperous Britain heave a sigh of relief and forget about Liverpool again?

Make no mistake, we are wasting the God-given resources of our nation by leaving three million people on the dole; and we are breeding a dangerously bitter spirit. In Merseyside long-term unemployment for many means a generation on the dole, often ten years, maybe twenty years without a job. We need something like a major programme of public works and public service.

I am not saying that the Government should buy off threats by immediate deals. No good government could do that. I hope that against all the evidence, disadvantaged people in Liverpool will determine to give peaceful, democratic change another chance. And I hope that, once this present difficulty is over, the Government will listen to the cry of pain which is certainly there behind the threats.

We have moved into a new technological age. The free market will not require the whole labour force again for the foreseeable future. We should expect those who are lucky enough to have demanding and highly paid jobs to shoulder the major part of the burden by increased taxation, not to leave those with the weakest bargaining power to bear the burden of technological change for us all.

So what do I want Chichester and Chester to do – and all of us in more affluent Britain? Well, we must acknowledge that all of us are part of the problem. For example, who created the 'Inner City'? Not only those who live there today. Also, those who once lived there and 'went up in the world', as they say, and took away the self-confidence and talents which could have given so much to those communities. Also those who take their wealth from the City.

There will be no deliverance for the poor in the body of our nation, without some medicine being taken by the better off parts of the body. And the medicine really will do us good as well as the poor. If we start to look at the world from alongside the poor, we shall start to see what Christ can be to us in whole new ways. There are many Chichester and Chester Christians who have had their eyes opened by concerning themselves with 'Inner City' areas: recognising poverty there has opened their eyes to see hidden poverty among neighbours in more affluent areas – people who have been too proud to admit their needs, and have lacked any of the fellowship which 'Inner City' communities can offer.

I hope that Chichester and Chester will take the Archbishop's Commission seriously when it reports. There is bound to be some challenge about Church resources in manpower and money, and about resources in our country, too.

I have talked about a cry of pain and of the concern which the whole body should have. Wherever you are, Urban Priority Areas are your concern: no part of the body can be healthy while other parts are so sick. You cannot properly talk about having a high standard of living, if brothers and sisters – other parts of the body you belong to – do not share it.

When we have great experiences of belonging to the body, we catch a glimpse of how God wants the whole world to be. Last Sunday a thousand of us had such an experience in the Metropolitan Cathedral for the performance of the St Matthew Passion. It was performed by four choirs, two from either end of Hope Street. That was hope for 1984 – sharing together in the body of meditation and adoration of Christ, the Head of the Body. That sharing together of our different talents was indeed a glimpse of how God wants the whole world to be; as we meditated together on that sacred Head sore wounded, we knew He was calling us to have concern for every other member of the body, especially those who feel themselves excluded.

Jewish Understanding of Interfaith Encounter

Immanuel Jakobovits

To be included in this volume honouring Robert Runcie on his forthcoming retirement is for me a very special privilege. Among many other admirers the world over, I look upon him as a distinguished religious leader who has made a lasting impression on the spiritual fortunes of Britain. His tenure was marked by some of the most momentous events in human history, culminating in the sudden collapse of Communism, both caused by and leading to the yearning for religious freedom. The Archbishop's own role in encouraging this triumph of faith was not insignificant.

Other dramas, too, challenged his spiritual statesmanship more acutely than those faced by many a predecessor. For instance there was the Falklands conflict far beyond our borders, and the fierce debates on women's ordination and on homosexuality within its own Church. Whether one always agreed with his views or not, one could not but be impressed by his art in blending fortitude of conviction with moderation.

Historically notable too, was the report Faith in the Cities, *commissioned by him. This was perhaps the most influential Church document of its kind ever issued. It was at his suggestion that I prepared and subsequently published a Jewish response,* From Doom to Hope.

But both national and world-wide virtues apart, I have particular reason to appreciate his firm friendship, both communally and personally. His staunch support for the Council of Christians and Jews was and remains a major factor in assuring a specially gratifying relationship between our two communities. His remarkable address on Christian guilt for the Holocaust at the Kristallnacht commemoration in November 1988 will never be forgotten.

Personally he favoured me with extraordinary manifestations of friendship. He conferred on me the unique privileges of being the first Rabbi ever invited to deliver the Lambeth Lecture, and also to receive the Lambeth Doctorate of Divinity from his hands at a memorable ceremony.

With this contribution, based on the Lambeth Lecture, 25 October 1983, I humbly pay my respects to a treasured friend, an esteemed partner in promoting interfaith amity, and a noble champion of faith in action.

Understanding is a fountain of life to those who possess it (Proverbs 16:22)

Favour us with the knowledge, the understanding and the insight that come from You (Jewish Daily Prayer)

Jewish history provides the original testing-ground for both strife and healing in the interplay between different faiths. The Jewish experience encompasses the entire gamut – from sectarian divide through persecution to reconciliation – in the cycle of estrangement and rapprochement. It pioneered virtually all other trends and movements in this sphere.

One example bears testimony to this pioneering role. In the vocabulary of 'man's inhumanity to man', such terms as racism, genocide, holocaust, pogrom and ghetto, now commonplace, derive from the Jewish experience, and were until recently used only in connection with the persecution of Jews. 'Ghetto', first used in 1611, is defined in the *Oxford Dictionary* as 'The quarter in a city to which Jews were restricted'. 'Pogrom' dates from 1905, when it was applied to the massacre of Jews in Russia. 'Racism' features only in the Addenda of the 1972 edition of the *Oxford Dictionary*, where its first use is dated 1942. It entered English usage from the earlier German 'Rassenlehre' which was used by German anti-Semites to denote the inferiority of Jewish people. 'Genocide' dates only from 1944 when the language was inadequate to describe the enormity of the Nazi crimes and a new word had to be coined. 'Holocaust' was until recently applied exclusively to the six million Jewish martyrs of Hitler's 'Final Solution'.

Naturally, it is not only words which have passed from Jewish to universal currency. The struggle of the Jews to secure equal rights through emancipaton largely served as the prototype for the human rights movements which brought equality to oppressed minorities. 'Let My People Go' signalled not only the Exodus from Egypt three-and-a-half thousand years ago; it rang for decades to secure the freedom of Jews in the Soviet Union and of deprived groups in other lands. Zionism could be regarded as the first national liberation movement. There can hardly be any more painful irony than that countries whose struggle for independence was preceded, if not inspired, by the success of the Jewish national effort, now often lead the implacable opposition to Israel in the United Nations and elsewhere. Their ultimate obscenity is to brand Zionism as racism – the very term coined for the oppression of Jews.

Despite setbacks to racial and interfaith harmony in recent years, enormous progress has been made over the past forty-five years. As we moan over declining morals and mounting perils we should also recognise some very solid advances towards social justice and human brotherhood, achieved at a speed and on a scale unprecedented in the thousands of years of humanity's tortuous evolution: the emergence of scores of newly-freed nations; the rise of the Welfare State providing care for the sick, and aged, the workless and the poor where they previously had to endure destitution and abandonment. The instant communications of the media we so often decry rouse millions to protest against injustices perpetrated thousands of miles away. The emphasis on human rights, now regarded as a major international concern, represents momentous advance in the cultivation of a world-wide social conscience. Whatever gaps between hope and reality have yet to be bridged human equality is now acknowledged as an ideal for which to strive in a way it never was only two generations ago. Broadly speaking the world is today more compassionate, more sensitive to injustice and oppression and louder in agitation against these evils than ever before. Our justifiable concerns – still numerous – should not make us impervious to our achievements in the overall refinement of human relationships.

This leads us to a paradox. Compassion, equality, freedom and brotherhood are basically the essence of religious teachings and aspirations. Indeed, they originate in the moral pioneering of ancient Israel, its faith, its Prophets and its persistence through centuries of spiritual loneliness when these ideals were shared by no other people. Subsequently Christianity and then Islam spread worldwide the seeds nurtured in the Holy Land. We might therefore have expected the major thrusts of moral conscience to have been generated primarily by religious forces. Essentially religious ideals should have been activated mainly by religious dynamics.

Yet this did not happen. The role of religion and religious leadership proved to be marginal. The technological wonder of television more than the spiritual marvels of religious faith has been responsible for people showing concern about hunger in Biafra, apartheid in South Africa, war in Vietnam, or desperate need in underdeveloped countries. Religion and morality are only casual, sometimes accidental partners. The public conscience is in the main stirred by secular rather than religious stimulants.

This phenomenon may even govern the revolutionary developments in Jewish–Christian relationships over recent decades. We may divide these advances into quite distinct parts: the treatment of Jews at civil level; and their recognition at religious level.

On the whole, Jews have been among the beneficiaries of the enlightened and tolerant attitudes bred by the emerging emphasis on human rights. Anti-Semitism has become and remains unfashionable. Neo-Nazism and extremist movements with avowed anti-Semitic tendencies, have shrunk and lost popular support.

In Britain this has been demonstrated at elections when the fringe parties committed to anti-Semitic programmes have failed to win any real support. Economic depresson attended by high unemployment did not turn Jews into scapegoats, as happened with such devastating results in the past. All European and Western governments are unequivocally committed to the suppression of anti-Semitism, in a manner which would have been inconceivable formerly. Regrettably, however, this progress can hardly be attributed to religious initiatives.

Alongside the relaxation of external pressures and the abatement of personal or social prejudice, there has been a significant détente in the religious tensions which for so long clouded Jewish-Christian relationships. Bridges of communication and understanding have been built where there was previously a gulf filled with suspicion or even hatred. Numerous declarations – from Vatican II to the Jewish-Lutheran Consultation in Stockholm and more recently the Lambeth Conference – have called for radical revisions of Christian teachings on Jews, inaugurating an entirely new era of interfaith harmony.

But even in this sphere, the stimulus came, and continues to come, largely from outside. Guilt feelings released by the Holocaust have much to do with it. So has the new climate of greater sensitivity to discrimination and injustice. Religious leadership readily reacts to these changes in social awareness. Catching the new mood of liberalisation, it frowns on vestiges of blatant anti-Semitism embedded in theological doctrines and liturgical texts. It promotes dialogue on the basis of equality and even encourages scholarship to rediscover the Judaic roots of Christianity. This process is now widely followed in numerous theological and academic institutions and is producing an increasingly impressive literature. Yet one wonders whether the initial impetus to the opening of these doors that were previously closed must not be attributed to secular factors, as much as to religious initiatives.

Perhaps Jewish expectations of the rapprochement with Christianity have been exaggerated in some circles, and misunderstood in others. The Orthodox Jewish community does not seek theological dialogue in the narrow sense of subjecting one faith to the critical scrutiny of the other. Nor do we aspire to joint religious services, or inter-faith activities of a specifically religious nature. There are other and better ways to show mutual trust and respect.

We do not have to *convince*, we have to *understand*, and the words of Isaiah 1.18 inevitably come to mind: 'Come let us reason together.'

There is much unfinished business on our common agenda. But modifications in our forms of worship and probes into one another's beliefs are not among its items. Traditional Judaism is hesitant on interdenominational activities and debates where religous differences impinge. I explained this in a sermon in 1971 subsequently reproduced in *The Times*:

> We regard our relationship with God and the manner in which we define and collectively express it, as being so intimate and personal that we could no more convey it to outsiders than we would share with others our husband-wife relationship. We feel it improper to expose one's innermost beliefs and mode of worship to the judgement and comparative scrutiny of those who do not share the same religious commitment.

Let me share with you a passage from an article entitled 'Christology in the Christian-Jewish Dialogue of Today' by Dr Paul Gerhard Aring, a

German Protestant theologian, published in *Christian-Jewish Relations* by the Institute of Jewish Affairs in London:

Today we earnestly ask in the context of the Christian-Jewish dialogue: is our affirmation of Jesus Christ, is our Christology really still credible? It is only a generation ago that in our country many Christians, in all subjective sincerity, acknowledged Jesus Christ as their Lord, while at the same time countless brothers and sisters of the Jew Jesus were destroyed like vermin! Can we, after all that has happened to the Jews during centuries of Church history and against the background of the Christian avowal of Christ, can we after all the injustices, the malice the violence and the crimes – really, legitimately claim that we are bound to a mission without in all seriousness questioning our right to the mission?

Having asked these questions, he calls for a thorough re-examination of some Christian teachings.

Now, Jews may be gratified to see such questions asked and such challenges faced. But it is not for me as a Jew, to pose them. It is not my business, or my right, to question the mission or the credibility of another faith, and I would not like such questions to feature in any Jewish-Christian dialogue. Pleas for more sympathetic attitudes, by all means; but theological criticisms – no. Any faith must be defined, questioned, and revised only by its own adherents and custodians. Dialogues should be bridges, not dams. The theological rivers to be spanned must flow separately, if their confluence is not to cause whirlpools of confusion and confrontation.

Instead of items which touch on our distinctiveness and integrity, we should devote our interfaith agenda to two major rubrics. One is the re-examinaton and, if necessary, revision of our pragmatic relationship; the other the exploration of common approaches to moral and social issues which challenge religious leadership and conscience.

In the first of these, priority on the Jewish side would be the centrality of Israel in Jewish life, and the ramifications of this fact in Jewish-Christian relations. A basic ground-rule governing interfaith parleys must be the right of self-definition by each partner. We can only be or believe what we freely choose to be or to believe, not what others might prefer as the parameters of our faith-commitment. In the self-definition of Judaism a major impact is bound to be the restoration of Jewish sovereignty in response to hopes and prayers over nineteen centuries of national homelessness, as inspired by the Jewish reading of the Hebrew Prophets and their promise. Corresponding to the emergence of Zionism, and the concern for Israel's security, as a leading dynamic of Jewish self-expression is the equal and opposite shift from anti-Semitism to anti-Zionism as the principal expression of anti-Jewish prejudice. Any redefinition of Church attitudes to the Jewish people which omits this fundamental change is dated and incomplete.

In stressing the importance of self-definition, I add another aspect of the ability to comprehend each faith only in its own terms. I am often asked whether and how our internal divisions between Traditional and Reform Judaism compare wth the denominational factions within Christianity. The short answer is that there is no comparison. In that reply lies the key to understanding Judaism.

Theologically and doctrinally, our divisions are in general much more far-reaching and fundamental than the corresponding differences between various Christian denominations. We differ on matters affecting the very foundations of Judaism, on some of the most cardinal principles of faith, such as the Divine authenticity of the Written and Oral Laws, the binding character of Biblical and Talmudic legislation and the role of these in private and public Jewish life. This touches the very heart of Judaism.

Yet, these differences, however profound, have not led to schisms even remotely comparable to the denominatonal divisions within Christianity. For cohesive factors unite us as one people: a common history, a common fate and a common destiny. These are expressed in corporate responsibility in which all Jews, irrespective of their beliefs or heresies, look upon this common peoplehood as a supreme expression of their Jewishness. Jewish peoplehood is itself an integral and indispensable part of Jewish religious identity. Any rapport with Judaism and the Jewish people must appreciate this unique combination of religion and peoplehood. Hence the crucial importance of Zionism and Israel, and hence the grey area on Jewish-Christian understanding in this respect which still calls for definition on the Christian side, unencumbered by any political considerations.

The second issue in the exploration of common responses to common challenge, is an assumpton analogous to what I have just said on religion and peoplehood constituting Jewishness. Just as the diversity of Jewish religious beliefs does not compromise the solidarity of Jewish peoplehood so differences of faith should not vitiate the universality of humanity. An interfaith declaration to that effect alone might be a most meaningful demonstration of our spiritual aspirations and purpose. It could be as important as the Charter of the United Nations which, if it had been upheld with conviction, would have prevented the many wars which have tormented the world since 1945.

One wonders whether the impotence of political statesmanship which lets us drift ever closer to a world of uncontrollable lawlessness does not offer collective spiritual leadership renewed opportunities to break the spiral of human degeneration. Yes, I did refer earlier to momentous gains, often overlooked, in the cultivation of a worldwide social conscience; and yes, these were achieved through secular rather than religious stirrings. However, they are now in danger of being swept aside by rising tides of terrorism, crime, vice, infidelity and extremism which are eroding national and individual values. The noblest campaigns for human rights can become demoralised through insensitivity to suffering, through a surfeit of violence in entertainment and the media, and by despair in human progress.

Strange inconsistencies now abound. In theory and ideology, we are now more egalitarian than ever before. Yet in practice the gap between the haves and the have-nots constantly widens. Hardly a shoulder is shrugged when we learn that millions are threatened by starvation, or that the industrial nations spend considerably more on armaments than on Third World assistance. Labour-saving technology now reduces the time spent on work or on travel. One would imagine that the time saved would make people more relaxed, more cultured and more inclined to devote themselves to spiritual pursuits. Yet, in fact, those who are busy are more harassed than ever and those who have time on their hands misuse it. They are in danger of turning excessive leisure into the greatest social menace of the future. Well-meaning reformers focus on the interests of criminals rather than their victims; the peddlers of pornography find massive support. The unfettered freedom of the press provides a platform for character-assassins and hate-mongers. Meanwhile the freedom and security of the law-abiding majority are under ever-mounting pressure.

Such discrepancies between fine ideals and harsh realities demonstrate a moral void which can be filled only by recognising and promoting the spiritual ingredients in the human condition.

In conclusion, I select one example to show how a religious initiative might help. I referred to the menace of leisure and idleness. Whatever one's work ethic, whether work enslaves or ennobles, the fact is that an abundance of free time tends to breed delinquency, feed the boredom of marriage, and induce anti-social tendencies through a feeling of not being wanted. This leads to many of the evils afflicting our society. It is a fact that, even if we desired to keep people busy for eight hours a day throughout their working life, there simply is not enough work to go round. Shorter hours and earlier retirement, if not prolonged unemployment itself, is likely to become increasingly commonplace. The problem may exceed both the resourcefulness of government legislation and the moral fervour of the popular demand for work.

How different things could be if education went beyond the training of professional and occupational skills, and perhaps even beyond the present school age to include not just instruction in civic virtues, but also the cultivation of such interests and skills as would encourage the potential latent in every one of us. Such training would keep people creatively occupied and would meaningfully stimulate their leisure time.

Here surely is but one crucial area where a collective national challenge uniting all faiths could have a major impact on raising a new generation to build a better society. I know of no secular agency which, aware that the full human being is a fusion of body, mind and spirit in the hostile environment of an increasingly mechanised world, could generate such visions and energies. They will be vital in a world where values and propensities remain constant while needs and circumstances change beyond recognition.

Oscar Wilde wrote: 'Truth, in matters of religion, is simply the opinion that has survived.' Nearly a hundred years on, I would say; 'Religion, in matters of truth, is simply the guide which will allow us to survive.'

So where do we go from here? Surely to the prophet Micah (6:8) who teaches that our joint Creator requires us to do justly, to love mercy and to walk humbly with our God.

One can do justly and love mercy; but if we fail to walk humbly with our God then those virtues are utilitarian and they lack a moral imperative.

For the person of faith – the full person – the third teaching is vital. Whether we translate as, 'humbly', 'modestly', 'decently' or 'in secret', i.e. even when no one watches (and the original text will support all these variations), we are describing the man in whose honour this sermon is dedicated. Robert Runcie, Primate of All England; 102nd Archbishop of Canterbury; President of the Council of Christians and Jews; my personal and much admired friend.

May he have a long and happy retirement.

Missionaries

Geoffrey Parrinder

Ease of communications in the modern world ensures that church leaders become figures of international standing and Dr Runcie must be one of the most travelled Archbishops. In addition to presiding over the Church in England, and over pan-Anglican conferences, he has visited many of the daughter Churches throughout the world which are the products of those Christian missions which are sometimes criticised. Further, at his enthronement in Canterbury Cathedral in 1980 there were present not only leaders of other Christian denominations but also Jewish, Muslim, Sikh, Hindu and Buddhist representatives, almost certainly for the first time. Visiting churches in Asia and Africa the Archbishop has urged Christians to respect local customs, and he has promoted the fellowship and dialogue between religions that is essential overseas and at home.

Television on Saturday evenings in Britain is often dreary, with endless chat shows, party games and many kinds of sport. So when the BBC announced a series on *Missionaries* it brought hope of fresh travel pictures with serious history and discussion. Unfortunately the programme contained many half-truths, and some half or full lies. In my local bookshop the printed version has been placed appropriately among works of fiction.

Of course no missionaries have been perfect, and anyone from the inside could have provided examples of foolishness or prejudice, but also of service and sacrifice. In these programmes the basic assumptions of mission, and its origins and history, were not examined carefully or fairly. Judaism, we were told, was hostile to the twelve apostles. What was this entity, Judaism? All the first Christians were Jews, from Jesus himself, and the programme risked falling into the old trap of regarding 'the Jews' as responsible for the ills of early Christianity. Then it was said that Paul and his colleagues were righteous and arrogant, without credit being given for their founding international communities, of Jews and Gentiles.

At the close of the Gospel according to Matthew the disciples are said to have been given a commission, translated variously as 'Teach all nations' or 'Make disciples of all nations'. Whether these words can certainly be attributed to Jesus or to the increasingly Gentile church, adding a Trinitaran formula, it can fairly be maintained that the principles of the Gospel imply application to all people without distinction of race, colour or sex. The commensalism which Jesus practised with publicans and sinners found natural extension in commensalism of Jews with Gentiles which Paul developed in correction of Peter (Gal. 2:11).

In fact, mission seems to be natural to most of the great religions of the world, which have wished to share with their fellows the truth and way of life that they have discovered. The three largest historical religions were missionary from the outset, in this order: Buddhism, Christianity, Islam. Later Sikhism and Bahaism took up the world mission. And in modern times the most active political ideology, Communism, has been virulently missionary, until it became 'the god that failed'.

However, it has been said that some religions were not missionary, being tied to race or land, and Judaism has been cited as an example. Yet there are many instances in the Hebrew prophets of the people being called to be 'witnesses' and 'light to the nations' though in the present era travail and restrictions on activity brought a diminution of the mission until it seemed to be abandoned. Thirty years ago Rabbi Isidore Epstein, in his Penguin book *Judaism*, wrote that his community had withdrawn 'from the missionary field and was satisfied to leave the task of spreading the religion of humanity to her daughter faiths', that is, to Christianity and Islam. But Rabbi Leo Baeck under the Nazis insisted on the rights of Jewish proselytism, and now all groups of Judaism welcome converts. The attack on the missionary principle, then, is not only a criticism of Christianity but of all the major faiths.

Supposing there had been no Christian mission to England, what, one could speculate, might the chief priests be at Canterbury today? Gibbon suggested that if the Arab Muslims had beaten the Frankish armies at Poitiers in 732, the way would have been opened for building a mosque on Ludgate Hill and expounding the Koran instead of the Bible at Oxford. And we might guess that in the previous centuries if there had been no Celtic and Roman missions to these islands the alternatives to Augustine might have been Druids, and the religion of Britain today could be a mixture of nature worship and fertility festivals, perhaps with a dash of Stoic morality. With all its faults, Christianity brought better ideals and practices than these, and if we are the beneficiaries of mission work, should we deny it to others? Missions begin at home but then, unless there is racial prejudice, they must go overseas.

'Just think, they tell people their gods are false, their idols must be destroyed, their ancestors are in Hell.' So declared the programme on *Missionaries*, according to my notes. First of all it must be said that in sixty years of personal acquaintance with missionaries, I have never once heard such statements. The programme paid much attention to American fundamentalist evangelists, whose meetings were photogenic but whose activities may be ephemeral. It paid little heed to the older established missions of the larger Churches, and none at all to their long record of study and understanding of the traditional religions of Asia and Africa. Only in the final episode was it hinted that perhaps at last a few orthodox missions were learning to adapt their ways to beliefs and customs of other peoples. In fact, this process had been initiated from the beginning and developed at intervals over the centuries.

When Paul preached from the Areopagus in Athens, according to the account in Acts 17, he quoted Greek poets who said that we are the offspring of God. To find common ground with his hearers he went from the unknown God to the known, and declared that in Him we live and move and have our being.

It is true that there are exclusive statements in the Bible, as there are in most religions and ideologies. But the Bible is an anthology, from many different hands and times, and rather than singling out exclusive texts the positive elements need to be taken into account, and all of them expounded in the light of the highest Biblical teaching of the love of God for all people.

Any Christian speaker about other religions is liable to be challenged with the words attributed to Peter, speaking to the priests and elders of his people and declaring that 'there is salvation in no one else, for there is no other name under heaven given among men by which we must be saved' (Acts 4:12). This account was probably written down fifty years or more after the event described, and it indicates one strand of early Christian preaching. But a later statement, also attributed to Peter, affirmed that 'in any nation any one who fears God and does what is right is acceptable to him' (Acts 10:35). This is in the context of welcoming God-fearing Gentiles into the Church, and it shows that Acts is not a book of systematic theology but indicates attitudes in different circumstances.

Similarly we may be confronted with the verse, 'no one comes to the Father but by me' (John 14:6). But the fourth Gospel is a complex and subtle book, drawing out implications from the remembered or idealised words of Christ and meditating on them. There is a wider view in the first chapter (verse 9), 'the light which lightens every man'. A former great Archbishop of Canterbury, William Temple, in his *Readings in St John's Gospel*, developed this statement by recognising the inspiraton of the Word of God in great teachers and religions of Asia of which early Christians had been ignorant. He wrote, 'By the word of God – that is to say by Jesus Christ – Isaiah and Plato, Zoroaster, Buddha and Confucius, uttered and wrote such truths as they declared. There is only one Divine Light, and every man in his own measure is enlightened by it.'

Isaiah of course, since Christianity is unique among the world's religions for incorporating the scripture of its parent religion into its own canon of the Bible. The Greek Plato has long since been adopted as the father of Christian philosophy. Zoroaster was the Persian prophet whose teachings of angels and spirits, heaven and hell, judgement and life after death probably influenced inter-testamental Judaism and early Christianity. The Buddha and Confucius and other teachers of farther Asia had very different teachings, but they are known and appreciated better in the West today than ever in the past and their truths, said Temple, must come from the Divine Light which enlightens everyone.

During the Dark and Middle Ages there were exclusive declarations of salvation made by theologians, with restrictions to membership of the Church, and to certain kinds of Church, but changes appeared again among the very missionary movements which went along with European explorations from the fifteenth century onwards. Missionaries to China found it difficult to obtain an entry into that empire, let alone a hearing. But the Italian Jesuit Matteo Ricci in the sixteenth century entered China in Buddhist dress, was received at the court of Peking, and allowed his followers to continue veneration of Confucius and their ancestors. A little later Roberto de Nobili pioneered studies of Indian religion and sacred language. The lives of these men have been written up in popular form by Vincent Cronin.

The BBC programme made slighting reference to the great Baptist missionary William Carey, without recognising that he studied and taught Sanskrit and translated into English the popular epic of the great Hindu god Rama. In the nineteenth century it was a Wesleyan missionary in Ceylon who first translated some of the Buddhist texts. Many other missionaries, Roman Catholic, Anglican and Free Church, learnt oriental languages and translated Arabic, Persian, Sanskrit, Pali, Chinese, Japanese and other Scriptures into European tongues, and so they made known writings of eastern religions which have now circulated across the world. No doubt such translations were made for missionary purposes, to aid in apologetics but also to learn what other religions teach and do. In addition they have been used by Hindu and Buddhist groups in the West. And such texts have been taken for impartial and academic study, and for mutual understandng and dialogue.

An expansion of Temple's statement may be seen in the latest book of the philosopher-theologian John Macquarrie (*Jesus Christ in Modern Thought*, 1990). Continuing and adapting the list of heroes of the faith from Heb. 11, he suggests: 'By faith Mohammed . . . brought them the message of the one invisible God. By faith Gautama Buddha . . . taught the multitudes of Asia to restrain desire and to learn compassion for one another. By faith Krishna brought the presence of the high God.' And so on to include Confucius, Lao-tzu, Zoroaster and Nanak and others.

Definitions of 'mission' in the *Concise Oxford Dictionary* indicate a 'body of persons', sent to a 'foreign country', by a 'religious community', to 'convert heathen'. 'Heathen' is a derogatory word, suggesting countrified or illiterate people whereas the religions of many countries have been highly cultured and literate. The 'foreign country' suggests exotic places, but a feature of today is the presence of different religions in our own country.

The mission has traditionally been a 'sending', by a religious community. Basically it is a desire of that community to share its knowledge and to serve the needs of the rest of humankind. But clearly the methods and approaches differ in every age and place. Matteo Ricci and William Carey acted differently in disparate circumstances, but both of them sought to understand and serve the peoples among whom they lived. In modern times Christian ashrams in India, or anthropological studies and vast educational works in Africa, or dialogues in the Islamic world, have sought to bring understanding and reconciliation.

In our own land, without sending to foreign parts, the mission is to understand and help people of other ways of thought and practice. How misunderstood, misrepresented, persecuted and alienated Islamic communities in Bradford have felt, has been revealed vividly in the Rushdie affair. The Churches have been among those who sought to calm Muslim fears and the Interfaith Network, with Jewish and Christian co-chairmen, stated publicly that *The Satanic Verses* contained 'passages which were bound to cause deep offence to Muslims'. Missions should be services addressed to people's needs, in neighbourliness concern, dialogue and help, following one who said, 'I was a stranger and you welcomed me'.

Christian Unity and Human Unity

Lesslie Newbigin

Questions of Church unity are often dismissed by 'activists' as being irrelevant to the great issues of peace and justice, and therefore a deviation from the main business of Christians in the contemporary world. As Primate of All England and as leader of the world-wide Anglican Communion, Robert Runcie has combined a deep love for the Church and a longing for its unity, with a wide vision of human responsibility for the great issues of our time. I would like to hope that this sermon, written in January 1976, will in some measure reflect his own vision for the Church and the world.

I, when I am lifted up from the earth, will draw all men to myself. (John 12:32)

Today is the last day of the week during which Christians of all confessions and in all lands pray together that God will give to His Church that unity which is His will, when He will and how He will. And this word of our Lord himself, spoken as He looks forward to his Passion, is a reminder that the unity of the Church only has meaning if it is the sign and instrument and first-fruit of the unity of all mankind. It is because we have often forgotten this, and pursued Christian unity as though it were an end in itself, that so many people have written the whole enterprise off as an irrelevance. The Nairobi Assembly of the World Council of Churches, from which I have recently returned, was a powerful reminder of this fact. Its theme was Jesus Christ as both liberator and reconciler of all mankind. It was an Assembly where, as never before, the conflicting concerns of peoples in every part of the world, rich and poor, black and white, capitalist and socialist, Western and Eastern were held together in the common confession that it is in Jesus Christ alone that both freedom and unity are to be found. The ecumenical movement is not simply the effort to unite the divided Churches; it is, in the words of Dr M.M. Thomas at Nairobi, the adventure of discovering the significance of Jesus Christ for our time, and that means the significance of Jesus Christ for all men without exception.

And one thing that can be said about our time is this: that we desperately need – even if we do not desire – the unity of mankind.

We know that, for better for worse, we belong together, squeezed ever more tightly together on this small and vulnerable space-craft which is our planet. We know that we are now so dependent on each other that none of us can solve our problems except in co-operation with the rest, and so closely packed that none of us can move without jostling the rest. We know too that our space-ship is at this moment on a collision course with ecological disaster. Yet our togetherness and our shared danger do not create unity. We do not have to study the behaviour of rats crowded into a cage to know that closer crowding tends to produce not harmony but aggression. As each of us feels more threatened, each is driven to assert his identity more forcefully. And so – absurdly – we develop more and more aggressive tribalisms in smaller and smaller units, just at the time when the facts require wider and wider co-operation. And, lest we should be under any illusions, let it be remembered that, whatever is done now about population control, the world's population is going to double from its present 4,000 million to 8,000 million in the next twenty-five years.

We know that unity is imperative if we are to survive. But on what basis? Human history could be told as the story of successive efforts to impose unity on wider and wider areas of our world. The name we give to these efforts – at least when they are practised by other people – is 'imperialism'. *My* attempt to establish unity is seen by *you* as a threat to your freedom – and you are right. But of course *I* see it differently; I see it as the beneficent enterprise of offering to all mankind the blessings of peace, order and civilisation. My devoted and disinterested labours for unity appear to you as a threat to your liberty; your assertion of liberty appears to me as a crime against unity. You call yourself a freedom fighter, but I call you a terrorist; I am a missionary statesman, but you call me a colonialist. Here is our tragic human dilemma: that freedom and unity, the demand for justice and the longing for peace, confront each other as opposites. Can they ever pull together? Is there a place where 'righteousness and peace have kissed each other'? Is there one, to use the title of the Nairobi Assembly, who *both* frees *and* unites?

Let us first be clear about one point. Put bluntly it is this: every programme for unity, if it does not explicitly state the centre which is offered for that unity, is in fact a concealed imperialism. If I do not point to an explicit centre for unity, I am in fact by implication offering myself and my ideas and interests as the centre of unity. Let me illustrate this from one particular sphere, the question of unity among the religions. This is a specially important example, because religion is among the powerfully devisive factors in our world. It is not surprising that there are many programmes on offer for unity among the religions, programmes which invite each of them, including and perhaps especially Christianity, to drop their exclusive claims and recognise their fundamental unity. But if one

examines these programmes one always finds underlying them
some idea – generally not clearly acknowledged – about what is
important in religion, what matters, what is central. In other words
the programme contains within it a religious view which its pro-
ponents regard as obviously what everyone ought to accept. The
imperial claim is there even when it is concealed. For none of us
has a point of view which is above all points of view, and all of us
– this is part of our human situation – confuse our point of view
with the ultimate truth, confuse our interest with the interest of all
mankind.

Is there, in truth, a given centre around which humankind in all
its vast diversity can be made one in a unity which does not domi-
nate but liberates? Is there one who both frees and unites? There is
indeed. The man Jesus, crucified, risen, regnant, is the one who
alone can draw all men to himself. This promise of his which is our
text takes up the central thread of the biblical vision of world history,
the faith that the one living and true God would gather all the
nations to be his own people. But this messianic hope had also
become an imperialism: The Messiah would be a military leader and
Jerusalem would be his imperial capital. Once again the vision of
human unity has been transformed into an imperialism. How then,
and with what right, does Jesus claim that in him the promise is to
be fulfilled? Only because it is coupled with the promise that he will
be lifted up from the earth, that he will die for the sin of the world.
He will be nailed to a Cross like a common criminal, with the title
'Messiah' hung in mockery over his head. Those who will fix that
notice will do so thinking that this is a nicely ironical way of settling
the messianic claim. But God has His own irony and in fact the
crucified one will be the one through whom the promise is fulfilled.
It will be so, because it will be the place – the one place – where
there is a final dealing with the central corruption of human nature
which turns every programme of unity into a new imperialism.

What is that corruption? It is in simple terms the fact that man
consistently puts himself at the centre of the universe. Man made
in the image of God, made therefore with desires and imaginations
which nothing less than infinity can ever satisfy, man finite and
fragile, yet made for infinity and eternity is driven both by his
desires and by his anxieties to put himself at the centre and to see
the universe as the sphere of his knowing and doing and other men
as rival centres of knowing and doing. And when man thus takes
the place of God he becomes the plaything and the victim of that
which is not God. The universe which God has given to him to be
his home becomes the fate that threatens him, and the neighbour
whom God has given to be his companion becomes the enemy who
tortures him.

The Cross is the place where the depths and height of human
greatness and human misery are matched by a deed which goes to

the heart of the human situation. The Cross is the place where man who has tried to put himself in the place of God is met by God who has put Himself totally in the place of man. It is the event in which the true centre of human affairs displaces the false centre, so that the one who understands and accepts it can begin to live from another centre. It is no longer I that live but Christ who lives in me. The life that I called my own is forfeit; the life I now live is his gift, the gift of his life given that I might live.

No words can ever do more than hint at the meaning of the Cross. It is the central event of all human history, the hinge upon which all things turn. It is the place where all men without exception are judged as enemies of God fit only for destruction, and all men without exception are accepted as the beloved of God, called to a new creation. It is therefore the place where human unity is offered not as a programme to be fought for, but as a gift to be received in faith. It is as Dag Hammarskjold said in his memorable address to the 2nd Assembly of the World Council of Churches, the one place where nations could truly be united nations.

'A gift to be received by faith.' It is, of course, easy to disbelieve. There are always good excuses for scepticism. But the community which does believe, and which lives by this faith, must obviously understand itself not as an end in itself, but as sign, instrument and first-fruit of the unity which is God's will and His gift for all men. It is a *first-fruit* in the sense that it is the place where we are able to enjoy now a partial and provisional but real unity transcending all the divisions of mankind. The reason why a world Assembly like the one in Nairobi is not an expensive luxury but a necessity is that it is the place where we can test and bear witness to the reality of which I am speaking. At such a meeting all the sharp conflicts between nations, economic interests, cultures and traditions are present and active, but we learn afresh that there is given to us in Christ a unity strong enough to hold together in mutual respect and forgiveness those who take different positions, because we are able to accept one another as forgiven sinners who stand together under the Cross of Christ and whose best efforts can only be the faltering obedience of sinful men and women, who can never identify their own programme with God's purpose for the unity of mankind.

The community is also an *instrument* which may be used as God sees fit to set forward the unity of mankind. Its relation to human unity will be that of servant and not that of managing director. It will not imagine that it is the only instrument God has. It will be sufficient for it if God gives it opportunities from time to time to be the unobtrusive instrument of reconciliaton between opposed groups, and of that liberation without which there cannot be true reconciliation.

And the community will be a *sign* of the unity which God intends for mankind in the sense that by pointing men constantly beyond itself to Jesus and his Cross it will enable them to believe the promise of God and to have hope. It will point to the crucified and risen Lord, knowing that the Holy Spirit can in his own way and time use its words and deeds to bring men to faith. It will be a sign in the sense that it points credibly to what is invisible – invisible not because it does not exist but because it is beyond the horizon – and therefore give men the courage and the sense of direction which will enable them to move towards the true destination.

In the large volume of reports which the delegates to the Nairobi Assembly had to read, covering the work of the WCC over the past seven years, one of the most impressive was the chapter dealing wth the work of the Churches' Commission on International Affairs. The staff of this Commission is inevitably a rather hard-boiled group of people, who have to spend their days dealing with professional diplomats and politicians. There have been numerous testimonies from the professional world of international diplomacy to the value of the Commission's work. But in the Commissioners' own report they said that, in their experience, the most significant thing they had been able to do was simply to be the means of keeping hope alive in situations where there was, humanly speaking, no hope. That is indeed an essential function of the Church, to be the sign that ensures the traveller who has given up hope of ever reaching any worth-while goal, that there is a road and that it leads to home.

'I, when am lifted up from the earth, will draw all men to myself.' The Church is in the world – in all the world – to be sign, instrument and first-fruit of that unity which God wills and for which Jesus died and rose again. We pray for the unity of the Church not for itself, but in order that it may be more credible as a sign, more effective as an instrument and more recognisable as a true first-fruit and foretaste of the unity of mankind.

The Conversion of Paul

Grace Jantzen

Throughout Archbishop Runcie's time in office, the Church of England has been considering the ministry of women. Some progress has been made: women are now ordained deacons and the exercise of 'Making Women Visible' has raised awareness of the exclusively masculine language still frequently dominating the liturgy. Yet women still cannot be ordained to the priesthood of the Church of England; and some of its leaders are aware of the disaffection and alienation many women feel at this perceived injustice. Furthermore, the issue is not simply one of accepting women into pre-existing structures, but of using women's insights from a position of marginalisation and oppression to make the structures themselves more open to the liberating Spirit of God.

This sermon was preached at Exeter College, Oxford, in January 1990.

This week the Christian calendar commemorates the conversion of Paul. From my perspective as a feminist theologian, I confess that I find the commemoration strongly ambivalent. On the one hand, it cannot be denied that it is because of Paul's conversion and subsequent missionary activity that the Christian Gospel spread from being a tiny sect centred in Jerusalem and its surroundings to being a major influence in the Roman Empire. Were it not for Paul, Europe might never have been Christianised and the civilisation we know would have been unimaginably different.

Furthermore, Paul can be acclaimed as the great preacher of liberation. It was he who stood out against the Jerusalem Church when the question of circumcision, the external observance of the law, came up. It was he who insisted that righteousness is not found in meticulous keeping of tradition or doing the expected thing, but is found in the joyful freedom of the Spirit, the liberation that refuses to be bound by ecclesiastical and societal conventions, no matter how time-honoured and respectable. Against those in his time who prayed daily, 'I thank my God that I am a Jew and not a Gentile, a freeman, not a slave, a man, not a woman,' Paul presented the great charter of human liberation: in Christ 'there is neither Jew nor Greek, there is neither slave nor free there is neither male nor female; for you are all one in Christ Jesus.'

Yet it is also true that this same Paul, preacher of the Gospel of truth and love, and champion of the freedom of the Spirit of God, wrote and taught some things, and had things written by others in his name, which have been used to perpetrate the anti-feminist, anti-Semitic, racist, power-mongering attitudes for which the Christian church is rightly derided. 'Let a woman learn in silence with all submissiveness . . . for Adam was formed first, then Eve; and Adam was not deceived, but the woman was deceived and became a transgressor. Yet woman will be saved through bearing children, if she continues in faith and love and holiness, with modesty . . . ' Well, perhaps this was written not by Paul, but by someone claiming his authority; and just perhaps Paul might have taken a less misogynist line. But what about the way in which he takes the institution of *slavery* totally for granted, issuing commands to slaves to be obedient to their masters 'with fear and trembling, in singleness of heart'? And what about his certainty that every person should be subject to the governing authorities, because 'there is no authority except from God, and those that exist have been instituted by God'? One can hardly imagine a greater gift to the propaganda campaign of every corrupt regime and authority in Christendom – and there have been many. It is arguable that Paul himself would not have approved of all the uses to which he has been put; but it would be going much too far to hold our hands on our hearts and say that this is all misinterpretation of Paul, and what he *really* meant is of course nice and liberal and ideologically correct.

So the commemoration of Paul's conversion fills me with ambivalence. What are we celebrating? Liberation, justice, compassion and hope for the oppressed? Or the very ideology of oppression against which we struggle in ourselves and in our society?

My guess is that the answer is not either/or. Surely it is salutary to remember the conversion of a man who is, like the rest of us, committed to liberation and justice, and yet is, like ourselves, at the same time an instrument of oppression, partly through ignorance, partly through weakness, partly through our own most grievous fault. And surely it is no accident that the commemoration of this conversion falls in Epiphany, the time when we remember the visit of the magi to the infant Jesus. For they, too, were well-intentioned blunderers, stumbling into Herod's palace enquiring where Christ should be born, and thereby setting in train the wholesale murder of the innocents. The liturgy and Christian Tradition have largely suppressed the dangerous memory of their bungling, making it seem wonderful that they found and worshipped the Christ child, and shutting our ears to the anguish of Rachel, weeping for her children, refusing all comfort, grieving at their needless slaughter. And yet is it not precisely this that we need to recall: that for all our good intentions, we can generate untold injustice and anguish, not only in our perversity, but even in our efforts to seek the Christ? We struggle for liberation and find ourselves oppressors; we work for peace and encounter our own violence; we are placed in positions of success and authority and find ourselves powerless, entrenched in patterns of injustice.

Yet in Paul's conversion we commemorate one occasion when all this was reversed. What exactly was Paul's conversion? Well, first, it was not a conversion from secularism to God: Paul had been a devout Jewish believer from his youth. Neither was he lax in observance. Nor was his spirituality in doubt: he had a pattern of devotion and prayer that would leave most Christians standing. Nor could Paul's intentions have been questioned: he was a Pharisee of the Pharisees, filled with zeal for truth and for the righteousness of God, and therefore determined to stamp out that which he saw as contrary to true religion. We first make his acquaintance in Scripture as a young man who looked after the coats of those who stoned Stephen, the first Christian martyr; and when we encounter him now, he is 'still breathing threats and murder against the disciples of the Lord,' quite sure that he is doing God a service in his oppression of the persecuted Christians. What happens to him on the Damascus road cuts straight across all that. As the Scriptures record it, 'A light from heaven flashed about him. And he fell to the ground and heard a voice saying to him, "Saul, Saul, why do you persecute me?" And he said, "Who are you, Lord?" And he said, "I am Jesus, whom you are persecuting . . . "'

Here is a total reversal, not of Paul's intentions, or spirituality, or belief in God, which were never in question, but in what he recognises as their practical consequences. Suddenly Paul is confronted with the fact that God is not to be found in the structures which he had been serving, no matter how sincerely pious and righteous they were; but in the persecuted, in the oppressed – and not only abstractly, but in the very people whom *he himself* was persecuting. Paul saw that Jesus, the one who had died in solidarity with the poor and victimised, was the clearest manifestation of the face of God. In Jesus, crucified with thieves, God is to be sought. And Jesus? Where is he to be sought? In the very ones whom Paul was seeking to stamp out. 'I am Jesus, whom you are persecuting'; look into the faces of your victims, and see my face, and see the face of God.

No wonder that Paul became the great apostle of reversals. If it is in the dying Jesus that we have the clearest manifestation of God, then it is in his foolishness that we see the divine wisdom, in his vulnerability that we must understand omnipotence, in his compassion that we must look for divine justice. Every attribute of God must be measured against the arms of the Cross. And every effort at human righteousness must be measured against its solidarity with the Cross, and with all who bear the Crosses of victimisation and oppression and persecution. It is not simply the recognition that Jesus too is a persecuted one; it is the shock of realising that the victims of the persecution *are themselves* the Christ, whom we will encounter in them, or not at all. 'I am Jesus, whom you are persecuting.'

What did this come to, for Paul? Sometimes Paul's conversion, like the experiences of such Christian mystics as Julian of Norwich and Teresa of Avila, is studied simply as a psychological experience, an encounter with God in the privacy of subjective consciousness: questions are then asked about its ineffability, its authenticity, its psychological qualities. But this, I think, is to miss the point completely, in Paul's case as in the others'. Paul's conversion, though profoundly personal, was not private: it was not his private religiosity that had ever been in question, but its political consequences. Accordingly, it is at the reversal of his praxis, his identification with the persecuted rather than his oppression of them, that we must look if we wish to understand his conversion.

Moreover, we miss the point if we suppose that Paul got everything right after this. He *still* sometimes championed the strong against the weak, the master against the slave, the male against the female, rather than championing their liberation and empowerment. Paul was converted, he underwent a profound reversal of his values and praxis, but he did not suddenly become perfect or wholly consistent. He remained, like the rest of us, capable of major blind spots with incalculable consequences for oppression, and in continuous need of the mercy of God.

But the point is that even though he did not always get it right, even though he could still be exasperatingly inconsistent, he *did* encounter Jesus as the persecuted one; he *did* recognise from that point onward, that the face of the persecuted is the face of God, solidarity with the victim must be normative for living before God. And it is *this* that we celebrate.

For Paul, the immediate consequence was that he had to stop what he was doing: he had been making a career out of oppression, and it had to stop. But what then? In the case of Paul, the first thing he did was to go and sit for three days quietly in a house. He didn't have much choice: he had been blinded and devastated by what had happened to him, and he had to take the first steps in assimilating the reversal that he had undergone, and finally submit to healing at the hands of one of the very people whom he had been persecuting, learning from his intended victim how to see again. But again, this is utterly appropriate. If the victim whom he has been persecuting is Jesus, then it is in the victim that Jesus comes to him with healing for his blindness, teaching him how to see. True vision is possible only from the perspective of the persecuted, the oppressed, whose perspective is necessarily the underside of the oppressor's, and reverses it. Paul had to spend a long time assimilating the new point of view, making it his own, and learning to see, to re-vision the world from the perspective of the crucified one; and it was his intended victim who would be his teacher. Only then could he emerge in solidarity with those whom he had once derided, and become identified with them, a champion of justice and liberation.

The celebration of the conversion of Paul must be for us renewed commitment to the same reversals: the reversals of values which identify power, wealth and success with the blessing of God, and which see the victims of the success culture as unenterprising and unworthy of esteem. Where are *we* to find Jesus? Where are *we* to look for the face of God? 'I am Jesus, whom you are persecuting': and it is in the persecuted, the victims, then as now, that we will encounter Christ, or not at all. The point is not that we need to do more praying, or more academic theology, or more churchy things; the point is that we need to start to listen to the voiceless, to recognise how we as privileged members of a success culture collude in societal structures of violence and oppression, to see in the faces of our victims the face of Christ, and to receive from their hands the healing of our blindness.

Like Paul, that may take us a while. And like Paul, we won't always get it right. But like Paul, we could do a lot worse than to spend three days in silence, shutting up, listening to our victims, or to those who are working in solidarity with them, really letting ourselves see what our society looks like from the underside. We might not like it; we might not even agree with them. But we could sit still for a while and just listen. We could sit for three days with the women at Greenham Common watching the movements of the still very active missile base. We could stay for three days at the London Lighthouse, or some other organisation offering active support to people with AIDS. We could spend three days – and three very uncomfortable nights – with the men and women sheltering under Waterloo Bridge; and see what the morning and evening rush hour of wealthy, successful commuters looks like from that perspective. We could spend three days learning from a group working for social justice in this society or in some other: a battered women's shelter, Amnesty, the movement for justice in El Salvador . . . The possibilities are endless. The point is not that we should immediately start rushing round setting the whole world to rights, again from our superior perspective and omnipotence; what we need to do is learn to attend, to listen, to see in the ones we have been victimising the face of Jesus, and to receive from them healing for our blindness and direction for our lives.

I should like to end with a collect for the Conversion of Paul, written by Janet Morley:

O God against whom we struggle,
you speak with the voice of the persecuted
and call the oppressor to turn to you;
confront in us the violence
that we enact or consent to,
that our strength may be made perfect in weakness,
and we may put our trust in you,
through Jesus Christ, Amen.

Leadership and Crisis

Jonathan Sacks

Religious leadership in a secular age is an unenviable responsibility.
Secularisation fragments religious communities. Some conclude that faith
must accommodate itself to the prevailing intellectual climate. Others insist
that the age's ethos must be resisted in the name of faith. A conflict is set
in motion between theological liberals and conservatives. Meanwhile,
religious affiliation declines.
   Under such circumstances it needs unusual courage to keep the
community of faith together while preserving the debate between a
timeless tradition and the time-bound society to which it must be applied.
Robert Runcie, as Archbishop of Canterbury, has consistently
demonstrated that courage. He has done so with grace and humanity,
compasson and resolution. The following sermon is a tribute to the values
by which he has lived and the example he has set.

Then the word of the Lord came to him: 'Why are you here, Elijah?' He
replied, 'I am moved by zeal for the Lord, the God of Hosts, for the
Israelites have forsaken Your covenant, torn down Your altars, and put
Your prophets to the sword. I alone am left, and they are out to take
my life.' The Lord said to him, 'Go out and stand on the mountain in
the presence of the Lord, for the Lord is about to pass by.'
   Then a great and powerful wind tore the mountains apart and shattered the rocks before the Lord. But the Lord was not in the wind. After
the wind was an earthquake, but the Lord was not in the earthquake.
After the earthquake came a fire. But the Lord was not in the fire. And
after the fire – a still, small voice (I Kings 19:9–12).

In the year 1165, an agonising question confronted Moroccan Jewry.
A fanatical Muslim sect, the Almohads, had seized power and were
embarked on a policy of forced conversions to Islam. The Jewish
community was faced with a choice: to affirm Islamic faith or die.
It was not the first nor was it the last such occasion. Throughout
the Middle Ages, periods of relative tolerance alternated with phases
of fierce religious persecution. Under both Christian and Islamic
regimes, Jews had to make the fateful choice: conversion or death.
   Some chose martyrdom. Others chose exile. But some acceded to
terror and embraced another faith. Inwardly, though, they remained
Jews and practised Judaism in secret. They were the *conversos*, or as
the Spanish were later to call them the *marranos*.

To other Jews, they posed a formidable moral problem. How were they to be viewed? Ostensibly, they had betrayed their community and their religious heritage. No less seriously, their example was demoralising. It weakened the resolve of Jews who had been determined to resist, come what may. Yet many of the *conversos* still wished to remain Jewish, secretly fulfil the Commandments and when they could, attend the synagogue and pray.

One of them addressed this question to a rabbi. He had, he wrote, under coercion declared his allegiance to another religion. But he remained at heart a faithful Jew. Could he obtain merit by observing in private as many of the Torah's precepts as possible? Was there, in other words, hope left for him as a Jew?

The rabbi's written reply was unambiguous. A Jew who had embraced Islam had forfeited membership in the Jewish community. He was no longer part of the house of Israel. For such a person to fulfil the Commandments was meaningless. Worse, it was a sin. The choice was stark and absolute: to be or not to be a Jew. If one chose to be a Jew, one must be prepared to suffer death rather than compromise. If one chose not to be a Jew, then one must not seek to re-enter the house one had deserted.

We can understand and even admire the firmness of the rabbi's stance. It is one model of what religious leadership must be. He sets out, without equivocation, the moral choice. He refuses to cloud the issue. There are times when heroism is, for faith, a categorical imperative. Nothing less will do. His reply then, though harsh, is not without courage. But another rabbi disagreed.

The name of the first rabbi is lost to us. But that of the second is not. He was Moses Maimonides, the greatest rabbi of the Middle Ages and one of the most formidable Jewish thinkers of all time. Maimonides was no stranger to religious persecution. Born in Cordova in 1135, he had been forced to leave along with his family, some thirteen years later when the city fell to the Almohads. Twelve years were spent in wandering. In 1160 a temporary liberalisation of Almohad rule allowed the family to settle in Morocco. Within five years he was forced to move again, settling first in the land of Israel and ultimately in Egypt.

Maimonides was incensed by the rabbi's reply to the forced convert and was moved to write a response of his own. In it, he frankly dissociated himself from the earlier ruling and castigated its author whom he described as a 'self-styled sage who has never experienced what so many Jewish communities had to endure in the way of persecution'.

Maimonides' reply, the *Iggeret ha-Shemad* ('Epistle on Forced Conversion') is detailed, a treatise in its own right. What is striking, given the vehemence with which it begins, is that its conclusions are hardly less demanding than those of the earlier response. Those faced with religious persecution must leave and settle elsewhere. 'If he is compelled to violate even one precept it is forbidden to stay there. He must leave everything he has and travel day and night until he finds a spot where he can practise his religion.' This is preferable to martyrdom. None the less, one who chooses to go to his death rather than renounce his faith 'has done what is good and proper' for he has given his life for the sanctity of God. What is unacceptable is to stay and excuse oneself on the grounds that if one sins, one does so only under pressure. To do this is to profane God's name, 'not exactly willingly, but almost so'.

These are Maimonides' conclusions. But surrounding them and constituting the main thrust of his argument is a sustained defence of those who had done precisely what Mamonides had ruled they should not do. Above all, the letter gives *conversos* hope.

They have done wrong. But it is a forgivable wrong. They acted under coercion and the fear of death. They remain Jews. The acts they do as Jews still win favour in the eyes of God. Indeed doubly so. For when they fulfil a Commandment, it cannot be to win favour in the eyes of others. They know that when they act as Jews they risk discovery and death. Their secret adherence has a heroism of its own.

What was wrong in the first rabbi's ruling is his insistence that a Jew who yields to terror has forsaken his faith and is henceforth to be excluded from the community. Maimonides insists that it is not so. 'It is not right to alienate, scorn and hate people who desecrate the Sabbath. It is our duty to befriend them and encourage them to fulfil the commandments'. In a daring stroke of interpretation, he quotes the verse: 'Do not despise a thief if he steals to satisfy his hunger when he is starving' (Prov. 6:30). The *conversos* who come to the synagogue are hungry for Jewish prayer. They 'steal' moments of belonging. They should not be despised, but welcomed.

The Epistle is a masterly example of that most difficult of moral challenges: to combine prescription and compassion. Maimonides leaves us in no doubt as to what he believes Jews should do. But at the same time he is uncompromising in his defence of those who fail to do it. He does not endorse what they have done. But he defends who they are. He asks us to understand their situation. He gives them grounds for self-respect. He holds the doors of the community open.

One could be forgiven for thinking that so complex a moral strategy would read like a study in ambivalence and equivocation. Nothing could be further from the truth. There are few documents in Jewish literature which so blaze with religious passion as Maimonides' *Iggeret ha-Shemad*.

The argument reaches a climax as Maimonides quotes a remarkable sequence of midrashic passages. Midrash was the classic form of early rabbinic interpretation of the Bible. It is characterised by an extreme daring, both exegetical and theological. In this case the common theme of the sources is the idea that a prophet must be a defender of his people before God. God chooses as His prophets those who have the power to transform justice into mercy. To be sure, the voice of Heaven speaks in the language of justice. The people have sinned and must be punished. But at the same time, God sends His prophets to speak in the people's defence. If the prophet adopts the perspective of justice and he too condemns the people, he has betrayed his mission.

So when Moses, charged with leading the people out of Egypt, replied, 'But they will not believe me' (Exod. 4:1), ostensibly he was justified. According to rabbinic tradition, the Israelites in Egypt had sunk into depravity. The biblical narrative itself suggests that Moses' doubts were well founded. Before the exodus and after, the Israelites were a difficult people to lead. But the midrash insists that God replied to Moses, 'They are believers and the children of believers, but you [Moses] will ultimately not believe'.

So too Isaiah was justified when he called Israel a 'sinful nation, a people laden with iniquity' (Isa. 1:4). But the rabbis interpreted the later episode in which an angel touches Isaiah's lips with a burning coal (Isa. 6:5–7) as a punishment for the prophet's slander of his people.

Maimonides cites a series of such passages and then rises to a crescendo: If this is the sort of punishment meted out to the pillars of the universe, the greatest of the prophets, because they briefly criticised the people – even though they were guilty of the sins of which they were accused – can we envisage the punishment awaiting those who criticise the *conversos*, who under threat of death and without abandoning their faith, confessed to another religion in which they did not believe?

There is nothing equivocal about Maimonides' defence of those who yielded to pressure. Nor is there any ambivalence about his latter analysis of what, in fact, is the right way to behave. He invests both with equal seriousness. There *is* a moral dilemma. There *is* a correct response. But the terms of the dilemma are such that those who choose another response are to have their integrity respected without, at the same time, having their decision endorsed.

In the course of his analysis, Maimonides turns to the biblical hero, Elijah. Elijah, we recall, risks his life in being a prophet. Under the reign of Ahab and Jezebel, Baal worship has become the official cult. God's prophets are being killed. Those that survive are in hiding. Elijah none the less risks a direct confrontation with the king which results in the great public challenge at Mount Carmel. He faces 400 of Baal's representatives. Elijah is determined to settle the question of religious truth once and for all. He addresses the assembled people and tells them to choose one way or another: for God or for Baal. They must no longer 'halt between two opinions'. Truth is about to be decided by a test. If it lies with Baal, fire will consume the offering prepared by his priests. If it lies with God, fire will descend to Elijah's offering.

Elijah wins the confrontation. The people cry out, 'The Lord, He is God'. The priests of Baal are routed. But the story does not end there. Jezebel sends a message to him: a warrant is out for his death. Elijah escapes to Mount Horeb. And there he receives a strange vision. He witnesses a whirlwind that shatters rocks; then an earthquake; then a fire. But the vision leads him to understand that God is not in these things. Then God speaks to him in a 'still, small voice', and tells him to appoint Elisha as his successor.

The episode is enigmatic. It is made all the more so by a strange feature of the text. Immediately *before* the vision, God asks, 'What are you doing here, Elijah?' and Elijah replies, 'I am moved by zeal for the Lord, the God of Hosts . . . ' (I Kgs. 19:9–10). Immediately *after* the vision, God asks the same question, and Elijah gives the same answer (I Kgs. 19:13–14).

The midrash turns the text into a dialogue:

Elijah: 'The Israelites have broken God's covenant.'
God: 'Is it then *your* covenant?'
Elijah: 'They have torn down Your altars.'
God: 'But were they *your* altars?'
Elijah: 'They have put Your prophets to the sword.'
God: 'But you are alive.'
Elijah: 'I alone am left.'

To which God replies that instead of hurling accusations against Israel he should have pleaded their cause. The meaning of the midrash is clear. The zealot takes the part of God. But God expects something else from His prophets. They must pray on behalf of humanity.

The repeated question and answer is now to be understood in its tragic depth. Elijah declares himself to be zealous for God. He is shown that God is not disclosed in dramatic confrontation: not in the whirlwind or the earthquake or the fire. God now asks him again, 'What are you doing here Elijah?' Elijah *repeats* that he is zealous for God. He has not understood that religious leadership calls for another kind of virtue, the still, small voice. God now indicates that someone else must lead. Elijah must hand his mantle on to Elisha.

Once again we are struck by the moral complexity set forth by the midrash. It is clear that God was with Elijah in the confrontation on Mount Carmel. He sends His fire. He vindicates His prophet. Elijah is one of the Bible's religious heroes. He is not content to hide and save his life while Israel lapses into idolatry. Yet the midrash insists – and in so doing is faithful to the intimations of the text itself – that religious leadership is not so simply reducible to the either/or of good and evil. To be sure, the Israelites have been unfaithful.

They have 'halted between two opinions'. But if they served idols, they did so at the bidding of their king and under fear of death. If Elijah believes he is the only person of faith left alive, he is wrong.

We are far from the days of Maimonides, further still from those of Elijah. But their conflicts are ours. They repeat themselves whenever religious leadership must be exercised at a time when faith is under threat. There is no simple equation of idolatry in the days of Ahab, forced conversion in twelfth century Spain, and secularisation today. But in each case, a religious tradition is overwhelmed by forces antithetical to it, and faith is forced into heroic postures.

At such times, there is an almost overwhelming temptation to see religious leadership as confrontational. Not only must truth be proclaimed. Falsehood must be denounced. Choices must be set out as stark divisions. Not to condemn is to condone. The rabbi who condemned the *conversos* had faith in his heart, logic on his side and Elijah as his precedent.

But the midrash and Maimonides set before us another model. A prophet hears not one imperative but two: prescription and compassion, a love of truth and an abiding solidarity with those for whom that truth has become eclipsed. To preserve tradition and at the same time the unity of those addressed by that tradition is the difficult, necessary task of religious leadership in an unreligious age.

A Moonie Challenge to the Churches

Eileen Barker

Dr Runcie is one of those who accepts challenges rather than dismissing them or denying their existence. He believes in trying to find out the truth and facing up to its implications. He believes in respecting individuals' rights to their own beliefs, while being well aware that some actions that follow from some beliefs may be unacceptable. For these reasons, he was an obvious person to turn to when, a few months after I had delivered this sermon, in January 1987 at Great St Mary's, Cambridge, I was considering founding an organisation that would try to help people by providing information about new religious movements that was as objective, up-to-date and relevant to their concerns as possible. Dr Runcie's enthusiasm convinced me that we should go ahead. He became the first Patron of INFORM (the Information Network Focus on Religious Movements) and has given it his unstinting support, taking up the challenge of the movements in his own intellectually honest yet deeply pastoral way.

> If any man come unto me, and hate not his father, and mother, and wife, and children, and brethren and sisters, yea, and his own life also, he cannot be my disciple (Luke 14:26)

A jealous Christ; a demanding Christ; an uncomfortable Christ – but a *challenging* Christ.

Sun Myung Moon was born in Korea in 1920 to a family which converted to Presbyterianism when he was ten years old. He claims that in 1936 Jesus appeared to him and told him that God had chosen him (Moon) to perform a special mission. For the next few years, we are told, Moon prayed hard and, with the help of discussions with God and various religious leaders in the spirit world (such as Buddha, Mohammed and Jesus), he arrived at a special interpretation of the Old and New Testaments. The outline of this interpretation, along with some further revelations, is now to be found in the Unification 'Bible', the *Divine Principle*.

Despite considerable opposition, Moon built up a small band of followers. The Holy Spirit Association for the Unification of World Christianity was founded in 1954. In the early 1970s, Moon moved to the United States and his followers, popularly known as Moonies, became visible throughout the West as clean-cut young men and

women selling candy, candles, roses, literature – and their beliefs –
in shopping precincts and other public places.

By the mid-1970s, organised opposition to the movement had
grown and Unificationists were regarded with suspicion and distrust. Questions were asked about activities arising from their
vehemently anti-communist stance, and about their ever-expanding
financial empire. In 1984, Moon was sentenced to eighteen months
imprisonment for tax-evasion. And like most new religions, the
Unification Church was accused of brainwashing its converts into
accepting a bizarre new heresy.

The *Divine Principle* offers what is arguably the most comprehensive theological position to be found among the new religious movements that have emerged during the latter half of this century. It
contains a cosmology, theodicy, eschatology, soteriology, Christology and its own interpretation of history.

According to the *Divine Principle*, God created Adam and Eve so
that they might partake in a loving 'give-and-take' relationship with
Him. Unfortunately, the Archangel Lucifer, being jealous of God's
love for Adam, and forming a rather stronger attachment to Eve
than he should have done, initiated a (spiritual) sexual relationship
with her. Eve then had a physical sexual relationship with Adam
before they were ready to be Blessed by God in marriage. Consequently, their union was not God-centred, but Lucifer-centred, and
their children (and their children's children) inherited 'fallen nature',
the Unification equivalent of original sin. The Fall is thus interpreted
as being the result not only of disobedience, but also of the misuse
of the most powerful of all forces: love.

The *Divine Principle* interprets history as God's and man's struggle
to restore the world to the state that God originally intended. Various methods are employed in the restoration process, but one crucial
factor is the coming of a Messiah who will assume the position of
Adam, establish the God-centred family and have children born
without fallen nature. Although sinless this Messiah is born of
human parents and, if people do not follow him, his mission can
fail.

With the help of several Old Testament figures, God prepared for
the advent of such a man: Jesus. However, once again, things failed
to go according to plan. Largely through the fault of John the Baptist,
Jesus was killed before he could get married and accomplish his
mission. He was able to offer the world spirtual salvation, but physical salvation was not yet possible.

The *Divine Principle* claims that history and the Bible point to the
Lord of the Second Advent being born between 1917 and 1930 in
South Korea. Although each individual is invited to make up his or
her own mind on the matter, Moon's speeches to his followers make
it clear that he is the Messiah, and practically every Unificationist
accepts him as such.

In 1960, Moon married his present wife, thus, it is believed, laying the foundation for the physical restoration of the world. Since then he has conducted several mass Blessings (marriage ceremonies) when literally thousands of couples are married to partners whom he has chosen for them – sometimes only a few hours beforehand. Children born to Blessed couples are believed to have original (not fallen) nature.

Conversion to the *Divine Principle* demands commitment to the Unification movement: if one believes the Messiah is here, one has a duty to meet the challenge and *do* something – even (especially) if sacrifices have to be made.

And rank and file Unificationists do tend to lead a pretty austere life. The movement is organised as an authoritarian hierarchy with Moon at its apex. Unmarried (and some married) members sleep in single-sex dormitories; food is perfectly adequate, but hardly luxurious; alcohol is frowned upon; drugs and tobacco are forbidden – as are sexual relationships outside marriage, and for some time after marriage.

Members frequently rise before dawn and continue working for around sixteen hours a day. They are taught that three-year periods of 'fundraising' (getting money) and 'witnessing' (getting new members) play an integral role in their spiritual development – as well as contributing to the establishment of the Kingdom of Heaven on earth.

How could anyone agree to lead such a life? How could people in their right minds accept the *Divine Principle*? How could they work for little more than subsistence for a Korean millionaire and allow him to choose them a marriage partner who might not even share a common language? Can the key be found in the *Daily Mail*'s successful defence of a libel action after it had accused the movement of brainwashing under the heading: *The Church that Breaks up Families*? I think not.

My study of the movement led me to conclude that if Moonies *do* use brainwashing techniques, these are extraordinarily ineffective. Over 90 per cent of those who attend the notorious residential workshops (which are said to be irresistible) have been perfectly capable of walking away unscathed. Of those who do join, the majority leave of their own free will within a couple of years.

It is true that membership of the movement has on occasion, led to the tragic break-up of previously happy families. Some members use the movement as a means of escaping from 'difficult' or over-protective parents, but many more have become so absorbed in their urgent task of kingdom-building that they have little time to spare for erstwhile interests or commitments.

Moon does not tell his followers that they have to hate their mother and father if they want to follow him, but he does challenge them to get their priorities right. Making excuses because one has 'bought a piece of ground, or five yoke of oxen, or married a wife' – or, to update the story by 2,000 years, because one has exams to sit, a sister's wedding, or an ailing mother – may be interpreted as not getting one's priorities straight.

If not obviously brainwashed, why are people willing to accept such commitment? They are not pathetic, uneducated or drop-outs. Membership of the Unification Church is drawn disproportionately from the middle classes. No one joins under the age of eighteen without parental permisson; the average age of joining is twenty-three. Members are of above average intelligence, have received well above average education and usually come from what would, by most criteria, be termed a 'good home' in which religion and the ideals of duty and responsibility have played important roles.

Almost all of those who joined in Britain had believed in God at the time of joining; indeed, *not* having a belief in God was one of the most reliable predictors that a person would *not* join – having a very strong commitment to a particular faith was another one, although this was not as reliable as atheism or agnosticism.

Despite (perhaps because of) the fact that most Unficationists had attended a place of worship more frequently than their peers, many had become disappointed and disillusioned with what they saw as the apathy and hypocrisy of the mainstream Churches. Generally speaking, the Roman Catholic Church elicited the most accusations of hypocrisy; the Nonconformist Churches were the recipients of slightly milder expressions of ambivalence or rejection; the Church of England was most likely to be viewed with contemptuous indifference.

Many young people seem to find difficulty in talking to *anyone* about religious matters. The once taboo subject of sex is an easier and safer topic to risk discussing in contemporary Britain. One is more likely to tell one's fellow students whom it was that one slept with last night than to confess to having had a vision of the Virgin Mary while saying one's prayers.

Even theology students have admitted to me that they wouldn't dare mention their religious experiences to their mentors for fear that they might be labelled excessively evangelical, or over-imaginative. Yet a surprisingly large proportion of the population has had something that they think of as a religious experience – and which they have hesitated to tell anyone about.

The potential Moonie is no exception. Many claim to have been unsuccessful in attempts to have a serious discussion with clergy about religious questions. I felt a certain sympathy with some of their complaints when, on the occasion of her confirmation, I asked my god-daughter's vicar what provision was made for the youth of his parish after they had been confirmed. He looked utterly blank. Then his face brightened as he remembered: 'There's ping-pong on Tuesday evenings.'

Although it is true that many young people are put off religion by the apparently remote intellectualising of theologically inclined clergy or the boredom of 'sweet-old-ladies-in-the-pews' congregations, it is also true that many have felt that the trendy, beer-drinking cleric, discussing 'Top of the Pops' in his leather jacket, doesn't help much either.

The Unification Church has offered a number of opportunities that its members claimed they had found lacking in the churches they had explored in their religious quests.

Spiritually, Unificationists claim that they felt they had 'come home' when they first met the movement. They found themselves in a context in which not only could they talk about their religious experiences and aspirations, they were expected to do so at breakfast, while fund-raising, while washing dishes – whenever; throughout the day they were expected to pray, to communicate with God and to surrender to His wishes.

Socially, within the movement they felt they had found a loving caring fellowship – a community with decent standards in which enthusiasm, rather than apathy, abounded.

Politically, Unificationists tend to have been idealistic young people who were disturbed about the state of the world; they had wanted to *do* something to make the world a better place, but had not known *what* to do or *how* to do it. They didn't feel that the mainstream Churches were showing the way forward, even if their leaders were not as corrupt as the politicians for whom most of them displayed considerable contempt. As Unificationists they believed their lives were given meaning and direction; they had accepted the challenge to sweat their guts out for something really important.

Intellectually, many of them found that the *Divine Principle* answered questions that had puzzled them. Why, for example, was the world still in such a state if Jesus had come to save it?

Of course, there are some Churches in which young people are offered the religious expression, enthusiasm and certainties that the Unification Church offers. And, of course, one can argue that Unificationists are looking for answers that are too simple, and that the movement is unlikely to fulfil the promise that it offers.

And, of course, as I have already indicated, the membership of the Unification Church is tiny – no more than a few hundred in the UK. Fewer than 4 per cent of those who *leave* the mainstream Churches become fully committed members of *any* new religious movement. But many of the complaints that Unificationists make about the Churches are echoed by others who are not prepared to go quite so far as Unificationists in their search for *both* helping to improve the world *and* leading a religiously inspired life.

It is not inconceivable that, by looking at what the Unification Church offers and what at least some people find attractive for at least some part of their lives, the Churches could become more sensitive, not merely to the needs of those who have never crossed their portals, but to those of people who have been brought up within them.

It is not inconceivable that the Churches could become more sensitive, not merely to the questions of those who do not care about God, but to those of people who are desperately seeking for ways in which to find Him.

It is not inconceivable that the Churches could become more sensitive, not merely in order to satisfy the whims of those who are interested only in themselves, but also to find employment for people who are prepared (desperately want) to sacrifice a great deal in order to try to make the world a better place.

That there are well-educated young people of above average intelligence who are looking for *religious* guidance and who want to improve the world is a fact that goes far beyond the phenomenon of the Unification Church. If the Churches consider that Moonies are mistaken in their enthusiasms, if they believe that there are truer answers, more desirable goals, more effective means of getting closer to a Kingdom of Heaven on earth, then perhaps they should try to make the alternatives clearer.

In this sense, the Moonies present a challenge to the Churches. And it is, very largely, a challenge to the Churches to challenge them.

The Whole Armour of God

Hugh Montefiore

I have chosen this sermon because of Dr Runcie's famous address at the Falkland Islands Thanksgiving Service at St Paul's Cathedral which aroused fury among Jingoists, but for which many others were devoutly grateful – and I use the word devout intentionally. The occasion of my address was very different – a service for the North East Area of the Burma Star Association at Sheffield Cathedral on 31 August 1990 at which, over forty years after the Second World War, hundreds of veterans still turn up. The points of connection will be apparent. These occasions are played down by some purists as mere concessions to folk religion. They are important, however, because they express a form of popular but genuine Christianity, and they help people who are distanced but not alienated from the Church to articulate their feelings of dependence on God, and their attitudes towards their fellow men; and they are a way in which such people can express their Christian faith.

> Wherefore take unto you the whole armour of God, that ye may be able to withstand in the evil day (Eph. 6:13)

I wonder whether that list of army equipment which St Paul mentions in his epistle rang any bells with you. I suppose the 'sword of the Spirit' might have brought back memories of your *dah*, and the 'helmet of salvation' might have made you think back nearly fifty years to the days when you wore a tin hat, or more likely your bush hat. 'Your loins were girt about' not, alas, with truth, but with that ghastly green webbing and your feet were shod not 'with the preparation of the Gospel of peace', but in heavy black Army boots. We had nothing for a breastplate except a khaki shirt, and nothing for a shield except the good earth in a slit trench. And it was an evil day, with humid heat and monsoon, with jungle sores and malaria and an absolutely impossible terrain. But all the same, those of us who are here not only survived, but withstood and won.

I am sure that you will agree with me that, after giving thanks to God, our first duty at this service is to honour the dead. Most of us here today must have come close to death out there: but some were taken and we were not. It was not that we were better, or even that we were worse than they were: *their* number was on the bullet or the shell, and *ours* was not. We who were left behind will ask ourselves what we have been doing during those fifty years to show our gratitude to God; but despite such introspection, let us first honour the dead.

This came home to me personally with redoubled force a few months ago when I went into a house which I had not entered since I was thirteen years old, and that's quite a few years ago. The first thing I saw inside the porch was a photograph of Colin, an old friend with whom I had been at school, who had been a fellow Gunner officer in my regiment, killed by a sniper as we made our way from Kohima to Mandalay. He had been the hope of his family, with a brilliant record, but his life was cut short, and his body lies now with all those thousands at Kohima Cemetery, and his brother and his sister still grieve over him. I'm sure that all of us could tell a similar tale.

We remember too the fellowship which we had together in those difficult days. How could we know if we would ever again set eyes upon our loved ones? How could we be sure that we would even win the war? What we did know was that we relied on one another totally for our very lives, and in that atmosphere friendships were fashioned and a totally different attitude prevailed from those that characterise our nation in these present days of affluence and ease. There was a spirit which bound us all together – we might almost say 'Holy Spirit'. Most of us at that time I suppose would hardly have described ourselves as religious people – that was certainly the case with me, although the experience convinced me that after the war I must be ordained if ever I survived. Outwardly irreligious as we might have seemed, I do believe that when a man is deprived of the usual props of family and the distractions of civilian life, his life in the armed forces can bring him face to face with the living God as few other professions can. That is why military men are almost always basically religious people.

The reading from St Paul which we heard reminds us that our spiritual fight is not against flesh and blood, but against cosmic powers, against the authorities and potentates of this dark world, against the superhuman forces of evil in the heavens. How are we to put that into modern language today in a way which makes sense in today's world? In an obvious sense we were fighting against Japanese soldiers and very brave enemies they were, many of them family men simply doing their duty with great courage: that came home to me when we overran a Japanese field post office in the jungle, and there was all their mail with snapshots of their wives and little ones. Yes, we were fighting them, but our real enemies were not they, but those great structures of evil, Japanese traditions of militarist expansion, Japanese imperialism, Japanese blind obedience. I do think that these were evil, and we knew it, and that was why we fought with a will, and won. We may perhaps contrast our war with a later Far Eastern war, in Vietnam, where American troops could not find that same sense of purpose, because their motivation was so very different.

Nearly fifty years later, what we do really feel about our enemies, the Japanese we fought against? Surely we ought to forgive them as much as we need forgiveness ourselves. But alas our feelings are not always at our own command: at least to my shame that is what I found myself. And so I hope you will let me share with you an experience I had last year. I was invited out on a lecture tour for five weeks by the Anglican Church in Japan – a small body, indeed only 1 per cent of that country is Christian and the Anglicans form one of the smaller churches. I thought that I must go, because I knew in my heart that I must make friends with those who were our enemies, and I could only do that if I went and lived among them. In Japan I came to realise how successful they are as a people: they had lost the war, they are still aware of that; yet there is almost a sense in which they have won the peace.

I had some moving experiences. I met a Japanese Anglican priest, now retired, who had been in Akyab in their Education Corps while we in 6 Brigade were preparing for a combined ops landing which mercifully never came off – mercifully, because after the war we discovered the strength of their underwater defences. We had a splendid Christian reunion; I a retired English bishop and he a retired Japanese priest. I felt this was real reconciliation, and it was the same in Hiroshima, when I had dinner with the Anglican parish, and there were thirteen people present who had actually been in the city when the atom bomb was dropped. I remember saying afterwards to a Japanese Anglican university Chaplain in Tokyo how ashamed we were in Britain about that bomb; and he astonished me by replying that he regarded it as a blessing, because unless it had been dropped in their midst the Japanese militarists would never have surrendered and the slaughter from a military invasion would have been far worse than it was. Whether you agree with him or not, you can hardly deny his generosity in saying it. Hiroshima is now a thriving city, and apart from the museum of horrors it is hard to believe what happened there; a kind of resurrection from the dead.

I have one more story. In Tokyo at Rikkyo University I met Professor Ogawa, now in his eighties. As a Japanese lieutenant in Singapore, he had made no secret of his Christian faith, and during the Japanese occupation, he had even joined the Cathedral congregation, driving there in his staff car; and he set the tone of compassion and thoughtfulness for those in Chang prison, until he was removed, when it completely changed. He told me that after the Japanese surrender Mountbatten had him sent to Sumatra, because his life would not have been safe at that time among his fellow officers. It was good to meet a contemporary Japanese saint.

What I am trying to say by these stories is that I do believe that the demons of Japanese militarism, Japanese imperialism and Japanese blind obedience have been exorcised; and that would not have happened without all that the British forces did in the Far East, together with our allies. We can thank God that, nearly fifty years ago, we did achieve what we set out to do by exorcising those demons. I do not mean that we can glorify our fighting, however tough it was – none of us wants to do that, and fighting always signifies an earlier human failure – but that, if we had to fight, we did achieve what we had to do. I do not mean either that each of us can be proud of our own individual performance – we know ourselves too well for that – but we can thank God with a full heart that those war aims were achieved.

According to the media, we are still the Forgotten Army: 12 August is thought of as the start of grouse shooting, not VJ day. To the young people of today it must seem strange that so many hundreds of us have converged on Sheffield to hold a religious service in memory of something that happened over forty years ago. Perhaps it is odd and yet we come here to worship for the best of reasons and with heart-felt feelings.

Finally, let me remind you of my text. 'Wherefore take unto you the whole armour of God, that ye may be able to withstand in the evil day.' I need not remind you that the spiritual fight is not yet over, and it will not be over so long as we are alive on earth. There are many people in our society who still suffer evil days. Think of our ideals for this country at the end of the war; and think where we are today. There are still wrongs to be put right, still evil structures to be cast down. We are not too old to have a go! We cannot fight them in our own strength: we need the whole armour of God; truth, integrity, peace, faith, salvation. These are lovely and beautiful words which St Paul used; and they stand for even lovelier realities. They are words for each one of us to make realities in our own lives; truth, integrity, peace, faith and salvation. They come to us through Christ from God.

Out of Tragedy

John Lawrence

*I share with Robert Runcie a love and veneration for the Eastern Orthodox
Church. I preached this sermon at Evensong on a day in spring 1989.
It was a very sad occasion in the life of that wonderful school, Christ's
Hospital at Horsham in Sussex. A much loved and respected boy had
unexpectedly committed suicide two days before. At the memorial service
the day before I arrived unsuspecting this tragedy, many boys and girls,
who had shown little interest in religion before, had come and very many
had made their communion. Many had come to Christ as a direct
consequence of this tragedy.*

The fierceness of man shall turn to thy praise (Psalm 76:10)

God can bring good out of a great tragedy. Some of you know that.
This evening I want to tell you something about the Church in
Russia, which has been through seventy years of such persecution
as has never been heard of in Christian history and has emerged
stronger than she was before. Russia has been a Christian country
for a thousand years, as we have recently been reminded, but much
of its religion was a mere conformity for the sake of appearance.
When Lenin and his Bolsheviks seized power in 1917 they launched
a most savage attack on all forms of religion.

Most of the Church leaders were shot or sent to a living death
in the Gulag Archipelago. Churches and monasteries were closed
forcibly and theological education was forbidden. Lenin personally
led this persecution. The mere fact of belief in God was sufficient to
draw down the wrath of the secret police. Icons were systematically
confiscated. But people did not cease to believe just because
churches were closed and they had no Icons. The persecution
increased in intensity for twenty years.

In Odessa, at a time when there were just a few churches open,
the people used to gather for worship at the usual time. Then a man
would step forward and be clothed in the robes of a priest. He
would then conduct the service which in the Orthodox Church takes
two or three hours. When it was over the KGB, which had its spies
everywhere, arrested the priest. No doubt he was tortured in order
to make him reveal what other priests might be in hiding. After that

he was shot or sent to the Gulag. This went on for a few months until there were no priests left.

On the eve of the Second World War there were only about two or three hundred churches open in the whole vast extent of the Soviet Union. Then came the first turning point. I was an eyewitness of this because I was Press Attaché at the British Embassy from 1942.

At this time Stalin needed the Church, without it he would have lost the war. It was a necessary element of national unity. So he allowed a certain number of churches to open and he allowed the Orthodox Church to elect a new Patriarch. Most of the Bishops were in concentration camps but enough were released to form a quorum. As an official at the British Embassy it fell to me to take a message from the Archbishop of Canterbury to the acting Patriarch. This was absolutely the first contact from the outside that anyone had had with the Moscow Patriarch. He lived in a log cabin on the outskirts of Moscow. He had a chaplain, and two nuns were in attendance. There was nowhere for him to keep any papers. He must have been cut off almost completely from his dioceses except those near Moscow.

The communists supposed that religion was an outdated way of thinking. It was even prophesied that the last believers would be gone by 1980 and communism would be seen as the wave of the future. So religion was still persecuted after the war but not so savagely.

Yet the Church continued to make progress, particularly among the young who had grown up under communism. Since the Second World War the Church has grown steadily with ever accelerating tempo. In 1985 with the coming of Gorbachev she was increasingly free to speak her true mind. There are still prisoners of conscience in the Soviet Union and local party bosses still make it difficult to get a church opened. At this moment there are about 2,000 congregations that have nowhere to worship. But there are already enough Christians to leaven the whole lump. Once again the blood of the martyr has been the seed of the Church.

Can Jesus Draw Us Together?

Marcus Braybrooke

As Joint President of the Council of Christians and Jews, Dr Robert Runcie made an important contribution to Christian-Jewish relations in Britain. With his agreement, the Joint Presidents, who include the Chief Rabbi, Cardinal Hume, and the Moderators of the Church of Scotland and of the Free Churches, started holding an annual private meeting to discuss the concerns of the Council and to give their advice. In an imaginative move, he awarded an honorary Lambeth degree to the Chief Rabbi. He gave an important talk at a CCJ AGM on our shared responsibility to treasure God's creation. In his moving address at the Kristallnacht Memorial meeting, he admitted that the poisoning of Christian minds by centuries of anti-Jewish teaching had prepared the way for the horrors of the Holocaust. During his time at Lambeth, the Second Official Anglican-Jewish consultation was held and also the Lambeth Conference agreed the important statement on 'The Way of Dialogue'. His concern for good Christian-Jewish relations was echoed by his concern for dialogue with people of all faiths. The Lambeth Interfaith Lecture has continued to attract distinguished speakers. Dr Runcie attended the World Day of Prayer for Peace at Assisi, spoke at the first Global Conference on Human Survival at Oxford in 1988 and, to mark the Fiftieth Anniversary of the World Congress of Faiths, he gave the 1986 Sir Francis Yonghusband Memorial Lecture, which has been described as a 'landmark interfaith statement'. 'We need', he said, 'courage to acknowledge religious diversity as a rich spiritual resource, rather than a cause for competition and tension . . . Our world is in desperate need of a new and larger vision of unity which transcends our differences . . . a new way of life, where we no longer see each other as competitors but as partners and fellow pilgrims called to bear witness to the same spirit among all people.'

This sermon was given at Great St Mary's, Cambridge, in May 1988.

'How is it', a Rabbi friend said to me, 'that God can make His presence known in both church and synagogue?' We were both convinced that He did this, that in both synagogue and church, God meets his people. 'It is a problem', the Rabbi continued, 'for both our theologies – although perhaps not a problem for God.'

In the same way, some Christian and Jewish thinkers are struggling with the question, 'How are both the Christian "yes" to Jesus and the Jewish "no", both within the purposes of God?' Only when we can answer this will we have finally lanced the poison that through the centuries has embittered Jewish-Christian relations. A German theologian has said, 'We will only have Christian anti-Judaism behind us when theologically we will have succeeded in making positive sense of the Jewish "no" to Jesus.' This is because so often when Christians have exalted Jesus, they have done so by negative and unfair contrasts with Judas. Indeed, an American Roman Catholic, Rosemary Ruether, has spoken of anti-Judaism as the left hand of Christology. We are sadly and penitently conscious of how Christian anti-Jewish teaching has contributed to the sufferings of the Jewish people through the centuries. Often, on the continent, on Good Friday, Jews would lock themselves in their houses 'for fear of the Christians'.

For centuries, Christians have stressed their belief in Jesus the Christ by contrasting him with unfair and unflattering pictures of Judaism. The Old Testament God has been pictured as a severe judge, as if He were different from the God and Father of Our Lord Jesus. There is One God of mercy and justice who reveals Himself through the whole Bible. The Psalms speak again and again of God's loving kindness. We have blamed the Jews for rejecting their Messiah when he came, we have blamed them for his death and we have spoken of them as 'children of the devil' – depriving them of civil liberties and, in the crusades and pogroms, depriving them of life itself. Martin Gilbert in his massive study of the Holocaust begins his book with these words: 'For many centuries, primitive Christian Europe regarded the Jew as the "Christ killer", an enemy and a threat, to be expelled or to be put to death with sword and fire.'

It is clear that this Christian persecution and the centuries of anti-Jewish teaching prepared the ground for the Nazi movement, although that attacked Christians as well as Jews. Some 11 million people were murdered, of whom more than 6 million were Jews – and a million of those were children. I can never forget a picture at Yad Vashem, the memorial in Jerusalem to the victims of the Holocaust, of a mother chevying along her two small children, as if to school, but in reality to the gas chambers. The terrible sufferings of the Jews in the Shoah, or Holocaust, have gradually awoken Christians to the hideous consequences of the way we have contrasted Christianity to Judaism and are a warning of the dangers of bad theology. It is to be hoped that the Lambeth Conference issues a strong statement on this.

Even now, when the Churches have made clear that it is wrong to blame the Jews for the death of Jesus, Christians exalt Jesus by belittling Judaism. This is most obvious in the contrast often made between Law and Gospel and the accusation that the Pharisees were only interested in trying to earn God's favour. Central to the Old Testament is the Covenant when God in his mercy rescued the Israelites from slavery in Egypt and in the Torah (or Way of Life) showed them how to live. Read Psalm 119, and you will see the Torah was a delight and joy, not a burden.

Some time before Jesus, the Pharisees wanted to encourage the whole people to be holy and to follow God's teaching. They therefore tried to apply the Torah to everyday life. The Pharisees were the spiritual forebears of the rabbis of today. They were the spiritual leaders of their time and it seems clear that Jesus was close to them. His linking of the commands to love God and to love our neighbour – both commands taken from the Old Testament – has parallels in Jewish teaching. The Pharisees in their attitude to the Sabbath also gave priority to saving life over all other Commandments. The arguments reported in the Gospels probably reflect the bitter polemic of a later generation. When some thirty-five years after the crucifixion, Jerusalem was destroyed by the Romans, there was bitter hostility between Jews who believed in Jesus and those who did not. About this time believers were put out of the synagogues and Christians responded wth angry comments on the Jews – and these arguments colour the Gospel records. And we have seen recently there can be bitter polemic within the Church of England! It was after the fall of Jerusalem that the parting of the ways occurred but, we must remember, that Living Judaism grows out of the same roots as Christianity.

Where many of his contemporaries disagreed with Jesus seems to have been over his belief that the long-awaited new age was dawning. It was not that he rejected Judaism. He was a faithful Son of the Covenant. According to Jewish expectation, the new age would be marked by a new temple, by the restoration of the Twelve Tribes of Israel, by the rescue of sinners and outcasts and by the gathering in of the Gentiles. Jesus proclaimed the 'kingdom is at hand'. He spoke of a new temple not made with hands, he chose twelve disciples and he sought for the 'publicans and sinners', the lost children of the house of Israel. It is significant that Paul's conversion was also a commission to preach to the Gentiles.

The new age was not a rejection of the past, nor a condemnation of Judaism, nor an abandonment of the Covenant. Rather it opened the mercy of God to all people.

There are today those who speak about a 'new age' – I am sure there are quite a lot of 'new age' groups in Cambridge. Are we at the edge of a new stage in the development of human potential and spiritual consciousness? We don't know and good people can disagree.

To many Jews the world is not redeemed: the wars, the violence, the hunger, the torture, the homelessness seem to confirm their view. With the coming of the Messiah all these evils will be done away. Jesus does not meet the Jewish expectation of the Messiah. The Christian believes that the inner change effected by Jesus will eventually result in worldwide change. Yet the Jewish 'no' is a warning to us not to spiritualise redemption and to forget about the need to change this world. I was disturbed recently when I asked a confirmation class what was their picture of the kingdom of God. They all spoke about angels and flowing white robes and thought of the kingdom only in terms of heaven and not of a changed world. Indeed they had little hope that the world could be changed for the better. In the Jewish 'no', we see a warning not so to spiritualise salvation that we forget about the redemption of society. There is warning also not to equate the Church with the kingdom of God, but to remember that it exists to make known God's love for the whole world.

Christians believe that, in Jesus, God acted in a new way to extend the knowledge of His saving love, but it was the same God of mercy and justice who acted. The New Covenant does not set aside the Old, but makes us also heirs to God's promises. Through the centuries our two communities of faith have developed their own values, their own response to God – often in rivalry – but now we see how greatly we can enrich each other by sharing these treasures.

And just as it was hard for many Jews to recognise God's mercy to the Gentiles, so many Christians today find it hard to welcome evidence of God's saving activity in other world religions. How easily we try to keep God's promises to ourselves. Some Jews felt that Paul's preaching to the Gentiles threatened their claim to election, while Christians responded by denying that Jews were still God's people; just as some Christians today feel that to recognise God's grace in the life of a Hindu or Muslim is to cheapen the value of Christian faith. Surely rather, we see that God, whose love we know in Christ extends to all His children, as the Hebrew prophets taught long ago.

A Muslim scholar suggested that the existence of more than one religion is to stop the idolatry to which all religions are prone. We are tempted to claim a monopoly for our picture of God – although God is always more wonderful. Some Muslim extremists, it has been said, are tempted to replace the cry 'God is most great' with the slogan 'Islam is most great', and some Christians have used their faith as a cloak for imperialism and racism.

We cannot fully know the mind of God, but we can at least try to ensure that our theologies do not perpetuate division; rather that they seek to encompass the reality of God's presence in other communities of faith, not least his continuing presence with the children of Israel. We begin to see too that Jesus, the faithful Son of the Covenant is he who makes known to us the faithfulness of the One God of our fathers, Abraham, Isaac and Jacob – the God whom we adore as Father, Son and Holy Spirit.

In the words of a prayer from the new Good Friday liturgy, we pray:

Lord God of Abraham,
   bless the children of your covenant, both Jew and Christian, take from
   us all blindness and bitterness of heart and hasten the coming of your
   kingdom, when Israel shall be saved, the Gentiles gathered in, and
   we shall dwell together in mutual love and peace under the one God
   and Father of our Lord Jesus Christ.

Religious Education

Mary Warnock

The Archbishop of Canterbury has, in all his actions and words, shown a profound interest in linking Christian doctrine to what people think and do and what they need in a contemporary, largely non-Christian world. It is plain that the question how to educate children, how to fill the still-compulsory RE slot in the National Curriculum is central to the concern with the lives of everyone, not just practising Christians. Christianity has, in my view, a central truth which should be presented to all children. Dr Runcie has always been determined to find ways to make this truth known, perhaps especially to those who might never have thought themselves interested in Christianity. It was to the manner in which Religious Education should be presented that I briefly addressed myself in the following sermon (given at Christ Church Cathedral, Oxford, in May 1990), and the target of such education is all children, whatever their religious or non-religious background.

> But when the Comforter is come whom I will send unto you from the Father, even the spirit of truth, he shall bear witness of me (John 15:26)

Religion, any religion, claims to deal in, and have privileged access to, the truth. Notoriously these days this poses problems for those who have to *teach* religion, and especially for those whose job is to purvey Religious Education in schools. I think there is no educational topic on which there has been so little coherent thought; and it is not surprising, because our notion of truth is far from coherent. Since there are children in school brought up to believe in truths which would conflict wth the truths supposedly referred to in St John's Gospel, it is often held that no 'truth' should be taught at all in Religious Education classes. Instead, RE lessons should be devoted to raising children's awareness of the need to be tolerant of other religions than Christianity, and to the discussion of moral issues, with the general, perfectly decent and respectable aim of making them think about other people, at home and abroad. Many School Assemblies as well as compulsory RE lessons are conducted on more or less these principles. The teacher is supposed, as far as possible, to stand back, and remain *neutral*, not, presumably,

on all moral issues, but on all those which are either political
or most particularly religious.

There is in my view something daunting in the concept of a wholly
neutral teacher, someone apparently without convictions, without
personal enthusiasms ready only to say 'some believe this, others
that'. And yet this is the attitude teachers of RE are often trained to
assume. Yet we all know that the best teachers are creatures of
passion and belief, even dotty belief. And, in any case, that apart,
to advocate such neutrality in the teaching of religion seems to be
intrinsically inadequate. I think the inadequacy stems at least in part
from the childish and narrow idea that many of us have of truth.

If we are to advance towards putting some real content into the
compulsory RE slot in the school timetable, it is necessary to reconsider what religious truth is, what it claims to be, and how it differs
from other kinds of truth, historical, scientific and literary, while
overlapping perhaps with all of them. The first aim of the teacher
must be to try to open the eyes of children to what religion, and
especially the Christian religion *is*; what it is about. After all, times
have radically changed for teachers. There was a time long ago when
they had to be extremely careful not to offend the parents of their
pupils by beng markedly High or Low. Now that most of their
pupils know nothing whatever about Christianity, high or low, the
teacher's task is quite different. Teachers have to introduce, usually
for the first time, the remarkable *phenomenon* of religion, and in
particular the force and power to endure and to inspire that is
characteristic of the Christian religion. All children living, even tem-
porarily, in Europe need to understand this.

I don't believe such teaching can be done without two elements.
First, teachers must make their pupils familiar with the story of the
life of Christ (and this they can obviously do, beginning when their
pupils are very young) and second, and with more sophistication
perhaps, they must set that story in the context of another story,
involving the Jewish belief in the coming of a Messiah and the
attitude, therefore, of the writers of the Gospels, their beliefs about
what it was they witnessed. Both these elements seem to me crucial
in the teaching of Christianity and to some extent they carry with
them necessarily the recognition that other religions exist and tell
different stories equally grounded in history, but with different
meanings.

Apart from anything else a totally non-historical teaching of
Christianity is extremely confusing for children. Educated as I was
in a highly religious school where we had two Scripture lessons a
week, denominated OT and NT, I could never work out any sort of
relation between them, any more than I could grasp the connection
between arithmetic and algebra, which as far as I was concerned
just happened both to be called Maths. Nor could I ever understand

why we constantly sang hymns about Jerusalem, a place I had no desire whatsoever to visit.

But, far more important than that, to teach Christianity as a story within a story will begin to bring out the intrinsic nature of religion, its concern with creation, birth, life, death and the relation between humans and the universe as a whole. Not only children but all of us from childhood upwards essentially depend on stories to allow our imagination to have scope to grasp and explore truths about the world and humans in it. The question whether a story is true or false, did it really happen so or was it invented, is always ambiguous and the more we are brought up on stories, the more we come to appreciate the ambiguities.

A story essentially has a *point*; and the story of the life of Christ, from his birth to his crucifixion and beyond is, obviously, no exception. The story would not persist, to be told and retold every year, in the Church, through all the festivals of the Church, deploying all the narrative means of literature, painting and music, if it did not contain a point, a *meaning* to be interpreted and reinterpreted every time it was told.

We have, gradually, to introduce children, first to the story itself and then to the meaning attached to it, variously, at various times, by the Church. If this also involves a bit of Church history there is far from harm in that. For I believe that one cannot teach Christianity, even teach *about* Christianity, wthout teaching about the Church, and that this kind of teaching is what is most lacking in school. There is, it seems a kind of timidity, which makes the very idea of a Church and a liturgy suspect. Teachers are trained to be thus suspicious, and there are many who completely divorce the concept of Christianity from that of the Church.

Religious education can be justfied in two ways. First, if we do *not* undertake such education, then I fear that the world will be increasingly divided between those who have no notion of religion at all and no interest in it . . . for whom it is not a serious subject of discourse or speculation; and on the other hand those who embrace some creed or other in an anti-rational, anti-intellectual way, as conveying a literal truth which must be asserted though it flies in the face of everything else that we know, either as common-sense humans or as scientists. Such fundamentalism is, I believe, a genuine threat at the present time, quite possibly increasing, simply because of the timidity of the Church and of teachers with regard to the flexible and various nature of the truth . . . and especially the truth to be grasped by imagination and through metaphor, myth and story. To be wholly literal in thinking about religion is as disastrous as to be wholly unhistorical.

Second, if we *do* undertake the teaching of religion in school in some such manner as I have suggested, then we shall be offering children something they may otherwise altogether miss. One could,

I suppose, refer to what this is by calling it a 'spiritual' dimension to their experience; but I myself hesitate to use this word because I have never been certain of its meaning. I have a half-fear that to use it to justify introducing children to the idea of religion is a tautology, in that the spiritual and the religious are often taken to be identical. We would thus be saying no more than that we must teach religion because we must introduce people to religion. We need a different justification for taking religion seriously as part of education.

I believe that the justification must come through the concept of the imagination, the faculty which humans alone among animals have to enable them to consider their own lives *as a whole*, the *significance* of what they do, their birth and life and death, and their relation with other animals and other humans, their place in their own and future environments. It is historically through the attempt to understand these issues that religion came into existence, and, amazingly, has persisted as a way of thought.

Moreover, however strong a religious person's belief may be in a direct revelation of truth to him, or other believers, from a personal God, nevertheless everyone must acknowledge that the *language* in which such a revelation would be made, the language of religion itself, is essentially metaphorical. No one has seen God face to face. We see through a glass, darkly. And as the philosopher Kant put it, to suppose that when we speak of God we speak literally is to be guilty of gross anthropomorphism. The language of religion, and all religious thought, is essentially *symbolic*. But the understanding of metaphor and symbol, its possible power and truth, its ability to convey a truth inexpressible by other means – such understanding is a function of imagination; and it is to the enlargement of imagination that I believe all education should be directed, whatever the immediate subject-matter of that education. This is, in my view, the justification of including religious education in the school timetable . . . that it is essentially, not just accidentally, imagination-enhancing and therefore it opens children's eyes to a *different*, not everyday, notion of possible truth.

For the great enemy of the imagination, and thus of an enlarged understanding of the world, is what Keith Thomas, the President of Corpus, has called 'present-mindedness'. Whether they are concerned with science, with literature, music or history, children need to be shown that things have not always been as they are, and will not and need not remain as they are in the future. The twin ideas of continuity with the past and hopefulness for the future are essential to an understanding of what it is to seek the truth. The developing and changing interpretation of the Christian story is a supreme example of how 'present-mindedness', and with it the related disability of 'literal-mindedness', may be avoided. Through education, both at school and in church, people may learn to embrace what they see as the truth, not discarding the past, but joining with it, through the Church and all its symbolism, to *celebrate* the continuity and the hope of Christianity. Such, as I understand it, is the Paraclete, the spirit that will not leave us comfortless but will bear witness to the truth of Christianity and to which St John refers. It is to open the eyes of their pupils to such a spirit of truth that teachers of religion in this country owe their first duty.

Those who are Left Behind

Anthony Harvey

In the autumn of 1983 I was appointed to the Archbishop's Commission on Urban Priority Areas (ACUPA). This proved to be one of the most awakening and maturing experiences of my life. I had been for some years Examining Chaplain to the Archbishop, which had meant little more than giving occasional advice on theological matters. But now he offered me a challenge of a different order: that of formulating an appropriate theological response to what our Report called 'a grave and fundamental injustice' in the 'Inner Cities' and municipal housing estates of England. For the privilege of taking part in this work and for the experience of seeing so many instances of the triumph of the human spirit over the degrading constraints of material deprivation, I shall always be profoundly grateful.

'The problem of the poor', we used to say among ourselves, 'is the rich'. That is to say, one of the most disturbing features of Britain at that time (which is by no means absent now) was the extent to which the majority of our fellow citizens and fellow Church people was simply unaware of the conditions under which a substantial minority was living. It seemed a necessity to use the pulpit of Westminster Abbey and elsewhere to challenge this lack of awareness and to stimulate reflection and concern. This sermon is one which I preached on a number of occasions with this object in view.

I wish you to imagine a country – a fairy tale country, I am afraid, but also perhaps in some ways more real than a fairy tale – bounded on three sides by the sea. It has a large coastal plain, and its fourth side consists of a very steep and difficult escarpment, beyond which is a much larger stretch of rich open country. The majority of people live on the plain; but the more fortunate are in the open country beyond the escarpment, either because they were born there, or because they were fit and agile enough to make the difficult climb out of the coastal plain and up the escarpment. Meanwhile, the government of the country consisting mainly of well-born and vigorous people, has also moved from the plain up into the better country.

For a long time things remain fairly static. The people on the plain are overcrowded and have only limited resources. Many of the things they need are scarce and become very expensive. But their more fortunate fellow citizens beyond the escarpment are not oblivious of their plight. Indeed, because the people of the plain are relatively so numerous, and because the country is a democracy, they have a powerful voice in the government and can often ensure that the better off up there are sufficiently taxed to provide necessary amenities on the plain. The better off do not much care for this. But in fact they depend upon the plain people to do a lot of jobs they don't wish to do themselves, and so they are reasonably content to contribute to their welfare.

One day a government is elected which has a different approach. The reason, it believes, why there are so many people on the plain is that they haven't the initiative, the skills and the strength to climb up the escarpment. Accordingly, it devotes considerable resources to providing aid for just this purpose. Training, ropes, strong shoes, maps – all these are provided, and a surprising number of people succeed in accomplishing the climb. And they find it is true, there are more jobs, more opportunities, a better life in the open country up there.

But from time to time people go back to the plain to see how things are down there, and are surprised and distressed to find what a lot of people are still there. There are those who simply have not the strength or the agility to make the journey. There are also many who seem obstinately to prefer staying where they are, just because they think of it as home and don't want to move and there are a few – these are the oddest of all – who don't feel it is right for them to move unless all their friends can come too, and who insist on staying to share the life of those who are left behind.

But perhaps the most distressing thing about this community on the plain is the effect upon it of all the fittest and most vigorous people having left. Take their schools for example. The best teachers are of course the kind of people who can climb the escarpment; so the schools up there have gone on getting better while those on the plain are left getting worse. And look at all those workshops and factories standing empty. The sort of craftsmen and businessmen who made a success of them have left now; and anyway the successful people up there don't seem to need their products any more. Perhaps they can get them cheaper from abroad or something; at any rate the orders from up there have a way of just coming to an end without warning and the factories and workshops have to close. Worst of all, the people on the plain have lost their voice in the government. So many people who used to be with them have climbed up the escarpment that those who remain have now become a permanent minority. Which means that they can never again have any real say in the policies of the ruling party. They are beginning to feel that nobody cares for them.

Now this isn't actually true. Those who have climbed the escarpment are decent people. They *do* care about those who are left behind. But what can they do? The going in the open country, though much better than on the plain, is not as easy as all that: many of them have to work hard to keep going, and a number are in difficulties and have to be helped along. They haven't got much over to help the plain people with. Moreover their government is doing what it can. It is sending back more ropes and tackle and climbing equipment and trainers; and a trickle of people are still coming up over the escarpment. But this of course only makes things worse for the rest. The few fit and able people who were left among them are departing, leaving the rest who cannot, or as it seems obstinately will not, attempt the climb, still more bereft of any resources to improve the misery of their condition. The more aid the government gives to potential climbers the more hopeless the plight of those who can never attempt to climb.

This parable may be judged by some to fit the present situation of this country. I have recently spent a short time in a city of the North East with ACUPA. I was staying with a young priest who lives and works on a housing estate where the unemployment rate is 80 per cent. The fathers and grandfathers of these people worked in the shipyard on the edge of the estate. The shipyard is now closed and no industry has taken its place. There is no work locally and a bicycle ride to another part of the city would end only at the back of a dole queue which is already longer than in most parts of the country. Local government is starved of funds to make any impact on the acute poverty of the area; and those who are doing better in other parts of the country do not seem to care.

But I repeat, they *do* care. In other words, the parable is not intended to make a political point. All governments are concerned about those left behind, and none has found a sure method of solving the problem. In one form or another, the problem of poverty has been with us always and the parable speaks, not, or not only, to the world of politics, but to the Church.

For what does the Church do for the people of the plain? The Church is, by definition, compassionate and caring. It will not abandon the poor to their fate. But what does it do? Ironically, it contributes to that very process which causes the trouble. It helps the fittest and ablest to climb out of the plain into the better country beyond: indeed, if it does anything else it is accused of meddling in politics. In the last century missionaries who went to India were appalled by the poverty and illiteracy. They started schools among the very poor. The schools were good, their pupils did well and sent their own children. The schools got better still and were soon out of reach of those poor illiterate people for whom they were founded. Within two generations the schools had moved from the plain to the open country; and the Church was seen, correctly, to be an institution for the privileged.

Or similarly. A parish works hard and well in an 'Inner City' area. Its school is good, better than its neighbours. Its congregation is encouraged to have a better family life, the children do better than their neighbours, soon the families become more prosperous and move into better-class housing – but they still support their old Church which, once again, becomes identified with those who are successful, respectable – in short middle-class. Yet another group has climbed out of the plain, this time with Christ on their banner.

I repeat, no one is to blame. There is nothing sinful about success. There is nothing wrong in doing something well. It is not a part of the Gospel to give a bad conscience to those who have climbed up to a better life. And for the most part Christians who have done so are still deeply concerned about those left behind. But they cannot see what they can do.

A religious order in India has seen the problem with its schools. It has handed over those it founded, which are good and now privileged, and is starting again among the very poor. Doubtless the same story will repeat itself: the new school will be as good as the old, and in due course will be a place of privilege. But at least at this moment the chance has been taken to bring the caring of the Church back where it belongs among the poor. Such moments do indeed come. In the Western world, in modern times, it happens perhaps about once a century. In the eighteenth century Methodism moved into the world of the very poor in this country. In the nineteenth century the Tractarians and others did the same. All have now inevitably (as it seems) moved up into the open country. The twentieth century is still waiting for a major initiative from the Church, and the time may well be now.

But there is a further factor. The open country may offer a better life in many ways. But it has turned out to be less godly than was expected. Morals and religion have not flourished notably among those who have climbed. Too often, indeed, they have climbed on the backs of others and lost their sense of human brotherhood under God. Where then is Christ to be found? In our churches? Yes surely, for he is faithful, amazingly faithful, to all who call upon his name. But not only there. He is present, as he has always been present, among the poor, the unemployed, the deprived. He inspires, as he has always inspired, their resilience, their loyalty, their generosity and their humanity. And if we can learn to see him there, then our eyes can perhaps be opened to some of the things that prevent him being seen in ourselves. If it enables us to know Christ better, we may even be able to face becoming a little poorer ourselves.

Telling Tales

Julia Neuberger

This sermon, written in 1984 in the wake of Clive Ponting's revelations about the sinking of the Belgrano, was one that seemed in accord with the Archbishop's own sentiments about the Falklands War, and to express a principle he himself has held dear, that even when there will be public opprobrium, one must speak out.

The role of conscience is difficult to grapple with as an ethical principle, because of the easy excuse that one's conscience forced one into a position which in fact turned out to be to one's advantage. Throughout Robert Runcie's time as Archbishop, his speaking out has not necessarily been to his advantage and he has received a great deal of flak from government and from within the Church, for what he has said. But he has earned the undying admiration of others, and it is in that spirit that this sermon is now included in this volume.

Yom Kippur Morning 5745

In this afternoon's Torah portion, Leviticus, chapter 19, there is a sentence which should have been attracting a lot of attention recently. It reads: 'You shall not go up and down as a talebearer amongst your people.' It was a prohibition taken extremely seriously in rabbinic thought, and it is interesting, since what is being singled out here is evil talk rather than deeds, and talk, one might innocently suppose, is nowhere near as damaging as evil deeds. Yet our Leviticus verse is usually read together with three verses from Psalm 34: 'Who is the man that desires life and loves length of days, to see good in them? Keep your tongue from evil and your lips from speaking guile. Depart from evil and do good; seek peace and pursue it.' And the answer as to why the prohibition on evil talk is taken so seriously is provided by a rabbi commonly known as the Chafetz Chayyim, Israel Meir Ha-Cohen, who said:

> It is quite obvious that if you accustom yourself to being careful of what you say, not to speak disparagingly of your fellow even when it involves no harm to him, and all the more so, if you damage his livelihood; similarly not to insult him by abusive talk nor to keep a controversy

going by your stories, all of which constitute evil in the domain of tongue
– you will certainly, automatically, steer clear of robbery and theft. For
have you not undertaken to be careful not to cause your fellow harm or
disgrace by word of mouth, let alone by actual deeds!

Although not all gossip is dangerous, much of it is thoroughly
reprehensible, particularly the three categories of gossip in breach
of confidence, gossip the speaker knows to be false, and unduly
invasive gossip, such as about people's private lives, for instance –
though the intimate details of how an individual treats his children
or what drugs he consumes may well be of legitimate interest to
others, despite the subject claiming that the discussion is unduly
invasive. There is not much that most of us would disagree with
here. All it leaves us with is an uncomfortable sense of guilt about
how often we have gossiped reprehensibly, for we all do and a
worry about the damage we have done, for we all have.

But let us go back to our original verse from this afternoon's Torah
portion. 'Do not go up and down as a talebearer amongst your
people . . . ' Does that always apply? Does it apply to Clive Ponting,
to Sarah Tisdall? To nurses and doctors reporting colleagues for
misconduct? To lawyers investigating a colleague's negligence? To
clergy trying to stop the suicide of a young person? Is that talebearing? And is *that* prohibited?

No easy decision, this. And it is one which most of us have had
to face at one time or another. Whistleblowing – making revelations
to call public or private attention to negligence, abuse or danger –
is hard to come to terms with. But however hard for us, it must be
harder for those who decide to blow the whistle. For only the
most innocent whistleblower would believe, as Dr Stockman does in
Ibsen's *An Enemy of the People*:

> All that pollution up at Molledale – all that leaking waste from the mill
> – it's seeped into the pipes feeding from the pump room; and the same
> damn poisonous slop's been draining out on the beach as well . . . It's
> positively injurious to health, for either internal or external use. Ah,
> what a blessing it is to feel that you've done some service for your home
> town and your fellow citizens . . .

That was in Act 1. By Act 5 he has been labelled an enemy of the
people at a public meeting, lost his position as the spa's medical
director, and suffered through the stoning of his house by an angry
crowd. But through it all he held his ground: 'Should I let myself
be whipped from the field by public opinion and the solid majority
and other such barbarities? No, thank you.' He started off an innocent, but learnt only too fast that whistleblowing was a hard act –
that people would not rush to act, to make repairs; that vested
interests were involved. But was he right? Or was he committing
talebearing so strongly condemned in our text?

Or take another example: the role of some (by no means all) of the clergy under Vichy France apropos the rounding up of the Jews. Though French co-operation with the Final Solution was considerable, summer 1942 saw a variety of clerics speaking out – blowing the whistle on the system they had previously, to some extent at least, supported. Hence Monsignor Pierre Marie Théas, Bishop of Montauban: 'I give voice to the outraged protest of Christian conscience and I proclaim that all men, Aryans or non-Aryans are brothers because created by the same God; that all men, whatever their race or religion, have the right to be respected by individuals and by States.' That was blowing a whistle, certainly. But the action of Père Chaillet and his group 'L'Amitié Chrétienne' was probably more useful, given hindsight. For they dispersed Jewish children among a number of religious houses and refused to give them up even when Père Chaillet himself was placed under house arrest in the Privas mental hospital in the Ardèche for three months. But public protests by clergy, who often had privileged information, were a form of whistleblowing on the régime. Were they wrong? We would surely argue not. We would surely say that they were right – and that they were too late and too weak. But if we say that, we go along the line which demands whistleblowing in a variety of situations.

Back to the Chafetz Chayyim who has no doubts on this matter:

> Nevertheless if a man sees that his fellow is guilty of misconduct, given to pride or anger or neglectful of Torah study, he should apprise his son or disciples of this and warn them not to associate with him so as not to be influenced by his ways. For the real concern of the Torah in forbidding evil talk even when true was the evil intent involved in wishing to disgrace our fellow and enjoy his discomfiture. But where the intention is to save our fellow beings from bad influences, it is plain that it is permissible and even obligatory. But, in these circumstances, it would seem that it is necessary for the speaker to explain the reasons for speaking ill of his fellow, so that the listener should not be misled into going too far or into being astonished at his apparently inconsistent behaviour.

Is that not too simplistic? Have we not avoided all the real ethical considerations here? For, first of all, whistleblowers expose themselves, and often their families, to considerable risk, as in the case of Dr Stockman. They risk the opprobrium of colleagues, and possible loss of job. They place in conflict collegial loyalty and absolute conscience. They play with their own peace of mind – and claim to be dealing in absolute truthfulness.

And, worst of all for some of them, they are caught in another conflict. For the prevailing ethic of the profession concerned will require above all else loyalty to colleagues and clients. But the formal code of professional ethics stresses responsibility to the public and general communal duty above that. The prevailing ethic is 'Do not go up and down as a talebearer.' But the formal code of conduct is about a higher sense of duty, to the public at large. It is about not keeping silent . . .

So how does it work? In most professions, there is a proper system. Doctors – in hospitals, at least – have the Three Wise Men (who have been women at times!) to whom one doctor can make a complaint about another. Private whistleblowing. And barristers could complain about each other, in cases of real negligence, to the Bar Council, although a self-interested motive might be suspected. So far, so good, but it is strange that when a judge, one Judge Campbell QC, was convicted of smuggling whisky and cigarettes, despite losing his job, he did not lose his pension. Who blew the whistle there? And when solicitors are complained of to the Law Society, the Law Society acts slowly, and it takes years before the most minor action is taken. No whistleblowing there either.

And, if you remember, in the Normansfield Hospital case in 1978, it took a strike by the nursing staff to secure the removal of the consultant psychiatrist in mental subnormality, because complaints on both sides had simply not been heard. One person there blew the whistle: a Mrs Mills, who taught the children and was stopped from serving them milk or orange juice in the morning by the consultant psychiatrist, who had, in any case, some strange views on diet. She complained both to the Health Authority and to the Inner London Education Authority. But she was ignored. And it was not until the strike that the whole sad story emerged in the Normansfield Report as a result of the Public Inquiry into the troubles at the hospital.

The consultant was not the only one to blame. The management situation was poor and morale generally low. Nursing standards were far short of what was acceptable and patients were understimulated, dirty and smelly. The Area Health Authority provided poor management and the Regional Health Authority failed to monitor the Area. But who was going to complain? The mentally handicapped patients . . . ? Or those staff who could no longer cope with the strain of crazy diets and patients put into solitary confinement? The Normansfield Report makes depressing reading. Nor does it stand alone: Ely Hospital, Cardiff, South Ockendon, Rampton . . . all places where mentally handicapped patients have suffered considerable neglect and abuse. Does the injunction not to go up and down as a talebearer apply here? Or should we *all* be blowing the whistle, non-stop?

Listen to the editor of the *Nursing Mirror* on the subject of Ely Hospital, Cardiff:

> More depressing even than the harrowing details of inept administration and resultant malpractice has been the message which emerged again and again in reports like these – that nurses who have attempted to put things right have suffered personal discredit as a result, and what is more, failed to alter the situation.

Ten years later two student nurses were forced to discontinue their training at Brookwood Hospital after staff and management united to discredit allegations they had made about serious patient abuse – allegations later upheld by an independent Health Authority Inquiry and the disciplinary committee of the General Nursing Council. Nurses are often left very much on their own, as a nursing assistant described before a GNC disciplinary committee in 1969 – explaining why she felt powerless to intervene when a SEN had repeatedly submerged a mentally handicapped child's head in the bath:

> I didn't say anything . . . because in the past you knew your role in the Manor House. If you are a NA you don't interfere with trained staff, because once earlier on I was very unhappy in myself, and another NA and myself went to see Matron about another incident, and we were promptly told that if we weren't happy with our job we weren't to come telling tales. We could go through the gate – so you learnt not to tell tales, and not to say anything.

Perhaps more depressing is the following testimony from a mental nurse looking back on his introduction to mental hospitals in the 1960s.

> The whole institution had been a worrying experience for me. It seemed a million miles away from the pit village in which I was brought up. The sick room was further away still. The whole atmosphere was repressive. The nurses were surly and seemed to have a deliberate policy of humiliating the patients, many of whom were both seriously physically ill as well as mentally ill.
>
> In one room, a long term syphillis patient howled his way to death. Two patients died more slowly from Huntington's Chorea. The tough charge nurse said: 'You've got to keep on top of these people. You have to show them who is master.'
>
> 'Difficult' patients were deprived of meals. Others were handled roughly; plasters torn off their wounds, bed pans not delivered when begged for. In the communal showers I saw, on three occasions, patients given the wet towel treatment. Hospital towels soaked in water (in one case urine) and the patient who had fouled his bed or wet all over the ward floor was lashed mostly around the thighs and buttocks.
>
> The hospital was a world of its own. I felt sick at the treatment patients received, but like so many did nothing. Who would believe a raw nineteen-year-old? It was several years before I could even talk about those days to friends and family.

And who was *there* to blow the whistle? Would *that* have been talebearing? Would *that* have been wrong? Dozens of examples come to mind, from the complicated ones of Rhona Prime with her husband's spying and Clive Ponting and the *Belgrano*, to the simpler ones of staff in hospitals and schools particularly those who care for the least articulate.

Ponting felt he had a duty to Parliament over and above his duty to government. A good argument, but inaccurate constitutionally, for he is a servant of the Queen and her ministers, and strange ethically, for leaking cannot be defended where resignation and exposing can be. Rhona Prime felt she had a duty to the State above her loyalty to her husband, but only after she had discovered about his sexual assaults on little girls. One can *always* smear; always worry about the motives. And yet . . . 'You shall not go up and down as a talebearer amongst your people . . . ' There is a verse to set against it: 'You cannot hide yourself.' You cannot allow abuse to take place without reporting it – at whatever cost to yourself. You cannot let collegiality override conscience and duty. Where lives and quality of life is at stake you *must* blow the whistle. You *may* not hide yourself. But only if you have already tried all other methods of complaint, the 'proper channels'. Sometimes you doubt your own motives: 'I don't like him or trust him.' Sometimes the victim is in fact the person about whom you are complaining where the complaint was unjust. But however unreliable the system, however possible that people might use whistleblowing for their own purposes and crush it when they see fit, a society which fails to protect the right to speak out opens the door to political and other repressions. 'Do not go up and down as a talebearer amongst your people . . . ' No idle gossip, by all means, but equally no innocent blood, no withdrawal from the scene. For the whistle has to be blown by us all at some point in our lives – and with the cry of 'Tell-tale tit, your tongue shall be slit' in our ears, we have to brace ourselves to it.

Academic Unity and Tolerance

David Say

Dr Robert Runcie has been Visitor of the University of Kent at Canterbury since 1980 by virtue of being Archbishop of Canterbury. He has been closely identified with the life of the University of which he is an Honorary Doctor of Divinity. As Visitor he has been consulted from time to time by both staff and students. As a former Cambridge don and as the Principal of an Oxford Theological College, Dr Runcie has long been closely associated with academic life and has been a welcome lecturer at universities all over the world. He holds honorary degrees from Cambridge, Oxford, Keele, West Indies, Trinity College, Toronto, Berkeley Divinity School, Liverpool, and the University of the South, Sewanee. In 1990 he preached in Canterbury Cathedral at the 25th anniversary service of the University of Kent at Canterbury.

I gave the following sermon at the Cathedral for the University anniversary five years earlier.

The light shines on in the dark and the darkness has never mastered it (John 1:5)

William Temple, whose enthronement here as Archbishop of Canterbury I attended in the darkest days of the Second World War, spoke in his sermon, on that St George's Day in 1942, about the City of God, and he took his text from the penultimate chapter of the Bible, 'The nations shall walk by the light thereof'.

Temple wrote his own commentary on St John's Gospel and among the many fine things he had to say about the opening words of that fourth Gospel, was this:

As we look forwards, we peer into the darkness and none can say with certainty what course the true progress of the future should follow. But as we look back the truth is marked by beacon lights which are the lives of the saints and pioneers; and these in their turn are not originators of light but rather reflectors which gave light to us because themselves they are turned towards the source of light.

We are gathered in this wonderful place which over the years has seen so many of the great events in the life of the University: the installation of Princess Marina as the first Chancellor; and the fantastically crowded and deeply moving Christmas Carol services and numerous Degree Congregations, none, perhaps, more memorable than the last one when Bob Geldof was given a Papal welcome. And we are here not only to offer our thanksgiving for the past and to reflect upon the complexities of the present, but also to look ahead into the darkness of the future and to derive strength from the Light which the darkness will never master.

It may be thought by some that it is rather presumptuous for us to celebrate a mere twenty years of existence, which in matrimonial circles would be regarded as no more than a china anniversary! Should we not have waited for a golden or a diamond jubilee, if not for a centenary?

Quite apart from the fact that many of us would not be present for any such celebration, there is perhaps a certain timeliness in giving thanks while some of our founders are still with us, and in looking ahead as the University emerges from its teenage years into adulthood.

Earlier this year the 450th anniversary was celebrated of the death of John Fisher, one of the most distinguished of my predecessors, as Bishop of Rochester. If his chief claim to fame is his martyrdom at the hands of Henry VIII, his life was chiefly notable for his service to university education.

Fisher went out of his way to provide not only better conditions and facilities for education, but also better education. He was Master of his College at the age of twenty-eight and by the time he was thirty-two, he was a DD and Vice-Chancellor of Cambridge University.

He saw that the old framework of the scholastic scheme of education was too small; that it was cramping for those who used it, confining within ridiculously narrow limits the minds of teachers and learners alike.

Fisher was a realist: as one of his biographers has written, 'he succumbed to neither of the two extreme views of conduct; he did not do violence to his principles in order to seize opportunities, nor did he allow himself to hold principles that forced him to ignore or do violence to the facts.' Erasmus ascribed to Fisher the origin of all the most hopeful signs of university life in the sixteenth century and the peaceful introduction of Greek studies.

Fisher, who was a godly man and a great and caring Bishop in West Kent, set out boldly to change the pattern of university education, and only his martyrdom brought his reforming zeal to an end. It is good that we should remember him in Kent four and a half centuries later, and in the same year as we mark the twentieth anniversary of the founding of our own University. For I believe that one day historians will record that the 1950s and 1960s were another creative period for university education in Britain.

In the twenty years 1948–68 no fewer than twenty-one universities came into being and the University of Kent at Canterbury was the twelfth new university to be founded in the post-Robbins era.

It is right that we should honour all those who took the lead in ensuring that Kent had its own University, who chose the site and the architect, who aroused the interest of the local community and who appointed the first Vice-Chancellor and gave him the support he needed to bring the University into being.

We thank God for the inspiration, the imagination and the dedication of such men as Stanley, Lord Cornwallis, Sir Edward Hardy, Major Andy Pym and supremely, of course, Dr Geoffrey Templeman, the pioneer Vice-Chancellor. They founded a University where all the disciplines could come together and where the Humanities and the Sciences could each make their contribution to what our Royal Charter describes as 'the example and influence of our corporate life'.

I believe that we should be thankful that they founded the University on a collegiate basis and named the four colleges after men of the modern world, whose names will continue to be honoured from generation to generation: Darwin, Eliot, Keynes, Rutherford.

Let there be no doubt that the original sponsors of the University were men and women who took a long view of the future. They looked far beyond the first twenty years. And I believe that they would have us do the same.

We may be tempted to feel that in 1985 we are like a boat caught in a gale, tossed to and fro by wind and storm, and that at times we are made pretty sick by some of the elements to which we are subjected. And let no semantics about the use of the word 'cuts' hide from us the scale of the re-ordering that all universities are being called upon to make at the present time. 'The light shines on in the dark and the darkness has never mastered it.'

As William Temple put it, 'the divine light shines through the darkness of the world, cleaving it, but neither dispelling it nor quenched by it'. And this gives us the assurance that we shall ride out the present storms and that we shall get to where we would be. But we shall do this with more confidence if we only carry with us the things that are most valuable for our life and learning.

Dare I say that I believe this should include making sure not only of our academic freedom but also of our academic unity – that the Humanities and Sciences go on talking to each other and that both resist the distortion of financial pressures.

I believe it means also taking deliberate steps to maintain the life of the colleges and not to allow the economics of catering to hinder the growth of the corporate life of mixed communities, small enough for those of differing loyalties and enthusiasms to get to know one another really well, and to talk far into the night or while walking from the North Foreland to the South Foreland.

And third, I would make a plea that we should all resolve that one of the marks of this University should be its tolerance.

It is fashionable to laugh at Old School songs and in many places they are now only sung by the former members of a School. I went to a school which fifteen years ago was the first one in London to open its doors to those of all creeds and of none. We used to sing:

> Back in the old time, the morning time, the brave time,
> Earnest hearts once laboured for the halls we tread.
> They laid intolerance low.
> Up, up and let us follow where our founders led.

And before you dismiss that as corny or nineteenth-century liberalism, ask yourself whether or not in recent months the saddest thing that has been happening in both Church and State is the growth of an insidious intolerance. If we cannot listen to one another in our universities and allow those from whom we differ the freedom to express their views freely, what hope is there for tolerance to grow in Toxteth or Tottenham?

Dean Acheson, one time American Secretary of State, has written of a momentous event which occurred on 19 May 1780 in Hartford, Connecticut. By noon on that day the sky had turned from blue to grey to deepest black, and by mid-afternoon it was as midnight. The Connecticut House of Representatives was adjourned, unable to transact business. In the Council of Safety – the Upper House – the motion to adjourn was put. Colonel Abraham Davenport rose to speak. He said: 'The Day of Judgement is either approaching or it is not. If it is not there is no cause for adjournment. If it is, I choose to be found doing my duty. I move therefore, that candles be brought.'

We too are called to live and to do our work in a day of darkness and no little danger. Let us not despair about the present, nor be nostalgic in our reflections on the past, rather let us take heart from the assurance of the Gospel and face the future with confidence and hope. 'For the light shines on in the dark and the darkness has never mastered it.' Thanks be to God.

A Message for Monday Morning

Lionel Blue

Archbishops of Canterbury are not just leaders of a denomination, they also speak for and to a whole nation. Their 'pulpit' for this is a radio and television studio, which gives them the means to do it. Robert Runcie was an outstanding Chairman of CRACK, the Central Religious Advisory Committee on broadcasting, even before he became Archbishop, when he was still Bishop of St Albans. He has been a powerful speaker over the air, conducting the Daily Service, and arriving early to give the country its early morning boost with his 'Thought for the Day'. No one will forget his New Year Meditation from the crypt of Lambeth Palace and his plea for Terry Waite. In view of all this, these thoughts on 'Thought for the Day' (23 July 1990) seem appropriate.

At Seminary I was taught how to give a sermon. Dressed in a special robe with prayer shawl, linen tabs, and high black hat, I processed up the aisle to the pulpit, while choirs sang. In the pulpit my feet were on the level of my congregation's foreheads, which did not make for cosy chat. My congregation looked special too, in their creaky Sabbath best. Not unnaturally, I was expected to say special things, wise things, profound things, holy things, to repeat the great truths of Tradition.

Giving the 'godslot' on the morning radio is not like that at all.

The alarm goes at 5.30. I like to get to the studio early, so I'm in a rush. There's time for cleanliness or godliness – a shower or morning prayers – not both.

I arrive, looking grubby, at Broadcasting House, and treat myself to a paper cup of plastic coffee. Some of the staff look pretty tired too. They've been up since the early hours, putting together their news programme. And as soon as they've got it sorted out and organised, someone hurls a bomb into a bar in Belfast and it not only blows up the bar, it also blows apart their programme. They have to start organising all over again. How they keep their cool I don't know, but they do.

No choirs sing while I process into the studio, and before I speak into the mike, I try to think of the listeners at the other end of it. What do they look like; what are they up to?

At ten minutes to eight, they are either putting one foot out of bed, or they are in the bathroom, or in the kitchen crashing into

274 Tradition and Unity

kippers or rashers. That is when my little sermon comes through their transistors.

Their attention is fragile, so I have to tell them stories. These stories need not be the holiest in the world, but they must be relevant to the bedroom, bathroom, kippers and rashers. They have to exist in the same world, because the listeners have a power rarely exercised by a member of any Sabbath congregation. If they don't like what they hear, they only have to extend a hand, twiddle a knob or turn a switch, and obliterate it.

I once knew a German Jewish nun who was able to stand up in the middle of a sermon and say 'Father what you have said is simply not true', but fortunately for my profession, such free spirits are rare.

All this means I have to approach religion in other ways, to deal with people as they are and where they are, not where they ought to be. (In the pulpit, I often told my congregation where they ought to be, without much guidance about how to get from where they were to where they ought to be.) I have to deal, not with the problems I think they ought to have, but with the problems they are experiencing. And the most immediate is not salvation but the courage to get out of bed and not dive back under their duvet.

It is no use quoting Scripture, because we do not share the same ones, and in a secular society for many there are no Scriptures, only old books. Also all traditional Scriptures share one drawback: they are about other people at other times, about 'them then', and what my listeners want is something about 'me now'.

So to make the ancient Scriptures speak, I have to show them how to compose the Scripture of their own life, and lay it beside the others – and then they speak.

Scriptures for secular people? Yes! People who are not card-carrying members of any religious Establishment still recognise a spiritual dimension to their lives. They know, for example, because they are quite shrewd, how to read and assess holiday brochures. It's part of popular experience. Such brochures can give a fair idea of the comfort situation because comfort means things, and these can be counted and listed. But listeners also know that contentment is not things but something inner and invisible, spiritual, say. Now sex also means things – bottoms, breasts and bulges – but love, which is what they really want, is in another dimension.

Now they are not coming to religion for ethics, or doctrine, but because they think (quite rightly) that there is a spiritual dimension to happiness, which is what they want. I don't mind this way of approaching religion. It seems to me that if you approach reality anywhere with courage and honesty, you will get to the spiritual bedrock on which it is based.

The answers to the happiness problem do not change with the centuries. They are as flinty as they ever were:

- If you chase happiness, it chases you, and you will never catch it up.
- If you forget it, it might come, because it is the by-product of giving.
- If you can give happiness to others, you will acquire it yourselves.
- In the spiritual world, the more happiness you give, the more you have. It is a paradox, but paradoxes are the hidden logic of spirituality.

No wonder I have to use jokes to make such an uncompromising message acceptable early on a Monday morning.

When listeners sigh and want a world built another way, I tell them this story.

A man fell down a ravine. As he hurtled down, he grabbed a small tree, growing out of the side. Hanging over the void, he prayed to heaven. 'If there's anyone up there,' he said, 'come to my aid. Put down a hand and save me.'

And to his astonishment a Voice did come from Heaven and it said, 'Do not fear', it said. 'I will answer thy cry and save thee. I shall put my hand beneath thee and hold thee. Just trust in me!'

There was a long pause, and then the dangling man prayed again, but much more quietly. 'Is there anyone else up there?' he said.

No there isn't – sorry! Security isn't on offer, only courage, and the only power God has is the love he inspires in us. You need humour to preach such a stark message on a Monday morning.

Great is Truth and Mighty

Edward Carpenter

*For many informed members of the Church of England the retirement of
Archbishop Runcie serves to remind them of the great debt that they owe
to him. The unique office which he has held, to quote the words of Geoffrey
Fisher, a former occupant of the Chair of St Augustine, 'is one of a
primacy of honour; but it is one that can claim nothing more than that.
It jealously rejects, and is zealously protected, from any claims to jurisdiction
of doctrinal interpretation.'*

*It possesses, however, a considerable and creative influence, and my
own view is that Dr Runcie will go down to history as a great Archbishop
who has used such influence to good and significant effect. He has read
rightly the signs of the time and has shown himself sensitive to the
contemporary winds of change but has refused to be blown off course by
them. During his Archepiscopate, he has shown himself, inter alia, quick
to recognise two things: that Christian Faith in the last analysis has to do
with truth; and that it must be the task of the Ecclesia Anglicana to
bear witness to its being a viably intellectual option. One does not need
to defy and annihilate reason – 'the candle of the Lord' – in order to make
an honest profession of faith. His public utterances on many and diverse
themes have been instinct with a wide liberality; and he has paid his
hearers the compliment of believing that they were prepared to think – and
rethink!*

*Archbishop Runcie welcomed the fact that by a quirk of history, or was
it by divine Providence, the Church of England in its origins, and
throughout its history, has been 'comprehensive' in character. Theologies
which on the Continent have generated separated Churches came into the
Church of England at the time of the Reformation as the Church of the
nation. That Dr Runcie, without blurring or compromising his own
position, used his archepiscopal influence to preserve a balance and a fair
representation of diverse strands, was certainly a considerable
achievement. Consistently he opposed the idea of a Church of England
myopically introspective, preoccupied only with its own domestic life and
shrinking into a sect. Rather he looked out from Lambeth towards a national
and world-wide scene. For example he was well versed in the theological-
sociological thinking of such as F.D. Maurice, Westcott, Hort, R.H.
Tawney and William Temple. Thus he saw Christian insights as relevant
in the economic and political areas of life. Hence he did not hesitate to
speak his mind on these wide issues: sometimes incurring governmental
rebuke. In many areas he gave positive leadership as, for example, in*

relation to other world faiths, as was seen at the last Lambeth Conference. Not least in this respect was his frank recognition that Judaism is an 'ongoing religion' not destined to fulfil itself only by losing its identity within Christianity. It is a religion in its own right.

History can be a hard taskmaster but I am confident that Archbishop Runcie's stature will grow as the years go by and a more objective and sensitive appraisal of his tenure of office is made possible.

'The truth shall make you free.'

Some of you may recall what the poet William Wordsworth refers to as 'shades of the prison house', that is, one's schooldays. If you do it may be that you will also remember Bacon's *Essays* the epitome of wordly wisdom which probably still deserve a greater attention than we now pay to them. I often linger over the pithy introduction to one of his Essays: 'What is truth? said jesting Pilate; and would not stay for an answer.' It was indeed a pity that he was in such a hurry since he was in the presence of one who might have been able to help him.

My intention, however, is to introduce you to another character, a near contemporary of Francis Bacon, whose attitude to the claims of truth was far different, more costly and rigorously demanding. I refer to William Whiston, who was Isaac Newton's successor in the Lucasian Professorship at Cambridge, but is now only remembered for his translation of Josephus. For him life was a perpetual quest and in its pursuit he browsed fearlessly in the perilous fields of unorthodoxy, typical of which was his treatise 'Primitive Christianity Revived'. As a consequence he was hauled before the Hebdominal Council and deprived of his Professorship. As a consequence he left for London and became a suppliant for support at the gates of Fulham and Lambeth Palace. When he died at a great age friends who had remained faithful speculated as to a fitting epitaph. A biblical quotation seemed somewhat incongruous, so finally they settled upon: *Quocunque veritas duxit ausus sequi* (Wherever truth led there I dared to follow). Could there be a finer epitaph? In one sense it seems to say almost everything. What for Pontius Pilate was a matter for jesting and hollow laughter was for the author of this Latin tag cause of a deep and reverential concern. He suggests that truth is progressively apprehended and that we must be on the march to keep pace with it. It is indeed a life-long quest. We must not get immobilised in the straitjacket of a past personal history, or, 'cribb'd, cabin'd and confn'd' in a self-constructed prison house from which it is not easy to escape. But our author goes further than this. To enter into truth demands daring and courage to tread new paths. 'Straight is the gate and narrow is the way that leadeth unto life', proclaims Jesus, 'and few there be that find it.' If wisdom 'cannot be gotten for gold', neither will her secrets be revealed to the casual, to those who are cavalier in her pursuit and lack seriousness. As Jesus said again: 'I have yet many things to tell you but ye cannot bear them now.' If the truth is to make us free we must be prepared for her to lead us off the beaten track; to require us to stand alone in her defence. There is something deeply moving in the humble response of Christian in *Pilgrim's Progress* to the question: 'Do you see yonder shining light?' 'Yes,' he replies, 'I think I do.' Our effort to make sense of and discover meaning in the flux and change of time gives dignity to our common human nature. If life is indeed but 'a tale told by an idiot full of sound and fury signifying nothing', then the honest man must accept it; but the religious man does not believe that the logic of facts drives him to this sombre conclusion: nor does he believe that his overall faith is other than a viable intellectual option. It may not be a searchlight illuminating the whole scene but it can be 'a lantern unto our feet'. What matters in respect of our faith commitment is that we have thought about it, prayed about it and put it to the test. A faith purchased at too light a cost, never submitted to patient enquiry and reflection, will not stand by us when we need it most. Alas! 'Easy come, easy go.'

It is within this context that one is right to question the validity of many of the fundamentalisms, whether in religion, economics or politics, which are springing up around us – systems which spurn enquiry, despise reason, and whose disciples lack the courage to follow whither the argument leads. Mistakenly they suppose that the strength in which a conviction is held is a criterion of its truth and validity. Thus who can but welcome in our day and generation the coming together of faiths and cultures which for far too long have been geographically and hermetically sealed off from one another? Who can but rejoice in their seeing each other not as rivals or competitors with a monopoly of truth but as offering their distinctive treasures to a common pool? Perhaps the ultimate truth is bigger than all of us put together, and for this reason maybe a pluralism of faiths enables us to discover greater riches in our own. Our *visio dei* is deepened and our sympathies enlarged.

Yes indeed! 'The truth shall make you free.' 'I have many things to tell you but ye cannot bear them now.' *Quocunque veritas duxit ausus sequi.*

Suffering

Lord Longford

The Archbishop of Canterbury of the day is probably more involved in
controversy than anyone else, except the prime minister. Robert Runcie
is no exception. I have found myself, if it is not impertinent to say so, on
his side in all the main public arguments. I have particularly admired
the inspiration that he has provided to all those who labour on behalf of
the poor in the inner cities. No single act of his, however, moved me so
much as his insistence after the Falkands War that we should pray for the
Argentine dead along with our own.

At all times he has been explicitly and implicitly aware of human
suffering in the examples given and in many others that can be provided.
In my eyes he ranks with William Temple as a very great Archbishop.

Speaking as a Roman Catholic (a lapsed Anglican) I am sure that his
reception of the Pope in England went straight to every Catholic heart.

This talk was given in Hertford Chapel, Oxford, on 6 May 1990.

My only real reason for speaking to you tonight on *Suffering* is that
I have written a book on that subject which is coming out in the
autumn. My sufferings have been trivial compared with those of
some whom I interviewed in writing the book, and of course vast
numbers of others whose names I do not know.

Nevertheless, to live is to suffer, to love may be to suffer intensely.
You cannot live for eighty-four years on this planet without some
measure of suffering. In my book I have tackled three questions:

1. How do we explain suffering?
2. How do we endure suffering?
3. How do we relieve suffering?

I go into the first question at considerable length, but I shall not say
much about it this evening.

We are all confronted with this everlasting question which is
particularly severe to Christians. How do we explain the existence
of an all-powerful, all-loving God whose Son died on the Cross to
redeem us with the enormous amount of human suffering? There
is a fairly easy answer as long as we are concentrating on evil. Man
was given freedom and has grossly abused it. But innocent suffering,

earthquakes, for example, or children born with hideous deformities, present a graver problem. There will always be mystery here, which will only be resolved on the other side of the grave. I can assure you, however, from my first-hand experience, that many Christians who suffer intensely, either directly or through those they love, find a profound degree of comfort and strength in the answers provided by their Christian religion.

I will refer to witnesses only. The first is Margaret Spufford, a Cambridge University historian, an Anglican Oblate, whose book *Celebration* is one that I venture to recommend to all of you with unqualified enthusiasm. She herself suffers from a chronic bone disease which leaves her span of life uncertain. But what has been still more painful is that her daughter suffered from birth from an incurable illness which handicapped her totally throughout her life and finally killed her when she was barely grown up. Yet Margaret Spufford, as she explains with much eloquence in her book, has found deep joy within her suffering.

How has this been possible? She has certainly managed to achieve what we are all told to aim at but most of us find so very, very hard. She has combined her sufferings with those of Jesus Christ on the Cross. But there is more to it than that, as is beginning to be stressed more and more by modern theologians, by great sufferers and by those who devote their lives to the relief of suffering – from AIDS, to take only one example.

My other witness is Dr Sheila Cassidy. Some of you will remember her as having been hideously tortured in Chile. She is now the medical administrator of St Luke's Hospital for the Dying in Plymouth. One of her books, *Sharing the Darkness*, gives the clue. People like Sheila Cassidy do not only think of uniting their sufferings to those of Jesus Christ who died two thousand years ago, they think of him and through him of God, as suffering every minute of every hour along with us now. That is the most valuable message that I have obtained from my work on Suffering and in all humility I am anxious to share it with you this evening.

Before I close, I would like to say a word about the relief of suffering in a connection with which I am more familiar. We must never for a moment suppose that our duty to relieve suffering is confined to innocent sufferers, although of course we must redouble our efforts to help them. There are also those who, in human terms, we are bound to consider are guilty – convicted criminals, for example. Jesus Christ told us, as we all know, 'I was in prison and you came to me'. He did not merely refer to political prisoners unjustly convicted by wicked governments; he referred to all prisoners, including those who have committed terrible crimes.

When one goes to visit such people, there is only one approach, in my opinion, which is worthy of the Master. It is not enough when one visits a prisoner, convicted perhaps of a serious crime, to say: 'There but for the Grace of God go I.' One must say rather: 'There by the Grace of God go I.' In a spiritual sense one must kneel down and wash the prisoner's feet, as Christ knelt down and washed the feet of his disciples.

The Sin of Pride

Jack Mahoney

It is a particular pleasure for me as a Roman Catholic theologian to contribute to this collection of sermons published in honour of Robert Runcie, and thus to acknowledge his unwearied work for unity between the Christian Churches in the light of their common Tradition. Since not the least of his qualities is his manifest and deeply Christian humility, the reason for my offering in tribute this annual Oxford University Sermon on the 'Sin of Pride' is to be sought elsewhere than as an implied rebuke! As I have found so encouraging Dr Runcie's consistent refusal to resort to what I term 'facile moralising', so I hope that he (and others) may find not uncongenial the theology of a 'new humanism' for which I argue, and may agree in regarding some such positive 'theological nerve' as essential to the effectiveness of the decade of evangelising upon which the Christian Churches in Britain are now embarked.

The annual sermon on the Sin of Pride, was preached in the University Church of St Mary the Virgin, Oxford, 24 November 1985, on a text chosen by the preacher from among those prescribed by the Founder of the Sermon.

In admonishing the troubled Christian community in Corinth that 'Knowledge puffs up, but love builds up' (1 Cor. 8:1), Paul the Apostle was raising for his contemporaries, as also for us today, the complex relationship between knowledge and love and the conflict which can sometimes arise between them to issue in the sin of pride, the subject on which I have the honour to be invited to preach this morning – though whether this is an inspired piece of type-casting, or an instance of the spiritual tradition that ailments are best treated by recourse to their contraries, is not a question which I can in all humility be expected to decide.

Paul, as founder of the Christian community in Cornith, was advising it on a variety of disputed points. And in the passage containing the text which I have selected from those prescribed for this annual sermon he had come to the question of whether Christians might in good conscience buy or eat the meat of animals which had been sacrificed to the pagan gods in a local temple before being offered for sale in the market place or served at dinner.

His own position was quite clear. Since the pagan gods had no reality, the carcasses of animals sacrificed to them were not contaminated by association and the Christian believer was therefore at liberty to purchase such meat or enjoy it at a friend's table without anxious questioning, so far as his own conscience was concerned. But not all the members of the local church shared such enlightened views, and their consciences also had to be considered. In other words, moral freedom brought its own responsibilties in the possible harmful effects of one's behaviour on others. If they were shaken or shocked in their beliefs, or embarrassed or otherwise influenced into imitating what they felt or suspected to be wrong, then Christian freedom became destructive rather than constructive and the knowledge and enlightenment which claimed to justify such freedom was giving rise to self-assertion, inflating the ego and one's self-importance at the expense of others. 'Knowledge puffs up.'

But 'love builds up'. For love, unlike pride, is outward-directed and other-centred. And Christian love, which is God's own love, directs all our energies to edify others, building them up into the complete edifice which God is in process of constructing. Paul's teaching to the Corinthians, then, is that knowledge can lead to an inflated sense of one's own importance and a proud disregard of others, whereas the applicaton of knowledge should be tempered by a loving regard for the needs and claims of others.

It is no large step to draw from this a moral for today's society, and to point to the explosion of knowledge with which we are faced, while deploring the absence of a corresponding explosion of love in the pursuit or application of this knowledge in such fields as nuclear energy, medicine, economics and sheer technological expertise. It could be attractive and heart-warming to prescribe a salutary dose of Reinhold Niebuhr for what he diagnosed [in *The Nature and Destiny of Man*, 1941, p.200] as modern society's 'pride of knowledge'. He was writing in the shadow of the Second World War, and we in our turn may be on the brink of the Final World War. Yet it appears only a partial reading of the signs of the times to conclude that we live in a technological and pre-apocalyptic age when the charity of men has grown cold. For the relationship between love and knowledge is much too complex for facile moralising. Love can no doubt preserve knowledge from being proud and self-centred, as Paul realised. And without love knowledge is in danger of becoming tyrannical. But without knowledge love can be helpless and impotent. Only knowledge can direct love in the truth, and enable love to be effective and beneficent. Augustine, the great, if flawed, psychologist of love, was clearly correct in observing that nothing can be loved unless it is known. Otherwise the benevolence of love can become at best sentimentality and at worst a force for unknowing distortion or destruction; for tearing down rather than building up.

There can be in fact, if not a fear, then at least a suspicion of newly acquired knowledge and a prevailing anxiety about its possible misuse, to which Christians appear particularly susceptible.

Man's first sin, after all, if we are to follow Augustine, Gregory and Aquinas, was a grasping at knowledge in an act of pride, in his first reaching above himself to pluck the fruit of the tree of knowledge and so rival God himself. It is not therefore surprising to find a recurring strand of Christian thought which appears disposed to view subsequent attempts by man to expand his field of knowledge or to increase his power over creation as yet further melancholy evidence of an ingrained ambition in him to trespass and encroach upon the preserve of God. Such a concern to draw a circle around man, outside which he steps only at his peril, appears to point to an underlying theology of what might be called inverse proportionality to be discerned in much of the Christian tradition. I think of the propensity to be found in various theologians, from Augustine through Calvin and Catholic Jansenism to Barth, to demean and diminish fallen and sinful man, sometimes to the lowest possible depth of degradation short only of extinction. A sympathetic reading of such writing may view it more as a rhetoric of humiliation, which is fundamentally concerned above all to magnify God and give glory only to Him, particularly in His loving mercy. After all, as the medieval axiom neatly expresses it there can be no mercy where there is no misery. And a theology which pushes to extremes the dramatic contrasts of Luke's Gospel will extol the divine goodness and mercy by weighing down the opposite scale as heavily as possible with the burden of human wretchedness and misery which Christ Jesus took up on our behalf.

Even apart from sin, however, or apart from any consideration of fallen man, the same theology of inverse proportion is to be seen at work in the viewing of man's relationship in general with God as a continual border dispute. What is gained by man is snatched from God in a Promethean rewriting of the gospel of creation. As the 'secular' expands among the society of men the 'sacred' is marginalised to the limits of life in a re-enactment of the proud defiance of Adam. An interesting illustration of this basically dualist theology is perhaps to be found today in the field of modern medicine, where man is accused by some Christians of playing at God. The Protestant theologian, Paul Ramsey, writing of the genetic future of man [*Fabricated Man*, 1970, p.138], protests indignantly that 'men ought not to play God before they learn to be men'. And he chides the Roman Catholic theologian Karl Rahner for clinging to the belief that men are wise enough to invent themselves and for seeking possible guidelines for man's self-creation. [Ibid. pp.139–42] But even Rahner, that most imperturbable of theologians, concludes on the same subject that genetic manipulation is governed by man's desire to banish the *fatum* from his existence. It is, he explains [in an article in *Theological Investigations*, 1972, IX, p.244], an unwillingness to accept one's fate in patience and humility, as the gift of an incomprehensible love. What the scientist, then, views as the *datum* of existence which he may feel himself summoned in love to improve upon, Rahner, no less than Ramsey, regards as man's fate, God's definitive shaping of the human condition with which proud man tampers only at his peril.

The basic weakness in what I have termed a theology of inverse proportionality and identified as underlying the rhetoric of sin as well as the charge of proudly playing God is that, in its bid to glorify God and even to protect him, it unwittingly depicts God and man as engaged in a continuing territorial dispute over the field of knowledge and even of being. In so doing it actually brings God down to the level of man, as a knower like any human knower, a cause like any human cause, a being like any other being. And in this lies the theological root of the problem of pride. For God is not a being in potential competition with other beings. 'God doth not need Either man's work or his own gifts', as Milton came to see. But no more does he need either man's sin or man's ignorance in some Mauriac-like mystique. As Charles Péguy once remarked, 'we do not exalt grace by decrying nature'. And no more do we exalt God by decrying man, nor God's mercy by denigrating His creature. Man is called to work with God in creation, not against Him. The God whom Paul preached to the quizzical men of Athens is not a God who is reduced to living in little enclaves of the sacred or who needs protecting by the bulwarks of human ignorance and impotence. He is the God who is Lord of heaven and earth and in whom we live and move and have our being (Acts 17:16–28). By the very fact of His generous creation of man, God has revealed that He is not by temperament a jealous or grudging God. And so the glory of God is magnified less by the puniness or wretchedness of His human creation than by the inherent dignity and powers for action with which He has graced it, and of which we have today become so conscious.

But that realisation is a difficult one to maintain for, of course, it appears to glorify man at the expense of God. Moreover, it took a long time in coming. Such action or casuality as is to be found in the Bible, or at least in the Old Testament, appears almost entirely occasionalist towards man in its discounting his activity and treating him as little more than an occasion for God's action as the sole agent in history, by turns punishing and relieving His people through hardening or softening the hearts of their enemies. The neoplatonism of the early Church, in its contemplation of created being, appears to concentrate more on its exemplary and final causes, the source and the destiny of man, than on the formal or efficient causality within man which would give due recognition to creaturely being and creaturely activity in their own right, and take in all seriousness the human capacities which God had seen fit to create. And pre-scientific man, as Gordon Dunstan has pointed out [in *Not Yet the Epitaph*, 1968, pp.4–5], sought to achieve his effects in the world through the moral causality of praying God to bring them about for him rather than through developing and directing his own and nature's resources to that end.

It required the incorporation of Aristotle into Christian thought, notably by Aquinas, to give some substantial theological recognition to human activity and human causality, and to offer some way out of the impasse which baffled the neoplatonist Augustine: If the sons of God are really driven by the Spirit of God (Rom. 8:14), how can they be said to be themselves truly active? For divine and human activity and, underlying them, divine being and human being, must be conceived as engaged in perpetual competition and in continual territorial disputes if they are thought of as existing and acting on the same plane of reality, almost like continental plates, which are forever pressing against each other and struggling to oust each other. It was the contribution of Aquinas to Christian thought to realise and to stress that God and His human creature exist and act on differing planes of reality, in the relation of agent to instrument, or of primary to secondary causes. It was the great intellectual strength of Aquinas to incorporate this notion of instrumental causality systematically into Christian reflection, and in the process to throw some fresh light on the Christian mysteries of Incarnation, sacrament and grace. In the case of human activity he viewed man as an instrument in the hand of God, but as a human instrument of a special intrinsic nature, endowed with a share in God's own power, a share in God's own freedom, and perhaps most astonishingly of all, an intelligent instrument endowed with a share in God's own providence for mankind.

To an Augustinian and a Reformation cast of thought no doubt such sentiments can sound all too reminiscent of an ever-present pelagian tendency to deny man's radical need of God and to vaunt man's own proud self-achievement, which would constitute the basis of Roman Catholicism's self-justification by works, and which would finally disclose its true nature in the proud self-deification of the Enlightenment which has left modern society so desolate, so God-forsaken, so post-Christian and so similar to the pagan society graphically described by Paul in the first chapter of his Epistle to the Romans. Now indeed our consideration of the sin of pride has brought us to the very heart of what Professor Henry Chadwick has only this week described [in the *Catholic Herald*, 22.11.85, p.6] as 'the most complex of all articles of faith' that of God's and man's righteousness, or what I have identified as the relationship between divine and human causality, and not only in man's graced acts but also in his 'natural' acts, if such there be.

For light on the nature of divine justification and on how it might be possible to justify the ways of man to God, we await with eager expectation the fruit of the deliberations of ARCIC II, the Anglican-Roman Catholic International Commission of which Professor Chadwick is, of course, a leading member; trusting that in so mysteriously intimate and personal a subject the Commission will have avoided treating God's and man's being and divine and human causation in a univocal manner, and will have considered in all seriousness the Roman conviction drawn from Augustine himself, enshrined in the Council of Trent, and regularly acknowledged in the Roman liturgy, that such is God's goodness that He has willed that 'His gifts should be our merits'. [See Augustine, *Ep.* 194, 5, 19 (*PL* 33, 880); Trent, *Decree on Justfication*, ch. 16 (DS 1548); *Roman Missal*, Preface of Saints I.] It is as if all man's initiatives, exertions and even successes are transacted always and ever within the saving brackets of God's love and omnipotence. But they are no less man's for that, whether we attempt to explain it in terms of Seripando's 'double justification' which Trent considered but laid aside, or in perhaps more Thomistic terms of man as God's free intelligent instrument, inert and dormant without the divine energy and yet when taken in hand by God, made capable of directing and refracting the divine omnipotence in a multitude of human ways which are mysteriously both God's and man's own.

Further, if one considers the place of the Enlightenment in European religious thought it can be argued that similar considerations may be of relevance. For the temper of the Enlightenment and of post-Enlightenment society to the present may be viewed, not as a rejection of Christianity, but as a rejection of what John Henry Newman was to describe in another context as a second Augustinian edition of Christianity; not so much an abandoning of the Gospel as a rejecting of a theological anthropology of inverse proportionality, such as I have sought to identify and explain. And it is in that respect a temper which may be seen as characteristic of the teaching of the Second Vatican Council, whose work after twenty years begins to be reviewed in Rome tomorrow by the Extraordinary Synod of the Roman Catholic episcopate. Such a conclusion appears, at any rate to follow from the statement of that Council that 'far from thinking that the achievements of human enterprise and ability are in opposition to the power of God, or that the rational creature is a rival to God, Christians [or, at least, Roman Catholics] are of the view that the successes of the human race are a sign of God's greatness and a result of His marvellous design. [See *Pastoral Constitution* . . . , 34.]

A major enterprise of the Second Vatican Council was, in its own words, to inaugurate 'a new humanism'. In the words of Cardinal Hume [*Catholic Herald*, 22.11.85, p.4], 'The Second Vatican Council taught that the Church must be open to the world, its aspirations and struggles and seek to provide it with a soul and a conscience'. And from that spirit of Vatican II and that statement of Cardinal Hume's two considerations at least appear to follow, which will no doubt occupy the attention of the Roman Synod in the next brief fortnight. First, was the Council in its teaching too open to the world and too uncritical of modern society, oblivious of the nature of evangelical salt, as some have suggested recently, both in Rome and elsewhere? It could, of course, be observed that when one is trying to make amends for one's past ungracious behaviour it is scarcely the time to draw further attention to another's faults. Yet the friendly warning proffered recently [in the *Tablet*, 16.11.85, p.1216] by Bishop Newbigin, that in being more open to the modern world the Catholic Church might, like the rest of us 'become too much at home in the modern world', is one which of course must be accepted and considered in all courtesy. But alongside it may be placed the refreshingly candid and self-confident statement of the Roman Catholic Episcopal Conference of England and Wales in preparation for the Roman Synod summed up in its concluding sentence that it 'looks to the Extraordinary Synod for a clear and positive reaffirmation of the spirit and decrees of the Second Vatican Council and wishes to hear a word of encouragement for all who have worked so hard for renewal in the life of the Church since the Council' [the *Tablet*, 3.8.85, p.819]. Perhaps, it might be suggested, the Catholic Tradition of Christianity, with its positive regard for man, rather more than the Protestant Tradition, feels itself at home in the world and is consequently more able to be open to the world in a dialogue of mutual respect and trust rather than mistrust. Perhaps also its long tradition of esteem for human nature and nature's resources can equip it more with the theological confidence and provide it with the theological nerve which are certainly required to evangelise the world.

This leads into my second question, while also hinting at its answer. In what spirit is the Church to approach the world in order to be as effective as possible in its preaching of the Gospel? Here I pick up not only Cardinal Hume's openness to society, but also the request of the Episcopal Conference – an organ so necessary to the catholicity of the Church – for 'a word of encouragement' for all those who have faithfully and loyally worked to absorb and implement the teaching of Vatican II. What that Council of set purpose inaugurated was, as I have said, the challenging programme of a 'new humanism' which would take the world and secular reality seriously and do justice to its Creator. Such a Spirit-led enterprise would be sadly contradicted by a reversal to a preaching which upbraided proud and sinful man and tried unsuccessfully to cow him back to a world of border disputes with a grudging God. What appears more called for from all the Churches is a saving word of building up an encouragement to man to marshal all his resources of God-given knowledge in the loving service of his fellows.

Is the sin of pride thereby expelled from our Christan moral dictionary as made obsolete by the abandonment of a theology of inverse proportionality? Not if the core of pride is seen to lie in independence, self-sufficency and individualism. Not if the Christian response does not invoke a mushroom-cloud of divine disapproval but appeals more to man's better nature rather than castigating his sinful nature. And not if the remedy prescribed is the encouragement and cultivation of a sense of human interdependence under God, a loving and enterprising care for the personal dignity of men and women, and the unremitting example and teaching that individuality, as in God so also in His image, finds its fulfilment only in the communion of persons. Then pride will be cast down, for knowledge and love will be conjoined in man for the fulfilling of God's own work of edification. Then too others will see your good works – and give the glory to God (cf. Matt. 5:16). To whom be praise and honour in the Church and among men, both now and forever. Amen.

Advancing the Kingdom

George Carey

I have chosen this address given to the Clergy of the Oxford diocese on 17 May 1989 as my contribution, because at the heart of Dr Robert Runcie's remarkable ministry as Archbishop has been the breadth of his theological vision. Not for him the narrow and confined limits of local and national Church, but the vison of God's kingdom in God's world. I myself have been stirred on many occasions by the way he has drawn our gaze to higher perspectives and this lecture has been shaped in part by the same theological framework.

The title of your Conference, 'Sharing in the Outgoing of God', is a splendid over-all theme, and the sub-title I have been invited to respond to – 'Building the Church and Advancing the Kingdom' – is an equally arresting topic. We all want to build the Church. But it is important to begin, not with the Church, but with the Kingdom. Long before the word 'Church' is mentioned in the New Testament the note of the Kingdom is trumpeted loud and clear; indeed, the Kingdom is even prior to the Cross and resurrection even though these two great events are locked into its meaning.

Although we all know a great deal about Jesus' teaching about the Kingdom, I want to remind you of just a few salient facts. First, the Kingdom takes physical form in the person of the Lord. It does not take shape as territory or as a powerful institution but in human action; Jesus translated God's action to human beings by caring, loving, restoring and redeeming. Second, the Kingdom is all about a new world in which suffering and evil are done away with, in which people are made whole and in which relationships are healed. Third, Jesus' life was a celebration of the rule of God, we could even call it a 'doxological' celebration of the rule of God, so that meeting Jesus meant that those who followed him found themselves transformed by his embrace and within the Kingdom itself. Fourth, the teaching pointed forward to the time when the Kingdom would be a reality for all people. We must understand that the Cross, the resurrection, the ascension and the coming of the Spirit are all elements within the advance of the Kingdom.

Now, in short, this means that the message and works of the Kingdom have taken physical form in the person of Jesus Christ, so that to meet him is to belong to his Kingdom. The implications of this are tremendous and indeed possess a five-fold shape: cosmic, global, international, national, and personal. And this inspiring vision should be the backcloth to our thinking about the Church because it gives to the Christan world view an ideology which is cogent and coherent.

The challenge of the Kingdom is indeed a very considerable one as far as the ministry of the Church is concerned. Indeed, it challenges three traditional approaches to mission. First there is the temptation of *Establishment-driven mission*. I mean by this 'mission' subordinated to the *status quo*. There are two levels to this. At the national level, there are forces in every society which want the Church to be just the Church and not an arm of the Kingdom. They desire our subservience to the State as a handmaid in the task of influencing its citizens to be good, kind and civilised. And so the Church's job is seen as providing a moral climate and being a spiritual backcloth. Now, there are aspects of that of which we would surely approve, but we must never be fooled into believing that these are our primary roles. The Church fails to become a harbinger of the Kingdom when its role is limited to shoring up the fabric of society or maintaining the *status quo*. The Church in Nazi Germany before the war is a terrible reminder of what may happen if the Kingdom is displaced by the Church. But at the local level the temptation is when the mission of the church on the corner is assumed to be to prop up accepted values or simply to reinforce 'what has always happened' – thus preserving a romantic idea of the past and, perhaps, maintaining an illusion that all is well with the world.

Second, there is the temptation of *Maintenance-driven mission*. Since becoming bishop I have seen a new view of the Church – from the centre of the Church's bureaucracy – the view, that is, of the Church from the perspective of Church House, from the diocesan offices, from the view of those who work so dedicatedly for us as diocesan secretaries, from our Diocesan Boards of Finance and so on. Of course the bureaucracy is necessary, but the danger is that, when this becomes the usual way of looking at Church life, it results in mission driven to survive. Things are well when the quota is paid, when the parochial structure is sound, when no one is rocking the boat, when the parishes are obediently doing what all good servants of the Church expect – that we keep to the rules. And I find myself asking: 'Where is the Kingdom in such maintenance-driven mission?'; because this appears to be a Church which, growing from organism into organisation, has lost its vision.

Then, third, there is the temptation of *Church-driven mission*. If I have been critical of the view of the Church from the centre I must be equally harsh of the view from the sticks, from that of many local churches, who view their ministry in equally static terms. The Church is fine if we are, in a year's time, where we are now. We are pathetically pleased when we have ten confirmation candidates to present to the bishop, when our numbers are slightly up and when the quota is paid. There is the spectacle of busy clergy maintaining the life of the parish, visiting the sick, bereaved, schools and, of course, the many busy lay people keeping the machine on the road, lovingly lubricating it and polishing so that others may enjoy the ride also. And we are not surprised that in many parishes, while there may be the illusion of success, there is often dull, unimaginative worship to which the young will certainly not come, no sense of adventure or sparkle, and no great sense of God. Yes, I am being hard and I will return to the local church and speak of its virtues later, but we must hear the criticism and brace ourselves to see ourselves as others see us. If we really want to participate in the out-going of God, we must see the failure of a great deal of Church life. Listen to what Micklem said years ago:

> Men at their best cannot do with the Church as it is, not because it bears witness to Christ but because it does not bear a clear and consistent witness to him. Men connect the Church, not with a disturbing and renewing encounter with a Holy God, but as someone has said with: 'unattractive services, tedious homilies, the smell of hymn books, the petty round of ecclesiastical functions, the collection plate, an oppression due to lack of oxygen and memories of Sunday School'.

Or there is Gore's famous definition of the Church of England as 'an ingeniously devised instrument for the frustrating of objectives it is supposed to promote'.

But now let me be more constructive. If I have spoken of the temptations of the Church what is the shape of *Kingdom-driven mission*? First we must define how I am using the word 'mission'. And we have to acknowledge its ambiguity. Many are made uncomfortable by the word since it conjures up images of missionaries putting Laura Ashley clothes on South Sea Island natives, or frenetic Jimmy Swaggarts, or similar American evangelists waving big fat black Bibles at indifferent urban dwellers.

But the word 'mission', coming as it does from the Latin root 'to send', invites us to share in the 'Out-going of God', to participate in His work of bringing in the Kingdom in all its forms. At the narrow end of mission it means, in that famous definition of evangelism, 'One beggar telling another beggar where to find bread'. At the broad end of mission, it means standing in Christ like solidarity with all who are hurt deprived, oppressed, whoever and wherever they are.

I believe that *Kingdom-driven mission* will take three main forms. First, it will be *the Church truly incarnating itself in the local community*. This was the form of Jesus' ministry. It was the form the Kingdom took through him. We often see posters outside churches or on railway stations which cry 'God loves you'. But Jesus did not say that to Zachaeus – he lived the loving. He went to Zachaeus' house, he sat down with him at table and by this liberating act opened up a communication which demonstrated love, showing quite specifically that God accepted him as he was. Now, the word 'incarnation' traditionally has been at the heart of Catholic theology and ministry. Growing up in the East End of London as an unchurched lad I was aware of the Anglo-Catholic priests who served so sacrificially in the many churches of the East End in those days. They 'incarnated' the love of God. And this is something we must return to in our theology of the Kingdom and our living of it.

Here is found the reality of our faith. The Church is authentically itself when it lives the Kingdom, when it suffers for the King, when it rises above the expectations of the world, when it does not conform to the *status quo*, when it is not controlled by money or numbers. It is always a bad sign, I must remind you, when the Church talks about itself and its problems. The lust for talk about work increases as the power for work declines. Conferences multiply when work fails – I am not necessarily thinking about excellent and important conferences such as this where there is a need to meet, to think and pray – as long as it goes somewhere and lives are touched and changed. But talk of incarnation is to bring in the reality of getting to know our people and parishes and there is no alternative than that of being involved in our communities and, yes, by that underrated ministry of door-to-door visiting.

So the task is commitment to mission. One of Tolstoy's famous stories outlines how a well-to-do lady in Russia went to the theatre on a cold winter's evening, and wept vicariously at the fictional suffering on the stage. But she was entirely indifferent to the needs of her own servants and was surprised to find her chauffeur frozen to death from waiting outside in the sleigh. Many Christians today are caught in a similar peril. We agonise over the plight of others – about the misson of Christ, about the poor of the world, but we perceive the problem to be 'out there', and away from where we are. Bishop Stephen Bayne addressed the General Synod of Canada some years ago with these words: 'The most frightening thing about the Church in our time is not the lack of organisation nor even the lack of prophetic passion. Rather it is the feeling that 'mission' is an option. At present we are organised so that our main energies are devoted to self perpetuation.' If that analysis is correct then God help His Church. But the principle of incarnation is that mission is not an option; it is the mark of the true Church, as indispensable a mark of the Church as the words 'One, Holy, Catholic and Apostolic'.

Then, second, Jesus taught the Kingdom; he preached it, he spoke of it, and he taught in arresting ways *the reality of the Kingdom of God*. But before it can be proclaimed it has to be accepted, believed, cherished and experienced. There can be no effective preaching which is not based on the reality of the thing itself. Unless we know what it is to enter the Kingdom we cannot take others there. There was a fascinating remark in a *Partners in Mission Report* some time back, on an English diocese, which commented cryptically on the failure of many congregations that: 'They were trying to communicate an experience they had not had themselves.'

So effective proclamation must begin with the preacher constantly being nourished by the truth he or she has received. What is it we offer the world? What is the message of the Kingdom to us and to them? We may feel a little like a cartoon I saw recently which depicted a monkey looking totally confused, scratching his head and the caption beneath proclaimed: 'Just when I thought I had all the answers, they changed all the questions!'

But let me mention just three things that still give me confidence and conviction in Christian preaching. First, *it offers meaning in a world that is distorted and confused*. The preaching of the Kingdom speaks of the presence of the King and therefore of the reality of order. Social scientists such as the American Clifford Geertz have suggested that, without religion to provide a basic meaning system, people cannot understand and accept problems like death and suffering and unexpected tragedies. They feel threatened and disorientated when confronted by a universe which they cannot interpret. Now obviously this does not imply that everyone is going to feel a need for God or a need to worship. We still have to recognise the existence of many who, in Karl Rahner's splendid phrase, are 'unmusical in religion'. But it does suggest that in an age of confusion most people need some sort of rough and ready answers to life's basic questions. We live in a society which sadly lacks an ideology and a framework to assist people to interpret their existence. I believe that the preaching of the Kingdom gives to us a marvellous opportunity to speak to people who have such inchoate awareness of spiritual needs.

Second, *the preaching of the Kingdom is all about reconciliation in a world divided and estranged*. We are sometimes told that the message of the Church is out of date. But how can it be when the themes of the Gospel are more topical now than they have ever been: reconciliation; hope renewal; restoration; forgiveness; life through death; the sacrifice of oneself for another – all these things and more go to the heart of human existence. What may be open to criticism is the way we often proclaim it – without passion, conviction or depth. And the preaching of the Cross and resurrection is at the centre of the Kingdom; that God's hope for the world starts from the gift of His Son, and this gift is commemorated every time we break bread together – surely the most vivid sign of this love and commitment! Ironically, I find that modern writers like John Fowles, Saul Bellow and John Updike are regularly working out such themes in their writings and lucidly expressing the need for these in the heart of the human condition but are lacking the Gospel to show how people may be redeemed.

Third, our faith celebrates a *sense of mystery in a world we do not fully understand*. The danger in Christianity is the subtle temptation to believe that because Christ's revelation is final and complete, there is nothing more to learn. This then degenerates into simplistic ways of looking at life, and failure to marvel at the wonder and complexity of life. The theologian Robert McAffee Brown divided his scientist friends into two groups. There are the 'So what?' and the 'Gee Whiz!' groups. The 'So what' brigade accept without surprise whatever their research uncovers. But the 'Gee Whiz!' scientists are perpetually amazed at the intricacy and delicate balance of nature. Even more, they are moved by a sense of wonder and awe that things are as they are.

I want to suggest that we too in our preaching, worship and celebration need to recapture this spirit of mystery. We celebrate the breaking in of God's Kingdom and the Church as the sign of its advance into the lives and hearts of people. But we do not know all the answers. We must attempt to incorporate in our teaching the elements that made Jesus the most mysterious and arresting teacher of all times: the telling of the story, the stopping short of the answers, the elusive unveiling of truth, suggesting, probing, stimulating, pointing towards a larger truth which lies in God. And doing this, not because of uncertainty but because our God is Creator of all things; Alpha and Omega, the beginning and the end.

But there is a third challenge for the Church which has a Kingdom-driven misson and that is the task to *renew the life of the church* – and I mean by this the local church. When 'church' is mentioned in the New Testament the local Christian community is meant. But we, in our thinking, automatically think of the Church as denomination – our Church of England. We begin from the large and move towards the small and local.

I think this is an encouragement for the small church of, say, twenty or so members. There are churches in my diocese – out there in remote country areas – who only get seven or eight on a Sunday. It is very discouraging when you are dealing with such small numbers as that and you may well wonder where the Kingdom of God is when this is the reality of the Church!

But, whatever size we are talking about, our task is to renew the life of the local church. What might that mean? Let me give a number of pointers. First we must focus attention on the local congregation and seek to support its life. I see that as part of episcopal responsibility and I personally have set myself the target of engaging in five teaching missions every year in various parts of the diocese. I do so because when I was an incumbent I remember being called in to see the Archdeacon because a member of my congregation had complained about the changes I was making to worship. I remember leaving the Archdeacon's study thinking, 'Why is it that people in authority seem only to take an interest in what I am doing when things appear to go wrong! Why is it that no one says "I hear that good things are going on. Now how can we help? How may the resources of the diocese assist you?"' Someone has commented that the Church could probably survive a whole generation of disastrous bishops; it would be weakened but not terminated. But there is no possibility that the Church could survive a generation of disastrous parish priests, or consistently indifferent laity! So, I plead for the discovery of plans which push out life from the centre; supporting effective local leadership and encouraging local initiative.

Second, and related to this, we must learn how to move out in witness and evangelism. There are churches today which are learning the importance of church planting; that is to say, the extension of church life beyond the frontiers of the church building. I know of churches in urban areas which have bought houses on council estates where Bible study groups meet mid-week and where social activities go alongside these spiritual activities. I know of churches which have planted new congregations in public houses, in welfare clinics, in social clubs and elsewhere. We must move out of the safety of our buildings into the community and I am glad to report that new ways are being discovered to do this.

Third, renewal is a desperate need of our worship. I am not a modernist trying to overthrow the Prayer Book. But much of our worship, even when we follow the ASB down to the ultimate comma, is boring tedious, long and mind-numbing. The miracle of Christianity, I sometimes think cynically, is that people still come in great numbers – so something must be going on! Of course something is going on, but we could do much better. And we have to beware of two opposite dangers. The first is that of 'out of touch' worship, unrelated to life and only a throwback to a secure past. The other danger is to go with the spirit of the age – and the world around becomes our model. When the Church is run on the same lines as a circus, there may be crowds but, I warn you, the mystery and the *Shekinah* will be gone. The spiritual Church will maintain the balance between relevance and tradition.

Fourth, we have to come to terms with the reality of church life; that a great deal of parish life is done by a small number of people. Even if you look at your bigger churches you will find the same fact that it is a minority which runs things. Our target therefore must be to extend the commitment wider than it is. I don't know if you have heard of the 80/20 principle. In the last century an Italian thinker, Parito, set forth his 80/20 principle. He contended that, on the average, 80 per cent of the results in any human situation can be attributed to 20 per cent of the possible cause. For example:

20 per cent of the drivers cause 80 per cent of all accidents.
20 per cent of a business's customers produce 80 per cent of the revenue.
20 per cent of any effort produces 80 per cent of the results.

Parito's analysis may be applied aptly to the situation the Church finds itself in. Of course, we want everyone to be totally committed all the time and that is important as an ideal. And yet our Lord himself stressed that God's Kingdom may begin in a very unpromising manner; such parables of the leaven and sower, yeast and seed, stress the smallness and hidden-ness of the Kingdom and yet in the end nothing can stop its growth. So we should not despise this principle. Because if it is true that only 20 per cent of our people offer 80 per cent of the prayers, or do 80 per cent of the work, or give 80 per cent of the money to the Church – then that is still good, and it may be all that God needs at the moment. However, our task must be to extend the base so that others can share in the joy of service and the urgency of mission.

The final thing I want to do is to put on my prophet's mantle, and forecast the shape of things to come. I believe we shall see the following trends:

1. The focus will shift from buildings to people, to church planting and the establishing of small Christian communities in schools, clubs and elsewhere. If this happens, maintaining an Anglican ethos will be crucially important and very difficult.
2. The acceptance of the variety of worship and life styles in the body of Christ.
3. Less of an emphasis upon a professional, ordained class which exists to do worship on behalf of others.
4. Parish organisation will become more democratic and functional.
5. Men and women will be more integrated in the ministry and mission of Christ.
6. The development of a bigger vision of ministry than that restricted to the present threefold pattern.
7. Greater acceptance of risks in ministry.
8. Greater confidence in the mission of Christ in the world as we all attempt to advance the Kingdom in the lives of all.

Most of us will have read C.S. Lewis' *Screwtape Letters*. The Devil you will recall, encourages Wormwood to dupe the Christian into believing the Church to be weak and divided. But then come these significant and encouraging words: 'As long as he doesn't see it as we see it . . . as an Army with banners.'

Contributors

Lord Hailsham of Marylebone was formerly Lord Chancellor.

Rabbi Dr Dan Cohn-Sherbok teaches theology at the University of Kent, Canterbury.

The Most Revd Desmond Tutu is Archbishop of Cape Town.

Sister Frances Dominica is a member and former Superior of the Society of All Saints, Oxford.

The Rt Revd David Jenkins is Bishop of Durham.

The Most Revd John Habgood is Archbishop of York.

The Revd Don Cupitt is Dean of Emmanuel College, Cambridge.

Miss Angela Tilby is a writer and television producer.

The Revd the Lord Soper was formerly Superintendent of the West London Mission.

The Rt Revd Richard Harries is Bishop of Oxford.

The Revd Professor Maurice Wiles is Regius Professor of Divinity, Oxford.

The Rt Revd Graham Leonard is Bishop of London.

Mrs Lavinia Cohn-Sherbok is Principal of West Heath School, Sevenoaks.

The Revd Nicolas Stacey was formerly Director of Kent Social Services.

The Revd Professor Rowan Williams is Lady Margaret Professor of Divinity, Oxford.

Dame Cicely Saunders is Chairman of St Nicholas' Hospice.

The Very Revd Alan Webster was formerly Dean of St Paul's Cathedral.

The Revd Canon Anthony Phillips is Headmaster of the King's School Canterbury.

The Rt Revd Kallistos Ware is Orthodox Bishop of Diokleia.

The Very Revd Peter Baelz was formerly Dean of Durham.

Professor Ursula King is Head of the Theology Department, University of Bristol.

The Revd Professor Leslie Houlden is Professor of Theology at King's College, London.

His Holiness Pope John Paul II is Leader of the Roman Catholic Church.

The Very Revd John Simpson is Dean of Canterbury.

The Revd John Witheridge is Conduct of Eton College.

The Very Revd Davd Edwards is Provost of Southwark Cathedral.

The Rt Hon. Enoch Powell was formerly a Member of Parliament.

The Revd Canon Eric James is Director of Christian Action.

The Revd Professor Owen Chadwick was formerly Regius Professor of Modern History, Cambridge.

The Rt Revd the Lord Blanch of Bishopthorp was formerly Archbishop of York.

The Rt Revd Michael Nazir-Ali is the General Secretary of the Church Missionary Society.

The Most Revd Derek Worlock is Roman Catholic Archbishop of Liverpool.

The Rt Revd Robert Hardy is Bishop of Lincoln.

The Rt Revd Stephen Sykes is Bishop of Ely.

The Very Revd Michael Mayne is Dean of Westminster.

The Rt Revd Michael Turnbull is Bishop of Rochester.

The Revd Dr Edward Norman is Dean of Chapel, Christ Church College, Canterbury.

The Revd Canon Christopher Lewis is a Residentiary Canon of Canterbury Cathedral.

The Revd Canon Christopher Hill is a Residentiary Canon of Westminster Abbey.

The Most Revd Metropolitan Anthony of Sourozh is Head of the Russian Orthodox Church in Great Britain and Ireland.

The Rt Revd Alec Graham is Bishop of Newcastle.

The Rt Revd Lord Coggan of Sissinghurst was formerly Archbishop of Canterbury.

The Rt Revd Mark Santer is Bishop of Birmingham.

Mrs Mary Whitehouse is President of the National Viewers' and Listeners' Association.

The Rt Revd David Sheppard is Bishop of Liverpool.

Lord Jakobovits of Regent's Park is Chief Rabbi of the United Hebrew Congregations and of the Commonwealth.

The Revd Professor Geoffrey Parrinder was formerly Professor of the Comparative Study of Religions, University of London.

The Rt Revd Lesslie Newbigin was formerly Bishop in Madras.

Dr Grace Jantzen teaches theology at King's College, London.

Rabbi Dr Jonathan Sacks was formerly Principal of Jews' College London and is the Chief Rabbi elect.

Dr Eileen Barker teaches Sociology at the London School of Economics and Politics.

The Rt Revd Hugh Montefiore was formerly Bishop of Birmingham.

Sir John Lawrence Bt is an authority on Christianity in Communist countries.

The Revd Marcus Braybrooke is Vicar of Christ Church, Bath and was formerly Executive Director of the Council of Christians and Jews.

The Baroness Warnock of Weeks is Mistress of Girton College, Cambridge.

The Revd Canon Anthony Harvey is a Residentiary Canon of Westminster Abbey.

Rabbi Julia Neuberger is a writer and broadcaster.

The Rt Revd David Say was formerly Bishop of Rochester.
Rabbi Lionel Blue is a writer and broadcaster.
The Very Revd Edward Carpenter was formerly Dean of Westminster.
The Rt Hon. The Earl of Longford was formerly Lord Privy Seal.
The Revd Professor Jack Mahoney is Frederick Denison Maurice Professor of Moral and Social Theology at King's College, London.
The Rt Revd George Carey is Bishop of Bath and Wells and Archbishop elect.